Social Inequality:
Class and Caste in America

Social Inequality:
Class and Caste in America

Lucile Duberman
Rutgers University, Newark

J. B. Lippincott Company
Philadelphia
New York / San Jose / Toronto

Copyright © 1976 by J. B. Lippincott Company
All rights reserved.

With the exception of brief excerpts for review, no part of
this book may be reproduced in any form or by any means
without written permission of the publisher.

ISBN 0-397-47345-1

Library of Congress Catalog Card Number 75-40327

Printed in the United States of America

Library of Congress Cataloging in Publication Data

Duberman, Lucile
   Social inequality.

   Includes bibliographies and index.
   1. Social classes—United States.   2. Social status.
I. Title.
HN90.S6D83   301.44'0973   75-40327
ISBN 0-397-47345-1

dedication

With love to my husband,
Ralph Kaminsky

A mania for stratification seemed to have seized this democracy, and a thousand anthropologists were busy sorting out classes by means of such physical criteria as automobile makes, window sizes and shirt collars. Americans studied their own everyday artifacts as though they were those of a civilization long vanished—an odd preoccupation for a young and robust country. How much sense did it all make?

(Peter DeVries, *Reuben, Reuben.* Boston: Little, Brown and Company, 1964)

contents

contents

preface

Both the methodology and the conceptualization prevalent in the study of social stratification leave much to be desired. Many issues are considered "dead" which should be exhumed; many other issues are still "alive" which should be decently buried. In addition, while there is a profusion of books of "readings," there is a paucity of interpretive studies and unquestionably a lack of textbooks.

This book is addressed primarily to undergraduate students in sociology, although it is certainly suitable for graduate students, and there is no reason why the general reader should not find it interesting and enlightening. Although most sociological terms are defined, a basic acquaintance with sociology is assumed.

No author can claim to be free of bias, and no such claim is made here. However, an attempt has been made to be dispassionate and detached, although perhaps not always successfully. The subject of social stratification in American society is so emotionally "loaded" that it is difficult to remain objective.

Social Inequality has a number of multi-faceted goals. One is to acquaint the student with the field of social inequality by presenting past and present theoretical positions and empirical findings. Hopefully, this has been done in such a way that some synthesis has been achieved and some order created out of chaos.

Furthermore, the book focuses on a relatively neglected area in the American stratification system—social caste. Most sociologists tend to ignore or to treat cavalierly the relationship between social ranking and race, age, sex, religion, and ethnicity.

acknowledgments

I am indebted to many people who helped in the preparation of this text. Holger R. Stub and Norval D. Glenn generously read portions of the manuscript and made innumerable and worthwhile suggestions. My colleagues at Rutgers University also were generous with their time and knowledge. Ralph Larkin carefully criticized the section on education and social class, and S. Priyadarsini helped me to make accurate interpretations of the caste system in India. Special thanks go to my dear friend, Clayton A. Hartjen, who patiently read every word of the manuscript and made valuable comments, corrections, and additions. I wish to thank him particularly for the schematic drawings he created.

My editor at J. B. Lippincott Company, A. Richard Heffron, is all anyone could wish an editor to be. His blue pencil frequently turned my awkward sentences to elegance, and this book would have been greatly impoverished without his help. In addition, Dick was always thoughtful and understanding when I needed his aid. I would also like to thank Evelyn Weiman, the copy editor, who caught all the errors my third grade teacher missed.

I, of course, am solely responsible for any misstatements and misinterpretations.

Lucile Duberman

October 1975

chapter 1

The Inevitability of Inequality

Historical Treatment of the Concept of Inequality

There is nothing very new or profound in the saying that "all human beings are equal, but some are more equal than others." People throughout written history and probably before that were aware that social inequity and social differentiation are constants in all societies. As long as there is a surplus of any commodity in society, whether material or spiritual, there has been and will be a struggle for the possession of all or part of it.

Plato was one of the first to acknowledge that inequality is inevitable, and to suggest ways in which the distribution of money, status, and power could be altered for the betterment of both the individual and the society. In *The*

Republic he tried to answer the question, "What is justice?" He wrestled with the problem of how social inequalities could be made to correspond to innate talents and abilities. Thus, he proposed that each man should be tested and classified early in life and assigned to one of three groups: (1) the artisans, craftsmen, workers, and merchants, who were to form the lowest ranking group; (2) the warriors who protected the state, who were to form the middle or second group; and (3) the philosopher-kings or guardians, who were trained to rule *The Republic*, and were to form the highest ranking and the smallest group. For Plato, then, justice in society is achieved when both men and states are able to use the best of themselves to the fullest; when there is harmony and balance between the personal, internal part of the human being and the social, external state.

Throughout the centuries many other philosophers have recognized the inherent inequality among people. Sir Thomas More, lord chancellor of England, humanist, and scholar, contended that the best society, the *utopia*, was a rural, communal one. He suggested a return to the land and the simple life, a community in which money would be useless, and each citizen would own property and have an equal voice in government. Thus, for More, classlessness was the ultimate goal which would produce the greatest happiness for the greatest number.

Rousseau, writing during the early eighteenth century, conceived of two different kinds of inequality. One was natural, because people are differentially endowed physically and mentally. The other was unnatural, or what he called political or moral inequality, established and authorized by people themselves. The first was unavoidable; the second could be obliterated because it is nothing more than an artificial, unjust human creation.

For all the idealistic writings of philosophers and scholars, however, every society continues to exhibit evidence that people are valued differentially in greater and lesser degrees. Gerhard Lenski (1966:30–32) attributes this human condition to several factors. First, people are motivated basically by selfish interests, and altruism exists only infrequently, when very little can be gained or lost by proffering it. Second, people are always striving to possess and accumulate not only money, but power and prestige as well, and since such commodities are always and everywhere in short supply, people always are competing to obtain more than their fellows. Third, human beings are not equally endowed by nature to fight for scarce goods and services. Some are either physically, mentally, or emotionally better suited than others. Thus, some people have the natural requisites needed to be successful in the struggle over others. In addition, other people are conditioned or socialized to accept inequality, even those who are getting less than their fair share of the pie; because human beings are creatures of habit, many believe that the way things are, is good. St. Augustine justified this view from a religious point of view when he wrote that the poor "are deservedly and justly miserable, they ... are ... in harmony with the natural order of things" (1950:690). Thus, while throughout human history philosophers and humanists have dreamed of societies in which all people would be equal, clearly this has never been the case, and probably it never will be.

The Sociology of Social Inequality

Despite the obvious, it was to take a very long time for American sociologists to recognize the existence of social inequality, and to study the phenomenon in a systematic fashion in the United States. As late as 1929, Lundberg, in *Trends in American Sociology*, did not include a chapter on social stratification, although soon after that date there were some theoretical speculations and several empirical studies on the subject (Page, 1940; Warner, 1936-1955; Lynd and Lynd, 1929 and 1937; Dollard, 1937). The first book of readings for students appeared in 1953 (Bendix and Lipset), and the first textbook was not published until 1954 (Cuber and Kenkel). Two more comprehensive textbooks appeared in 1957 (Barber; Kahl).

The reasons for this strange reluctance to deal with social stratification by American sociologists reveals several things about the discipline. For one thing, it almost seems as if sociologists had been unable to face up to the facts and to admit that in American society, as in "decadent" Europe, there were those people who did not have the good things in life, let alone the necessities. Second, before World War I the economy had been more receptive to individual initiative; people had been moving westward; it appeared that there were opportunities to get as far ahead as one desired for anyone who wanted to work. Third, many sociologists truly believed in democratic principles, that the majority could really rule by vote, and that any "boy could be president" if he pulled himself "up by his bootstraps." Thus, it appeared to them that

America really did not have a stratification system in the sense of rigid, inherited classes. The word "class" seemed old-fashioned, European, and inapplicable to the forward-looking young country. It took the depression of the 1930s to awaken American sociologists to the fact that a class structure was a real phenomenon in the United States to which they had better attend.

Today the study of social stratification has become an indispensable part of American sociology. It is taught in almost every sociology department in universities; it is also taught in thousands of high schools in elective courses in sociology; it is an intregal part of most empirical studies; and it is included in every introductory textbook on sociology. Yet the discipline suffers from several inadequacies, perhaps the most important of which is the absence of an explicit, agreed-upon definition of several of its most useful concepts: differentiation, stratification, inequality, and social class. Because the usage of these terms is not standardized, writers employ different words to mean the same thing, the same word to mean different things, or they use these terms interchangeably without regard to precision or to definitions established in the work of others. These problems will be discussed in detail in Chapter III; we will touch on them briefly here.

Milton Gordon defines social stratification as a "concept which refers to a vertical arrangement of persons—a hierarchy—a system of higher and lower, greater and lesser, superior and inferior" (1958:238). Gordon is concerned with individuals; other sociologists focus on positions.

Celia Heller sees stratification "as a system of structured inequality in the things that count in a given society, that is, both tangible and symbolic goods of that society" (1969:4). Heller's use of the word structured is important, because it indicates that inequality is patterned, relatively constant, and legitimated by ideology. Such an interpretation rejects any implication that social stratification is a "natural" societal condition. Rather, it is manmade and purposeful. Others, such as Kingsley Davis, contend that it is inherent in all social groups.

Gerhard E. Lenski rejects the term stratification altogether, saying that it oversimplifies a complex modern system, showing too much concern with structure and de-emphasizing the processes that generate these structures (1966:2). Instead he would substitute the concept of "distributive power," and direct attention primarily to one basic question: "Who gets what and why?" (1966:3).

Similarly, sociologists do not agree on a definition of the term inequality. Some theorists, such as Leonard Reissman (1973) and Bernard Barber (1957), discuss the concept (Reissman uses it in the title of his book), but do not bother to define it at all. Others, like Thielbar and Feldman, whose stated purpose is "to determine what we know about inequality and what we want to know" (1972:vii), also neglect to define the word. A few, like Melvin Tumin, declare there is no difference between the two terms, social inequality and social stratification, and define them identically as "the arrangement of any social group or society into a hierarchy of positions that are unequal with regard to power, property, social evaluation and/or psychic gratification" (1967:12).

In short, no clear-cut definition of social inequality can be found, despite the frequent use of the term. Rather, most often it is coupled indiscriminately and alternatively with social stratification. Yet there is a subtle difference, which Heller comes closest to making. Following Rousseau, the term stratification can be reserved to describe those societies in which there appears to be a deliberate, rationalized, and relatively permanent societal institution for ranking and rewarding people differentially in terms of power, prestige, property, and privilege. Inequality, on the other hand, should be used to describe those societies in which there are unequal opportunities to attain societal resources because of natural differences between individuals that cannot be overcome, as in India. In other words, stratification, what Rousseau called "political or moral inequality," is created; inequality is beyond the abilities of human beings to alter.

The term social class is even more difficult to clarify because it is widely and inconsistently used. It has weak theoretical underpinnings, and therefore conceptual definitions are usually vague and frequently ignored once they have been dutifully stated. Furthermore, it has a myriad of operational definitions. We will discuss both the conceptual and methodological problems related to social class in Chapter 3.

Gordon states the problem succinctly:

The term "social class"—often shortened to "class"—is used by sociologists to refer to the horizontal stratification of a population by means of factors related in some way to the economic life of the society. Within this general delimitation the concept of class has no precise, well agreed-upon meaning, but is used either as an omnibus term, designed to designate differences based on wealth, income, occupation, status, community power, group identification, level of consumption, and family background, or by some particular researcher or theorist as resting particularly on some one of these enumerated factors (1958:3).

Social Structure and Social Stratification

Gerhard E. Lenski has attempted to show how distributive power in society is based on the economics and the technological know-how of the society. He asserts that "power will determine the distribution of nearly all the surplus [of resources] possessed by a society" (1966:44); but without a surplus there can be little or no power differential among members. Lenski, to prove his theory, describes five types of societies: hunting and gathering, simple horticultural, advanced horticultural, agrarian, and industrial.

Hunting and Gathering Societies

The most primitive societies are the hunting and gathering societies, such as the aborigines of Australia, the Semang and Sakai of Malaya, and the Kubu of Sumatra. Such societies are usually very small, with populations averaging about 50 individuals. Furthermore, they are frequently nomadic, or at least seminomadic, because they tend to move on when they have exhausted the land and animal resources in an area. This constant mobility, combined with their low level of productivity, means that they are able to acquire few permanent possessions. Those that they have consist primarily of articles that are essential for survival.

In such societies, tools, weapons, and techniques for producing food are simple and often inefficient, and because of this the people live close to a subsistence level. There is never a lasting surplus of anything, and generally the society fluctuates between periods of feast and famine.

Hunting and gathering tribes are communal, that is, they generally are leaderless and all possessions, anything that is captured or gathered, are shared by all members. Because they have few and inadequate tools, because they are nomadic, and because they are virtually leaderless, the outstanding feature of these societies is that there is an almost total absence of surplus commodities. Thus there is no meaningful inequality in the distribution of goods. Everyone partakes when there is food; everyone goes hungry when there is none. The group could not survive under any other conditions.

The same principles do not operate, however, when it comes to the distribution of honor or prestige. These are commodities that hunting and gathering societies can afford to distribute unequally, because inequality in this sense cannot threaten the group's physical survival. One reward that people can safely compete for is prestige. Radcliffe-Brown (1948) reports that among these societies three groups usually are accorded special prestige: the elderly; those with supernatural powers; and those who have special personal attributes, such as great hunting skills or pleasant dispositions. Lenski calls this "functional inequality" because it affords the more dependent members of the society (those who are less skillful, very young, etc.) ways of rewarding others who actually help them and toward whom they feel gratitude.

One by-product of prestige is political power, but it is limited in these societies. Government hardly can be coercive when there are no means of enforcing rules. Furthermore, the leaders usually are part-time leaders because no one in the society can be exempted from participating in the food-gathering activities. Thus what government there is, is persuasive. People grant authority to those whom they respect and honor. Political power is only moderate, tenure is generally short as new heroes appear, and there is no real obligation to obey.

In short, hunting and gathering societies cannot socially differentiate their members in economic terms because they possess no surplus of goods. The only way in which people can be rewarded for special achievement or exceptional ability is by granting them prestige and political power, although in limited quantity.

Simple Horticultural Societies

The simple horticultural society is one technological step above the hunting and gathering society; that is, it is not nomadic and its economy is based on gardening, although its tools are primitive. Their basic tool is the digging stick. Occasionally a primitive hoe is used, but plows or more intricate implements are unknown. Nor do such groups use agricultural techniques such as terracing, irrigation, or fertilization.

In almost all other ways the simple horticultural society is similar to the hunting and gathering society; differences are merely matters of degree. These societies are also small groups, but usually much larger than 50 individuals. By modern standards they are unproductive, but they produce more than the nomadic groups.

There is egalitarianism in the simple horticultural society, but somewhat less than is found in more primitive societies. For example, the Cayuvava of eastern Bolivia has seven villages, some containing as many as 2000 people, all under one chief (Steward and Faron, 1959).

The size of the community is an important variable in accounting for the increased productivity of these simple horticultural societies. Of course, most of the additional produce is used to feed the population, but a small part of it constitutes a surplus. Thus the members acquire some leisure time, since it is not necessary to spend every waking moment collecting food.

Leisure is spent in producing nonessential goods and engaging in other nonessential activities. Buildings are constructed more solidly. There are more ceremonies and religious rituals. There is even time for war. Not that hunting and gathering societies are totally peaceful; but warfare is a much more frequent and important activity among these more advanced peoples.

Most importantly, the nomadic pattern of the hunters and gatherers almost disappears. The latter move approximately once a year, while simple horticulturalists tend to remain in the same place for as long as 10 to 12 years. This tendency to remain relatively stationary means that people can accumulate possessions—not only the essential tools needed to survive—but also such things as art objects, weapons, ceremonial equipment, and musical instruments. They also are enabled to specialize, so that people can achieve special statuses in the society. Everyone need not be a hunter or a gatherer; there are those who also are engaged in full-time religious, economic, and political statuses. Whole villages become specialists in producing or amassing one kind of product, so that trade is established between the villages; for example, one village may supply fish because it is plentiful in its particular area in return for bows and arrows, which may be especially well-made in another village.

The result of the differences between these two types of societies is that greater social inequalities exist in the simple horticultural society. One kind of inequality is political. The chiefs of simple horticultural societies often are freed of the need to provide their own livelihood. Further, power is often greater because they have small groups of second-level chiefs who can enforce their edicts.

Another kind of inequality in the simple horticultural society is economic, as measured in terms of numbers of wives, ornaments, and livestock. Wives are apparently the highest form of wealth because of their reproductive capacity, their labor, and because women are in shorter supply than ornaments and pigs. While men will part with many of their material possessions, wives rarely are given away.

Inequality is also based on social status in the areas of religion and magic. It will be recalled that hunting and gathering societies also recognize those with supernatural power; but these societies reward such individuals with prestige. Simple horticulturalists reward their powerful members in material ways and the *shaman*, or medicine man, can easily be the richest in the society because he charges for his services. Thus the priest generally ranks just below the chief, and in some groups the chief and the priest are one and the same person.

A fourth type of inequality is based on status according to bravery and strength. While the hunters and gatherers also reward such attributes, they bestow prestige on the best hunters of animals; the people in simple horticultural societies bestow honor not only on those who hunt well, but also on those who display similar abilities as warriors. Warrior status confers a type of prestige which barely exists in the hunting and gathering society.

Warfare leads to another form of inequality which is unknown in the more primitive tribe. People captured in war are enslaved. Male prisoners are either killed or adopted; female prisoners become integrated into the society. This is not true slavery as Americans knew it historically. Nevertheless, the slave is in a lower status category than others.

Thus, as soon as there is even a small economic surplus, social inequities tend to become greater and more institutionalized because people have more time and more opportunity to specialize. Formally defined positions, carrying recognized rights and obligations, become available to those qualified to fill them. Discrepancies and inequalities become more magnified. A man can acquire prestige because of what he *has* in addition to what he *is*; furthermore, such prestige may be perpetuated, since offices and property are transmitted to succeeding generations.

Although this inequality is greater than in hunting and gathering societies, it is still quite limited. Material possessions remain readily available; most men are able to cultivate a piece of land to adequately supply personal and family needs. In addition,•the amount of any surplus remains quite small. Prestige continues to be the commodity in short supply, and those with material possessions are likely to share or give away possessions in order to gain prestige. For this reason the custom of *potlatch* is found frequently. Potlatch is a ceremonial feast at which prestige is gained by giving away wealth, with the most magnanimous man outdoing his rivals in generosity to acquire the most prestige. "The individual finds that he stands to gain more by giving them [possessions] away than by keeping them, since in so doing he both enhances his reputation and puts those who cannot repay under moral obligation to him" (Lenski, 1966:135). Thus material (with the exception of wives) is exchanged for honor, which has a higher value. Potlatch, then, is really an exchange—of goods for prestige. Its effect is to reduce material inequality and thereby increase inequities of power and influence.

In short, while there are differences of distributive power between hunting and gathering societies and simple horticultural societies, they are not great. Most people have relatively equal basic material possessions, but there is greater inequality in the distribution of political power. Leaders have more special privileges, are accorded greater honor, and they are often relieved of the need to support themselves. In the more advanced society, prestige is the commodity that is in scarce supply and it is therefore more valued.

Advanced Horticultural Societies

Advanced horticultural societies can still be found in subSaharan Africa. The differences between these societies and simple horticultural ones are extensive, not only in terms of technology, but in almost all spheres of life.

The chief cause of the difference lies in the discovery of metals, and consequently in the use of more sophisticated tools. Unlike simple societies, advanced ones use metal hoes, axes, knives, and weapons, thus greatly increasing their efficiency in many areas. Second, they have much more varied diets made possible by plants which have been imported from other parts of the world. This diversity is important because it permits greater use of the land, since various plants require different soils and rainfall, and because the same land can be used over again for crops which grow during different seasons. Finally, advanced horticultural societies use irrigation, terracing, and fertilization. All this means greatly increased and improved food production, and consequently vast changes in human society.

Populations increase greatly; societies spread over wider territories; population density grows higher. These changes lead to the possibility of empire-building. An economic surplus makes sustained warfare feasible because military and political groups can be maintained. Many advanced horticultural societies, such as the Incas of Peru, the Yoruba of Nigeria, and the Chibcha of Colombia, achieved huge populations and controlled enormous territories because they were able to support large armies for long periods of time. Many were states which covered thousands of square miles and which had strong central governments. Most were able to absorb and assimilate the ethnic populations they conquered without the loss of these groups' identities.

With all these improvements, then, advanced horticultural societies tend to be relatively permanent. Better use of land and the development of empires make it unnecessary for such communities to change location. There is enough variation in the soil and in members' talents to permit them to stay in one place.

Not only do the advanced societies have greater varieties of foods and peoples, they also have greater occupational specialization, of which the most significant category is political power and the growth of numerous governmental official positions. Generally, within the ruling class there are between three and five levels in the hierarchy, from the king at the top to the village headsman. Each of these has his own "cabinet" of specialists, including priests, soldiers, tax collectors, entertainers, artisans, and others. Occupational specialization is linked with trade. Monetary systems become essential, although they still tend to be very primitive. Unlike the haphazard exchange arrangements in the societies discussed earlier, markets appear in specific locations and are open on particular days during designated hours. But trade is restricted because of lack of transportation. Wheel, draft, and pack animals are either unknown or not used. As a result goods are transported by human beings on their heads and backs, or by canoe when navigable rivers are present.

The most socially significant difference between simple and advanced horticultural societies is the development of real social inequality. The king often achieves an almost god-like status. Melville Herskovits (1938) reports that in Dahomey, for example, anyone approaching the king had to bare his shoulders, head, and feet and no one was permitted to sit, except on the ground, in his presence. In theory, at least, he owned all the land in the kingdom, and estimates are that there were as many as 2000 females in his harem (Herskovits, 1938:45). Furthermore, his approval was required for all public appointments; he had control over all religious groups; and he could order the death of any citizen on the slightest provocation. Even members of his own family could be put to death or enslaved at his command. Obviously, despotism was the order of the day in advanced horticultural societies.

At the opposite end of the stratification continuum in these societies were the slaves, who unlike slaves in simple horticultural societies who could become integrated into the group, had absolutely no legal rights and who, indeed, were often offered as human sacrifices in religious ceremonies. Most slaves worked on the king's farms under almost subhuman conditions.

In short, Lenski claims that once there is an economic surplus and occupational specialization, the resulting development of a strong, central government with a semidivine king with unlimited power leads to marked social inequality, with the king and his family and favorites in positions of control. Thus, "the power, privilege, and prestige of individuals and families is primarily a function of their relationship to the state" (Lenski, 1966:160).

Agrarian Societies

Agrarian societies represent even greater development than the advanced horticultural societies. The differences can once more be traced to technological improvement. New tools, new skills, new varieties of food, the domestication of animals, the use of metals, and power other than human energy are all important refinements. The overall effect of uncountable inventions and discoveries is a huge increase in the economic surplus, an equally large decrease in the amount of time spent in survival tasks, and a polarization of classes.

Perhaps the most significant advancement in agrarian societies is in military technology, in such things as fortification, improved weaponry, chariot and cavalry warfare, and protective armor. These developments mean that each man can no longer provide himself with weapons as effective as those possessed by others, so that power accrues to those who can amass manpower and wealth enough to build and operate relatively complex devices. Thus, political power becomes even more efficient, better organized, and more permanent than it had been in advanced horticultural societies.

An additional notable feature of agrarian society is the growth of urban areas, some with populations as large as several hundred thousand. Although urban dwellers never constituted more than 10 percent of the total population, Gideon Sjoberg (1960) claims that they dominated agrarian society culturally, economically, politically, and religiously because the urbanites controlled the power and the wealth. Once again a small minority acquires power over a huge majority.

The urban members of agrarian societies engaged in a wide variety of occupations. For example, Clough and Cole (1941:25) reported that the tax rolls in Paris in 1313 listed 157 different crafts within the textile industry alone. There were wool, flax, and hemp merchants, wool combers, silk combers, spinners, weavers, dyers, fullers, calenderers, shearmen, sellers, tailors, headdress makers, and secondhand clothes dealers, to mention only a few. Such workers founded guilds to consolidate their power and to protect their industries by controlling the number of workers, their salaries, the prices charged, and even by regulating their own standards of acceptability. Thus in the agrarian society, a distinct merchant class emerged for the first time. While money had been used in a modest sense in advanced horticultural society, it now became salient as a means of increasing and facilitating long-distance trade and as an additional means of control over the peasant class.

The development of written language was also instrumental in polarizing the classes. Literacy was, of course, limited to the ruling class, and served as a dividing line between the "intellectual" powerful few and the "superstitious and ignorant" masses. Literacy also intensified class consciousness by making people aware of the difference between those who "had and could" and those who "did not have and could not." This class division based on literacy can be seen even today in the kingdom of Nepal, where only 15 percent of the population can read and write, and where the literate minority displays great disdain and contempt for the illiterate majority.

The strengthening of national religions also served to augment the power of the few. While in the more primitive societies there was generally religious homogeneity or, in some cases, mutual tolerance and respect for the varied local sects, priests and rulers in agrarian society implicitly agreed to use religion to serve the state and to increase their own personal wealth and prestige by elevating the king to a divinity. Moreover, because of a growing ethnic class and urban-rural pluralism, tensions and hostility between different religious groups added to the divisiveness of the society.

To summarize, the agrarian society is characterized by decided social inequality—political power being the primary source. When the economic surplus grows large, in concert with expanding occupational specialization and advances in military technology, control of the state is the most direct avenue to power and privilege. According to Lenski, "The governing classes of agrarian societies [generally about two percent of the population] probably received at least a quarter of the national income of most agrarian states, and the governing class and the ruler together usually received not less than half" (1966:228).

Thus, landownership and political power grew together in agrarian society. One may be converted into the other. This is far less likely to obtain in capitalistic society, in which a person may be very wealthy and yet exercise no political power. "Landownership, when divorced from public office, was valued chiefly as a means to obtain prestige and economic security, while public office was used primarily for political and economic advancement" (Lenski, 1966:229). Thus, wealth and political power were in a reciprocal relationship in agrarian society.

There were, according to Lenski, seven classes below the ruling class in agrarian societies. One of these he terms the retainer class (about 5 percent of the population), which consisted of government officials, soldiers, and household servants, all of whom were completely and directly dependent upon the ruling elite. In return for faithful service, retainers were considered to be above the common people in status, and were allowed, in small measure, to share in the economic surplus. The retainer class was important because its members added numerically to the strength of the ruling class, and because they served as mediators between the elite and the commoners, thus diffusing the hostility of the populace which otherwise would have accrued to the rulers. Nevertheless, although as a collectivity retainers were important to the survival of an exploitative distributive system, individually they were highly expendable, making them a competitive, suspicious, noncohesive group.

The merchant class, which we mentioned briefly earlier, was in a much stronger position. Although the rulers constantly tried to gain complete control over any economic surplus, the merchants in an agrarian society always managed to frustrate such efforts by acquiring a major portion of available wealth and occasionally a degree of political power. One reason for their success was that, unlike the retainer class, the merchants, because they were a cohesive group, were able to wrest a certain amount of independence from the rulers. Since trade requires mobility, the elite could not maintain surveillance over the traders as they moved about. Furthermore, although they possessed wealth which the rulers may have coveted, traders, unlike the retainers, did not constitute a political threat because they usually were not directly involved in the politics of the society. Finally, the elite stood to gain from the activities of the merchants because profits could be legitimately taxed, and because the merchants brought them otherwise unobtainable goods. A ruling class always requires those special commodities that set them apart from the masses of people. In short, the elite and the merchants depended upon each other, and thus the merchants were permitted into the ranks of the privileged, although there was always some hostility between the two groups.

The priestly class was also among the privileged. Generally the upper segment of this class was recruited from the elite and lived in a fashion similar to it; the lower segment, recruited from among the common people, served the common people and lived among them. Those in the upper echelon were deeply involved in the political life of the society. As mentioned briefly before, the needs of the governing class coincided with those of the priests. The elite required the blessing of the priests to legitimate its rule; the priests were dependent upon the elite for wealth and prestige. In its own way, then, much like the retainer and merchant classes, the priestly class functioned to assist the governing class in its exploitation of the commoners.

The majority of the population of any agrarian society is the peasant class. Upon these people lay the real burden of supporting the society, and in return they received little but misery. They generally lived in tiny, inadequate, crude huts; their diet was unvaryingly dull and insufficient; and they worked long and thankless hours on the farms of the rich. In addition, they were totally at the mercy of the ruling classes. They could be beaten, sold into slavery, their families could be separated; in short, they were treated no better than beasts. Most stoically accepted this lowly status, mollified by religion and ignorance. Some tried to change things by evading tax collectors, avoiding work, or even running away. Those who were somewhat more adventurous or enlightened tried to organize outright rebellion. Most failed completely; others were successful only insofar as they succeeded in having the members of one ruling class replaced by members of another.

There was also a small class of artisans, who generally came from the peasant class and who, for the most part, were just as deprived economically and socially. Most artisans worked for the merchants, either as producers or as peddlers. Like the peasants, some tried to rebel in various ways, for the most part unsuccessfully.

The lowest two groups were the unclean classes and the expendables. The best-known among the unclean classes is the untouchable Hindu caste of India. Generally, such people were born into these castes and engaged in what were considered loathsome occupations, such as cleaning the streets in cities in which sewage systems were nonexistent, or burying dead animals. The expendables were the absolute dregs of the agrarian society—beggars, outlaws, and criminals—who lived entirely by their wits, surviving on what they could steal or beg.

Agrarian society, then, is the kind of society in which a tiny minority dominates, controls, and exploits a huge, helpless majority. Lenski maintains that only one thing can be said in defense of the despots—they maintained law and order. Anarchy in an agrarian society would have been intolerable, and the ruling elite at least prevented that.

Industrial Societies

Lenski considers that what can be called "industrial societies" have come into existence during the last two centuries. The same type of advances that we have noted in other kinds of societies, such as improved tools and weapons and newer uses of metals, are still being made. In addition, human beings now use electrical and mechanical energy, while in the past men and animals did most of the physical work. For example, as late as 1850, although the industrial age was well underway, 93 percent of the energy expended in work was done by men, animals, wind, water, and wood; only 7 percent was performed by newer energy powers (coal) (Dewhurst et al, 1955:905-906). In contrast, by 1950,

95.4 percent of physical work was carried out by fossil fuels and hydroelectric power. Today, of course, atomic and solar energies are being used more and more widely. Industrial societies, then, are still in transition. There will continue to be technological advances in the production of goods and services that cannot even be envisioned.

Such technological advances cannot help but change almost all other aspects of life. Economic self-sufficiency is a thing of the past and relationships of exchange are unavoidable. While in Durkheim's mechanical society one person could do the work of all other people, that is, grow food, weave cloth, raise animals, and thus be independent, in organic society, specialization increases the individual's dependence on other individuals. The farmer cannot do the work of the doctor; nor can the lawyer create an article of clothing. People need each other in order to survive. Thus cooperation and a complex monetary system become indispensable in industrial society.

Industrialization, then, has led to human mutual dependence, of both individuals and communities and even of nations; to the rising importance of money; to an increase in the size of communities, especially urban types; and to lowered birth and death rates because of improved technology in birth control and medical care.

Political power also has changed. Monarchies, especially in the sense of divine and absolute right, have almost disappeared and various types of republican governments have replaced them. This means the diffusion of political power. At the same time it means, especially in socialist countries, the increased concentration of power in the hands of the governing many, and not in the hands of few, or one.

Furthermore, in advanced industrial societies, literacy is widespread, mostly because there is a tremendous need for trained, skilled workers. A by-product of extended education, of course, is that it keeps young adults out of the job market and allows the middle-aged adult to monopolize it. Moreover, extended education, by isolating youth from the mainstream of the society for longer periods of time has helped to create a youth subculture to the point where the cleavage between those under 30 and those over 30 in our society is as deep as the old separation between the urban and rural residents in agrarian society.

This divisiveness between generations is one of many factors contributing to the emergence of a new kind of family structure.

Many of the family's former functions and obligations (Duberman, 1974:18–22), such as care of the aged, the provision of education, recreation, and religious training, have passed out of the family and into other institutions. Families are getting smaller in size as old people are sent to special "homes" and the number of children produced is limited. In addition, technology and the ideology of the feminist movement have provided new freedoms for women. In short, family functions are changing. They are now much less instrumental and much more expressive. Young people do not depend on their fathers for occupational placement, on their mothers for educational and religious training, or on their siblings for recreation and companionship. Women are not as dependent financially on their husbands. Men have fewer legal responsibilities for both their children and their wives. All institutions, including the family, are becoming more impersonal and heterogeneous.

Although on a superficial level one could predict that the hugely increased productivity and the widened control of the state would lead to even greater inequality than we described earlier, the reverse now seems to be true. "Inequalities in power and privilege seem usually less pronounced in mature industrial societies than in agrarian. In short, the appearance of mature, industrial societies marks the first significant reversal in the age-old revolutionary trend toward ever increasing inequality" (Lenski, 1966:308).

A comparison of the political systems of the agrarian and industrial societies illustrates this important trend. In agrarian society political power was held by one ruler, or one ruler and those few who were close to him. The masses of peasants had absolutely no power. In contrast, the majority of people in industrial society have two important political rights: (1) the right to vote; and (2) the right to organize in support of their particular interests. Naturally, this does not mean that members of industrial societies enjoy complete equality; but it does mean that there is a great reduction in political control by a few people and a diffusion of political inequality.

In addition, in industrial societies there is a decline in financial inequality. We noted earlier that approximately one-half of an agrarian society's wealth belonged to one or two percent of the population. It can hardly be claimed that there is an equalization of income in the United States today, or that there is even a decrease in the differences in income between certain classes. In 1962 the families in the top 5 percent of the population economically held 18 percent of the nation's total wealth (Miller, 1972:378). However, although the upper classes clearly are still receiving a large slice of the pie in industrial societies, the ordinary person has a much higher income than in agrarian societies, partly because there is greater equality and partly because there is general greater productivity.

Lenski attributes this change in the distributive system to a number of factors. One is that in industrial society the complexities of the culture make it impossible for one individual or a small group to understand or control all facets of it. Thus many people must have authority and power because they must each be "experts" in their areas of skill and responsibility. Second, a vastly increased surplus means that the rulers can only gain the necessary cooperation of the masses by granting concessions. Thus concessions are made and cooperation is sought to avoid such disruptions as labor strikes and slowdowns. Third, Lenski notes that after a great deal of money has been acquired, people turn to other rewards for satisfaction, such as prestige and honor. So that in industrial society "after a certain level of wealth has been attained . . . [people seek] to win for themselves a greater measure of respect and affection" (1966:315).

Fourth, the decreasing birth rates and rising educational levels reduce pressures to compete for the same jobs. With enormous specialization, there is little interchangeability of jobs, except at the least skilled levels, and a high demand for skilled technical people. These two factors together mean that the "governing elite," if it can still be called that, can no longer drive wages down and prices up at will.

In spite of the trend toward egalitarianism, those with political power still control and determine much of the direction and goals of the economic institutions, although not to the same degree as in the agrarian societies. This means, then, that political power is still the key to other kinds of power. "Where an individual stands with respect to [political] resources can have a decisive influence on his chances of obtaining many of the things he desires" (Lenski, 1966:327). True, those with political power can no longer use this power directly to the extent that it had been used before; nevertheless, it is still an instrument for obtaining other kinds of rewards such as honor, prestige, and wealth. However, the level of inequality in agrarian societies, although it was higher than in any earlier type, is lower than it is in modern industrial society.

Nevertheless, in all types of societies, from the primitive hunting and gathering tribes to the highly industrialized democratic or communistic nations, inequality is unavoidable. True, total equality is unattainable, and to strive for it as a goal can only result in frustration and failure.

Bibliography

Barber, Bernard, *Social Stratification*. New York: Harcourt, Brace, 1957.

Bendix, Reinhard, and Lipset, Seymour Martin, eds., *Class, Status, and Power*. Glencoe, Ill.: Free Press, 1953.

Clough, S.B., and Cole, C.W., *Economic History of Europe*. Boston: Heath, 1941.

Cuber, John F., and Kenkel, William F., *Social Stratification in the United States*. New York: Appleton-Century-Crofts, 1954.

Dewhurst, J. Frederic, *et al.*, *America's Needs and Resources*. New York: Twentieth Century Fund, 1955.

Dollard, John, *Caste and Class in a Southern Town*. New Haven: Yale University Press, 1937.

Duberman, Lucile, *Marriage and Its Alternatives*. New York: Praeger, 1974.

Gordon, Milton M., *Social Class in American Sociology*. New York: McGraw-Hill, 1958.

Heller, Celia S., ed., *Structured Social Inequality*. New York: Macmillan, 1969.

Herskovits, Melville, *Dahomey: An Ancient West African Kingdom*. Locust Valley, N.Y.: Augustin, 1938.

Kahl, Joseph A., *The American Class Structure*. New York: Holt, Rinehart and Winston, 1957.

Lenski, Gerhard E., *Power and Privilege*. New York: McGraw-Hill, 1966.

Lundberg, G.S., *et al.*, *Trends in American Sociology*. New York: Harper & Row, Harpers, 1929.

Lynd, Robert L. and Lynd, Helen Merrell, *Middletown*. New York: Harcourt, Brace, 1929.

——, *Middletown in Transition*. New York: Harcourt, Brace, 1937.

Miller, Herman P., "Recent Trends in Family Income." *In* Thielbar, G.W., and Feldman, Saul D., eds., *Issues in Social Inequality*. Boston: Little, Brown, 1972.

Page, Charles H., *Class and American Sociology: From Ward to Ross*. New York: Dial Press, 1940.

Radcliffe-Browne, A.R., *The Andaman Islanders*. New York: Free Press, 1948.

Reissman, Leonard. *Inequality in American Society*. Glenview, Ill.: Scott, Foresman, 1973.

St. Augustine, *The City of God*. Translated by Marcus Dods. New York: Modern Library, 1950.

Sjoberg, Gideon, *The Preindustrial City*. New York: Free Press, 1960.

Steward, Julian, and Faron, Louis, *Native Peoples of South America*. New York: McGraw Hill, 1959.

Thielbar, Gerald W. and Feldman, Saul D., eds., *Issues in Social Inequality*. Boston: Little, Brown, 1972.

Tumin, Melvin M., *Social Stratification*. Englewood Cliffs, N.J.: Prentice-Hall, 1967.

chapter 2

The
Classical Theorists

Introduction

In the first chapter it was pointed out that there are no known societies which do not have some recognized method of ranking their members, or their positions in the group, or both. People are aware that they are unequal. Some have more money, some have more prestige, some have more power. This book is concerned with systems of inequality, and in order to explore them we first must understand the work of three major theorists: Karl Marx, Max Weber and Vilfredo Pareto.

Karl Marx

Marx's Definition of Social Class

Karl Marx was the first to formulate a systematic theory of social class. As mentioned earlier, the definition of social class, as we will show, is still in dispute today. Marx himself was not very clear in his definition, but he identified three major distinct classes, all related to sources of income: (1) the owners of capital, whose source of income is profit; (2) the landowners, whose source of income is ground rent; and (3) the laborers, whose source of income is wages. As capitalism grows, however, landowners become less important until finally, in Marxist philosophy, there are really only two great classes: the capitalists, who own the means of production and to whom surplus value accrues, and the workers, who can depend only on their own labor for income, and who do not have access to the surplus. Marx was also aware of other social groups—artisans, merchants, intellectuals, and small landowners but only two great classes are importantly involved in the social order. Marx predicted, however, that eventually, when the revolution or the overthrow of one of these classes by the other began, the lesser classes would be forced to choose between the capitalists and the workers.

For Marx, then, a social class is a group of people which has a permanent relationship to the means of production. However, sharing the same economic status and the same style of life is not sufficient to mold a group of people into a social class. There must also be a sense of "we-ness," of unity, a psychological feeling of belonging together which will promote the desire for community and the knowledge of common interests. This means that to really constitute a class, an aggregate of people within the same economic stratum who recognize their sameness of condition and interest must feel themselves as separate from other classes, even as hostile to them. In his discussion of Marx's notion of class, Raymond Aron states:

But class, in the true sense of the word, is not to be confused with any ordinary social group. Social class, in the true sense of the word, implies, beyond a community of existence, the consciousness of this community and the desire for common action with a view to a certain organization of the collectivity. And on this level, it is clear that in Marx' eyes there are in effect only two great classes, because there are, in capitalist society, only two groups which have truly contradictory images of what society should be and have also a definite political and historical purpose. These two groups are the wage earners and the capitalists (1968:206).

Marxist Sociology

Marxian thought derives from three sources: German philosophy, English economics, and French history. In the tradition of German philosophy, Marx believed in social evolution, in the notion that social systems are successive, and that there are stages in the "life" of any society. The final and perfect stage is socialism. Marx also adopted many of the accepted theories of the nineteenth century English economists, particularly the law of the falling rate of profit and the labor theory of value.[1] Finally, he used the French historians' idea of the class struggle, modifying it by suggesting that the division of societies into classes is not a universal necessity and therefore can and will disappear (Aron, 1968:178-179). Capitalism is an impediment to natural evolution and revolution will be necessary to remove it so nature can prevail.

Thus, Marxist sociology is inclusive, in the sense that it attempts to comprehend the totality of social life, rather than just one specific aspect of it. It is also an historical sociology insofar as it predicts the future of society based on its present state. In addition, Marxist sociology is deterministic. Its predictions are grounded in the notion that the future is determined by a society's economic mode of organization (the means of production). Finally, Marx was progressive and evolutionary, contending that each social regime is superior to its predecessors and that the best, the classless society, is yet to come.

Karl Marx, philosopher, historian, economist, and sociologist, offered a conception of social development which even today is debated and argued. Few sociologists now believe that there will be a world-wide class war; and yet at a recent meeting of the American Sociological Association in Montreal, 7 sessions out of 139 were devoted to papers on Marxian sociology. For example, one paper presented by Herman Schmid was entitled, "Is There a World Society?—A Marxist Approach to the Conceptualization of International Relations," and another by Martha Giminez examined "Structural Marxism and Hegelian Marxism as Theoretical and

---

1. The law of the falling rate of profit means that with the passage of time and the growth of the economy, the rate of profit on capital investment tends to diminish as capitalists use up the most profitable opportunities and are forced to turn to less profitable ones, and so on.

   The labor theory of value holds that the value of goods and services which are produced is a function of the amount of labor employed in the production process.

Political Practices." Thus Marx's theory of economic determinism is still applied to present-day questions by some prominent social scientists.

Marx's work, because it was so voluminous and eclectic, is also somewhat contradictory and sometimes his meanings are more implicit than explicit. His writings can be divided into two distinct periods. The earlier period, between 1841 and 1848, includes the *Introduction to the Critique of Hegel's Philosophy of Law*, *The Jewish Question*, *The Holy Family*, *Economic and Philosophic Manuscripts of 1844*, and most important of all, *The German Ideology*. The second period comprises his most valuable writings, *A Contribution to the Critique of Political Economy*, *The Communist Manifesto*, and *Capital*, all of which contain the major aspects of his thought. The first volume of this latter period was published by Marx in 1875; the second and third volumes were published posthumously by his associate, Friedrich Engels, in 1885 and 1894.

Capitalism

Marxism is mostly an analysis and interpretation of capitalism. Marx attempted to show that the inevitable conflict between management and labor (or in Marxist terms, between the bourgeoisie and the proletariat) is the hallmark of modern capitalist societies—the essential quality of modern life. Capitalism is structured on the antagonism between the two groups. This antagonism led Marx to predict that inevitably capitalism could not survive because the contending segments of society *must* eventually engage in a class struggle which will destroy the system.

The Communist Manifesto, written with Friedrich Engels in 1848, was primarily a propaganda pamphlet. Its central theme was that the history of people is a history of class struggle between free people and slaves, lords and serfs, patricians and plebians. The oppressors and the oppressed have waged constant warfare, sometimes covertly and sometimes overtly. This idea of class struggle was one of Marx's seminal contributions. In effect, *human history is characterized by antagonism between social classes which have a tendency to become more polarized over time.*

In the preface to *A Contribution to the Critique of Political Economy*, Marx described in detail this relationship between the oppressors and the oppressed as it appeared through the stages of human history. Each stage is differentiated in terms of its characteristic economic structure, or as Marx called it, its mode of production. There are four stages: the Asiatic, the ancient, the feudal, and the bourgeois.

The Asiatic stage is apparently not characteristic of Western civilizations. Under this mode of production, all workers are subordinate to the state. Lenski called such societies agrarian because the entire society is exploited by the governing elite. Marx did not address himself to this mode of production at any length, but it has become a matter of increasing interest because present-day Marxists fear that a full socialist revolution could result, not in the downfall of capitalism and the rise of the classless society, but in the Asiatic mode of production (Wittfoger, 1957; Lichtheim, 1963), with all persons becoming subordinate to the state.

The other three modes of production are clearly seen by Marx as stages in Western history. Each is defined by the relationship between workers and owners. The ancient mode of production is typified by the relations between slave and slave owner; the feudal is dominated by the relations between serf and lord; and bourgeois is characterized by the relations between those who earn wages working for the owners of the means of production and the owners of the means of production. All three stages represent exploitation of one group by another. All are antagonistic relationships. In each the rulers or exploiters are few in number while ruled or exploited are the great masses of people. Thus all societies throughout history contain social classes at war with each other, which are destined to destroy the prevailing mode of production.

Aron (1968:156–159) has summarized Marx's economic interpretation of history. First, human beings are born into social relations over which they have no control. In Emile Durkheim's language, the relationship in any type of society between a person and the mode of production is a social fact, existing in its own right, independent of an individual's will, and capable of exercising coercion over individuals (Durkheim, 1968:13).

Second, every society contains an economic base or infrastructure, and a superstructure. The infrastructure (or social reality) contains the relations of production. The superstructure (or consciousness) contains the ideologies and philosophies or the ethos of the society, determined by the infrastructure, which is controlled by the ruling class.

Marx stressed that it is not people's consciousness that determines social reality; instead, it is the social reality that determines consciousness. In other words, it is the social world in which people live that directs their ideals and belief systems. The problem, however, is that the superstructure is under the control of the ruling class, who decide the ideologies which will be "fed" to the proletariat. Before the wage earners can revolt against the rules, they must discard the false consciousness imposed on them by their oppressors. Once they recognize their own reality and their own exploited social position, they will develop class consciousness, which will make revolution possible.

Third, Marx believed that social change depends on contradictions between the forces of production and the relations of production. The forces of production are the society's ability to produce, governed by its scientific and technological knowledge and by the way labor is organized. The relations of production include the distribution of income and the possession of property.

The fourth element of Marx's interpretation of capitalism is a consequence of the third. The class struggle will arise out of the contradiction between the forces of production and the relations of production. That is, one class will want to hold on to the relations of production (property, income, capital, and so forth), thus retarding development of the forces of production while the other, more progressive class will want to change the relations of production, thus facilitating the growth and development of the forces of production. The bourgeoisie or the capitalists represent the old order, and the proletariat or the wage earners represent a new order.

Fifth, a situation of tension invariably develops from this class struggle which, according to Marx, can be relieved only by revolution. Marx does not envision a revolution as a political event, but rather as an historical necessity, occurring when economic conditions are ready for it, when an existing social organization has outlived its usefulness. In Marx's own words:

No social order ever disappears before all the productive forces
for which there is room in it have been developed: and the new
higher relations of production never appear before the material
conditions of their existence have matured in the womb of the
old society (1859).

To summarize our discussion thus far: Karl Marx's theory of social change and class conflict begins with the assumption that the basic economic organization of any given society determines the organization of the rest of that society and the life style of its members. Everything else—the class structure, the value system, the religious dogmas, and the cultural goals—is merely a reflection of the economic relations between owner and worker.

In the past every economic system has faced an inevitable class struggle because each system tends continually to polarize and alienate its two major classes—the oppressors and the oppressed. The capitalist system is no different from the ancient and the feudal systems. Eventually, the subjugated working class will throw off the ideologies which have been imposed on it in order to foster the workers' false consciousness, freeing it to develop its own class consciousness and to overthrow the dominant class. Following this, for a period the proletariat will rule, but very shortly there will be an entirely new type of society—classless and stateless—with collective ownership of the means of production (see Fig. 2-1). In Marx's theory, "The nonantagonistic, post-capitalist regime is not merely one social type among others; it is the goal, so to speak, of mankind's search for itself" (Aron, 1968:178).

These, then, are Marx's major notions about the class structure in capitalist societies, and the inevitable result that will come about as the classes become more hostile toward each other. The idea of a classless, stateless society is an appealing one. The notion

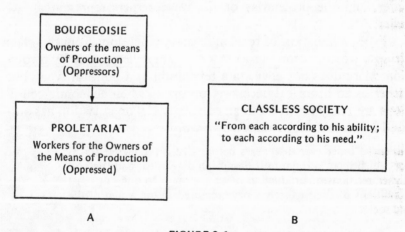

A   B

FIGURE 2-1

Graphic descriptions of Marx's theories of stratification: A, before the workers' revolution; and B, after the workers' revolution. *(The two-strata system of A was fashioned by Clayton A. Hartjen.)*

that each person should receive goods according to needs and should work according to ability is seductive. Yet most sociologists have already rejected Marx's utopianism, although, as mentioned earlier, it is still so attractive that social scientists continue to debate it and to attempt to utilize it. What, then, are the chief objections to Marx's interpretation of social class structure?

Critique of Marx

According to Aron, Marx's juxtaposition of the economic and political systems of society is the weakest part of his theory. It will be recalled that Marx predicted that after the revolution there would be a short period during which the proletariat would govern. Following this, since there will no longer be a need for it in a nonantagonistic society, the state will simply wither away. Aron writes that this is clearly impossible, since "in a modern society there are common functions of administration and authority which must be performed. No one can reasonably suppose that an industrial society as complex as our own can do without an administration, and an administration which is centralized in certain respects" (Aron, 1968:213).

Aron argues that Marx could not have failed to recognize that a modern society, especially with the kind of planned economy he envisioned, cannot exist without a state. Therefore, Aron believes that when Marx spoke of the disappearance of the state, he was speaking symbolically. What Marx really meant was that the *class character* of the state would disappear. When class hostility is no longer part of the social milieu, the administration or the state represents all of the members of the society and not just an elite ruling class. Thus, the state no longer dominates or exploits; there is truly "a government of the people, by the people, and for the people."

This seems a poor argument for Marx. If Aron cannot believe that Marx was unaware of the need for government in modern society, how can he think that Marx would suppose that a society with a large and diversified population could be in agreement on all issues? In his criticism of Marx, Aron seems to be kinder than the facts warrant.

Aron also points out that Marx was not justified when he reasoned that the replacement of private ownership of the means of production by public ownership would automatically guarantee the disappearance of class antagonisms. Decisions would still continue to be made by individuals in response to the needs of particular groups. "There is no preestablished harmony between the interests of different groups in a planned society" (1968:216). In short, the power of the state cannot diminish, even if the means of production are publicly owned, because without the state it is not possible to ensure that decisions will be made for the benefit of all, nor, for that matter, that all groups have collective interests. Perhaps, as Aron suggests, *class* antagonisms would disappear in a Marxist utopia, but surely other types of antagonisms would arise.

Marx presupposed that the political order would be reduced to the economic order. But some critics reply that this is not possible, since political problems remain constant, no matter what the economic system. People must decide who will govern, how the governors are to be chosen, how much power is to be permitted, how that power is to be exercised, what kind of relationship is to exist between the governing body and the governed. Aron succinctly summarizes this criticism of Marx's sociology:

> The mistake is to think that a certain way of organizing production and the distribution of resources automatically solves and does away with the problem of leadership. The myth of the state's disappearance is the myth that the state exists only to produce and distribute resources and that, once this problem of production and distribution of resources is solved, there is no longer any need for a state, i.e., for leadership (1968:217).

Aron addressed a second problem in the Marxist scheme of things. Marx discussed *ideology* as the false consciousness of a social class, which in turn was reflected in a false concept of its relation to the general society. These ideologies derive from the superstructure, which is controlled by the bourgeosie, and are "delivered" to the proletariat as divine truth. In order to escape its bonds, the proletariat must rid itself of false consciousness. Thus, false consciousness is related by Marx to class consciousness and, according to Aron, this raises two problems (1968:218).

First, if every class has a particularistic way of relating to the world, how does one ever discover which is the true way? Marx would have it that only the proletariat can learn the truth about the state of society. Why only this class? Actually, the "truth" is forever open to debate. Capitalist "truth" is no more or less suspect than proletariat "truth." Aron claims that all ideologies are "equally true, equally partial and partisan, prejudiced, and therefore illusory" (1968:219).

T. B. Bottomore (1966) is another thoughtful critic of Marxism. Bottomore concedes that, like most social scientists, Marx was a product of his own particular time and place—nineteenth-century England. At that time England was the most advanced industrial society in the world, and the situation which Marx observed certainly appeared to confirm his thesis that industrial development clearly tends to divide society into two socially segregated classes: a small class of wealthy capitalists and a large mass of propertyless wage earners. The middle classes of independent merchants, professional men, and small landowners seemed to be disappearing into factories and bureaucracies. Furthermore, during this same period in English history, the labor movement, the trade unions, and socialist politics all were developing rapidly, apparently supporting the Marxist notion that the workers were acquiring class consciousness and attempting to organize in order to gain political power.

Nevertheless, Bottomore claims that Marx's theories contain many indefensible errors, which he groups roughly into three areas. First, Marx assigned too much significance to social class and social class conflict in his conception of social change. In so doing he was prone to ignore other equally important social relationships. He did not take into account, for example, the growing nationalism and the conflicts between nations, which would be likely to have the effect of reducing any international affiliation of workers. Bottomore contends that class antagonisms were drastically reduced during World War I as individuals supported their nations, not their classes. Thus, what actually occurred during and after World War I was a strengthening of *national* bonds rather than of *class* bonds.

A second criticism is that although Marx's theory is reasonably sound when applied to modern capitalist societies, it fails to explain other types of social stratification systems. One reason for this problem is the different ways in which Marx himself used the term *class*. In *The Communitst Manifesto*, class refers to two major social groups—rulers and ruled—which are in conflict. In *The German Ideology*, Marx makes a more careful distinction between classes and estates,[2] claiming that true social classes can

2. Estate generally is defined as a social stratum which is less closed than a caste and less open than a social class. Although the rights and obligations of an individual are made mandatory by law, based on inheritance, there is some possibility of upward mobility. However, much of this mobility is within, not between estates, since each estate contains a wide diversity of occupations and socioeconomic statuses.

arise only under capitalism. Since he generally used the term social class in the latter context, he did not really confront the problem of using his theory to explain social inequalities in caste systems, estate systems, Asiatic or feudal systems. However, Bottomore does not hold Marx responsible for this problem. Marx did try to test his theory against what he considered the most important stratification system, the kind brought about by capitalism. Instead, Bottomore feels Marx's followers should have tested the theory under political and economic conditions other than capitalism before they so completely accepted his theories.

The third type of criticism is more serious and of greater concern to most sociologists. It centers around Marx's contention that the chasm between the proletariat and the bourgeoisie would continually widen as the conditions of their lives became more disparate, as the middle classes disappeared, and as the proletariat developed class consciousness. This antagonism would erupt finally in a revolution that would overthrow the bourgeoisie.

Bottomore claims that changes in modern social structure have invalidated Marx's predictions. The widening of the gulf between the two major classes has not occurred because there has been a general rise in everyone's standard of living resulting from the high productivity of modern industry. It follows that the working class has developed new aspirations and social attitudes which are not receptive to revolution. Furthermore, Bottomore asserts that the distribution of income has changed so that now the working class is receiving a larger share of the economic pie.[3] Finally, revolution has not occurred and will not occur because of expanded social services, greater employment security, and increased employment benefits. In short, Bottomore argues that the worker in the twentieth century is not alienated from either the work or the world.

Another of Bottomore's arguments is that Marx was wrong when he predicted that the middle class would disappear because its then relatively few members would join one or the other of the two great classes. Instead, there has been tremendous growth in the middle classes in very complicated ways (see Chapter 3). Thus, capitalism has not followed Marx's prediction that a more simplified stratification system of two classes would arise through the growth of technology. Instead, a much more complex and sophisticated system has evolved. Furthermore, these groups are coopera-

3. Many sociologists disagree with this contention, as we shall see in Chapter 3.

tive, conciliatory, and imitative, rather than being antagonistic and hostile toward each other. In short, Bottomore argues that the American stratification system is not dichotomized, but is on a continuum without sharp boundaries. Classes are not clearly defined nor discernible but blurred, thus diminishing class consciousness. The differences between them are based not so much on income and property as Marx expected, but rather on talent, education, and technical ability.

Bottomore contends also that the bourgeoisie is no longer the closed, cohesive group that Marx thought it to be. Diminishing property ownership and the breakup of enormous fortunes, increased social mobility, and the need in the business and professional sectors for real ability rather than for social status have all changed the composition, structure, and stability of the upper classes. Because of this loss of cohesion, because of the complexity of modern technological society with its demand for trained workers and managers, and because of the plurality of interest groups, the bourgeoisie can no longer be regarded as a ruling class.

These changes in the bourgeoisie have helped to invalidate Marxist theory; but so have changes in the proletariat. Marx predicted that differentials in skills and wages would be reduced as technology became more widespread, leading the working class to become more homogeneous, united, and revolutionary. The exact opposite has occurred. Occupations and levels of skills have become more diversified; there are fewer working-class people because of the growth of the middle classes; and there is greater social and geographic mobility which reduces the probability of worker solidarity.

Other writers have voiced similar criticisms of Marx. In general, five major arguments have been directed against Marx's ideas. Briefly summarized, they are:

1. Societies are not simply reflections of economic systems.
2. There are interest groups in societies that are unrelated to social classes.
3. Those who possess power in a capitalistic society are not always those with the highest income or the owners of the most property.
4. Conflict in a large modern society is rarely bipolarized.
5. Social conflict does not always lead to social change.

Nevertheless, Marxists continue to flourish and to follow and try to apply his theories. However, during the twentieth century Marxism has undergone three major crises.

Crises of Marxism

The first crisis was "revisionism," which occurred at the end of the last century and lasted into the beginning of the present one. A group of German Marxists, led by Eduard Bernstein, believed class antagonisms were not increasing in capitalist societies as predicted, and therefore the followers of Marx should revise their plans for the revolution. The revisionists were defeated by the orthodox Marxists of the Second International, led by Karl Kautsky.

The second crisis was the rise of Bolshevism. Led by Lenin, a group which considered itself Marxist won political control in Russia in 1917, and declared that it represented the victory of the proletariat. A dispute followed over the question of whether Soviet power was a dictatorship *over* the proletariat or *by* the proletariat. Kautsky maintained that since Russia was a nonindustrialized country with a small working class, the Bolshevik revolution was not a proletariat victory at all. The opposition of these two views led to the development of two distinct schools of Marxism. The Leninist school asserts that the revolution of 1917 in Russia was the fulfillment of Marx's prophecy; the second school believes that the prophecy remains unfulfilled because, although Russia has economic planning and some collective ownership of property, political democracy is absent.

The world is still in the midst of the third crisis, which centers on the question of whether true socialism as Marx envisioned it is represented by the Bolshevik version, the Western version as practiced in Sweden, or by something entirely different.

The Soviet version is that of a socialist society with central planning under the control of the almost absolute power of the state. The Swedish version also is a socialist society, but is characterized by a mixture of public and private ownership of the means of production, and great equalization of resources and income. Thus, in Sweden there is some central planning and some collective ownership, but socialism is diluted by the presence of such democratic institutions as several political parties, freedom of speech, and free elections. Aron refers to the first as "Sovietized socialism" and to the second as "Bourgeoisified socialism" (1968:223). Each group contends that it is the true Marxist.

However, there is a third group that rejects both of these versions. It would like to see a society which would combine the total planning of the Soviet structure with the liberality of the Swedish structure. This kind of society is nonexistent in our present world, and seems more utopian than possible. Perhaps it will come into being some day, but at the moment it is merely an abstraction in the minds of philosophers.

Marx once wrote that "religion is the opiate of the people." Raymond Aron (1968) has paraphrased Marx in chiding those who persist in beating the dead horse of Marxism: "Marxism is the opiate of the intellectual." The economist Paul Samuelson (1973:865) went a step further with his assertion that "Marxism is the opiate of the Marxists!"

Max Weber

Although Karl Marx is discussed in most books on social stratification, it is usually because of the historical value of his ideas. His theory is too monolithic, too polemical, and too difficult to test to be really useful in studying the phenomenon of social inequality. But Max Weber's theory is taken much more seriously by American sociologists because it is considered viable and reasonable. Weber's theory is contained in one essay (Gerth and Mills, 1946:180–195), making it readily accessible, and it is narrower than Marx's, lending itself more easily to empirical research. Weber's work on social inequality began where Marx left off.

In place of a single dimension, Weber presented a multidimensional theory. In contrast to Marx, Weber argued that social inequality has three aspects: class, status, and power.[4]

The Definition of Social Class

Weber's conceptualization of class is similar to that of Marx in that he defines it as an economic interest group and as a function of the marketplace. However, whereas Marx related class to the modes of production, Weber is concerned with the distribution of power within a community. Weber speaks of a class when: "(1) a number of people have in common a specific causal component of their life chances, in so far as (2) this component is represented

4. In the original translation, the German word "Herreschaft" was translated as "power" to designate Weber's third dimension of social inequality. Others have translated it as "party." Most sociologists use the terms interchangeably, since an exact translation is not possible.

exclusively by economic interests in the possession of goods and opportunities for income, and (3) is represented under the conditions of the commodity or labor markets" (Gerth and Mills, 1946:181).

⨉ For Weber, then, a class consists of a group of people who stand in the same relationship to the economic opportunity structure in a given society, and who live under similar conditions which are determined by the amount and kind of economic power they possess. His basic definition does not differ from the Marxist conception. However, Weber did not conceive of classes as self-conscious groups, but merely as aggregates of people in similar economic positions.

⨉ Weber devised a typology of classes which included: (1) a property class, whose situation is based on differential property holdings; (2) an acquisition class, whose situation is determined by the opportunity for exploitation of services on the market; and (3) a social class, "composed of the plurality of class statuses between which an interchange of individuals on a personal basis or in the course of generations is readily possible and typically observable" (Weber, 1947:424).

⨉ He analyzed the first two classes, property and acquisition, on the basis of privilege, dividing them into the positively privileged property and acquisition classes and the negatively privileged property and acquisition classes. The positively privileged property class lives on income deriving from the ownership of property, and is able to monopolize the purchase and sale of consumer goods and the opportunity to accumulate capital and to be educated. The negatively privileged property class is composed of propertyless people—the poor, the uneducated, the debtors.

⨉ Weber uses the same method to describe the positively and negatively privileged acquisition classes. Those in the positively privileged group monopolize the management of productive enterprises, and are typically entrepreneurs, bankers, financiers, and industrialists. These people not only control management, but they also influence the economic policies of the government. The middle privileged acquisition class includes independent farmers and artisans, minor public and private officials, and professionals. The negatively privileged acquisition class is categorized as skilled, semiskilled, and unskilled workers.

⨉ Weber suggested that classes may, at certain times and under certain conditions, act together in their own interests. He termed one kind of class action "communal class action" because it arises out of a feeling of belonging together; the other kind he called "societal class action" because it is oriented toward a change in societal conditions. However, unlike Marx, Weber did not believe class action is a universal phenomenon; or even that it is likely to occur often.

χ According to Weber, then, classes are not necessarily self-aware entities but are only economic in nature, and they are unlikely to unite into action groups to fight for their interests. A class is merely a group of people who are in similar economic positions in the marketplace. They experience the same life changes to acquire the things that are valued by the society, and only under very unusual conditions are they likely to develop "class consciousness" and to act in unison. If and when this occurs, according to Weber the class then becomes a "community."

In contrast to classes, status groups are normally communities. They are, however, often of an amorphous kind. In contrast to the purely economically determined "class situation," we wish to designate as "status situation" every typical component of the life fate of men that is determined by a specific, positive or negative, social estimation of honor. . . . In content, status honor is normally expressed by the fact that above all else a specific style of life can be expected from all those who wish to belong to the circle (Gerth & Mills, 1946:186–187).

Weber's Definition of Status

To differentiate between class and status group, Weber writes: " . . . one might thus say that 'classes' are stratified according to their relations to the production and acquisition of goods; whereas 'status groups' are stratified according to the principles of their *consumption* of goods as represented by special 'styles of life'" (Gerth and Mills, 1946:193).

In other words, Weber distinguishes between class, which represents life chances in the marketplace and status, which represents styles of life. Each is a different way in which people can be unequal. For example, a person can be in a high class if he is a gangster with a high school education who makes $100,000 a year; but he will remain in a low-status group because the society does not approve of his way of life. On the other hand, one can be in a low class if one is a minister with a graduate degree, earning $10,000 a year, but be accorded a good deal of status and honor because society values this vocation. At the same time, however, class and status frequently overlap. For example, a doctor is in a high class because he or she has a high income, and is in a high-status group because society respects the occupation.

"An 'occupational group' is also a status group" (Gerth and Mills, 1946:193) because each type of occupation generally yields a similar income to the people within it, enabling them to maintain a certain life style. Interest in the same occupation leads to friendships and marriages between those engaged in it. Members tend to live near each other, wear clothes of similar quality, enjoy the same kinds of recreation, and share values and goals. Finally, the members may form virtually a closed circle, as in the case of very high status groups who restrict their membership to "their own kind." In contrast to a class, which is impersonal and which is based completely on ability and economic position, the status group is personal and considers some people in the society "better" than others.

Power or Parties

Weber places classes within the economic order of the society and status groups within the social order. Parties, however, "may represent interests determined through 'class situation' or 'status situation' and they may recruit their following respectively from one or the other. But they do not have to be either purely 'class' or purely 'status' parties. In most cases they are partly class parties and partly status parties" (Gerth and Mills, 1964:194). In any event, "their action is oriented toward the acquisition of social 'power,' that is to say, toward influencing a communal action" (Gerth and Mills, 1946:194). Thus, although parties fall within the political order, power can accrue from many avenues: money, influence, authority, pressure. Although Weber makes subtle and important distinctions between the three types of inequality, undoubtedly there exists, with imperfections, a correlation between class, status, and party.

The graphic description (Fig. 2-2) illustrates Weber's scheme and also reveals its inadequacy in dealing with the modern American stratification system. Some categories, such as I, II, VII, and VIII, are still clearly present in American society, and can be said to represent two distinct classes: the upper and the lower. Most of the other cells probably comprise various status communities within the middle strata. While examples of cells IV and VI can be suggested, cells III and V probably cannot be found in present-day America.

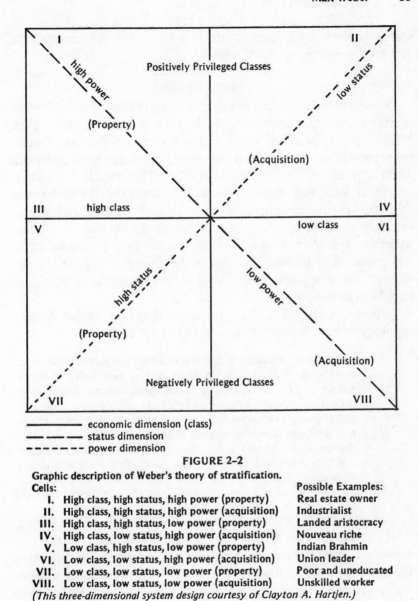

economic dimension (class)
—— —— —— status dimension
— — — — — power dimension

FIGURE 2-2

Graphic description of Weber's theory of stratification.

Cells:		Possible Examples:
I.	High class, high status, high power (property)	Real estate owner
II.	High class, high status, high power (acquisition)	Industrialist
III.	High class, high status, low power (property)	Landed aristocracy
IV.	High class, low status, high power (acquisition)	Nouveau riche
V.	Low class, high status, low power (property)	Indian Brahmin
VI.	Low class, low status, high power (acquisition)	Union leader
VII.	Low class, low status, low power (property)	Poor and uneducated
VIII.	Low class, low status, low power (acquisition)	Unskilled worker

(This three-dimensional system design courtesy of Clayton A. Hartjen.)

Thus, the complexity of Weber's model limits its use for studying stratification in modern industrial society. However, given the universality of his dimensions, the model may prove more viable for analysis when developing countries are included in the study. Nevertheless, the diagram does illustrate that stratum position is a function of all three dimensions: class, status, and power. Research is needed to demonstrate in which kinds of societies the various dimensions are most salient.

Critique of Weber

While there is no question that Weber's theory of stratification is widely discussed and accepted by most American sociologists, Weber has not been without his critics. One criticism has already been mentioned by pointing out that his scheme does not work when applied only to industrial society. The graphic description reveals at least two empty cells in this context (III and V), and some of the other examples given, such as in cells IV and VI, are certainly open to question. The chart illustrates that in modern society property ownership is no longer the clear avenue to status and power that it once was; nor is the ability to exploit the services of the marketplace as useful in acquiring status as it may have been in the past.

Oliver C. Cox makes this same point when he says that Weber's typology of class is nondynamic and too abstract, and

> . . . seems to be made to range over different social systems in an unsystematic way, with illustrations derived practically at convenience. . . . The amorphorous "social class" does not appear in his discussion of social action . . . [and] the concepts property class and acquisition class broken down according to positive and negative privilege cannot be applied in any single society. . . . Indeed the application of such concepts as "positive" and "negative privilege" to the whole status gradient in modern society is clearly misleading. There is no definitive description of social status in the social context of modern urban society as distinct from, say, social status in a feudal society (1960:227).

Celia Heller calls Weber to task for his discussion of the relationship between status stratification and economic stratification. On one hand, Weber declares that the two are empirically distinct; on the other, he says they are very often correlated. Heller states that Weber does not make explicit the fact that "one has to separate *analytically* the economic and status factors that *actually* are closely joined together, precisely in order to understand the nature of the connection in a given society at a given time" (1969:10).

In summary, although there are undoubtedly problems in Weber's theory of stratification, not the least of which may be one of language, it is a vast improvement over Marx's theory because it adds depth and subtlety to the unidimensionality of Marx's economic determinism. As Leonard Reissman noted, Weber's contribution "is broad, ranges far, and includes a variety of different manifestations of stratification under one roof" (1959:69).

Vilfredo Pareto

Power and Class Dichotomy

Unlike Weber and more in the tradition of Marx, Pareto's theory of the circulation of elites treats power in a dichotomous fashion. Pareto and Marx both see power as universal in societies, with two polar strata—the oppressed and the oppressors. But while Marx's concern is with the nonelites, Pareto's is with the elites. Since the term *elite* is used a great deal in the study of social inequality, it is important to understand Pareto's usage.

Pareto makes explicit the fact that there is what he calls "social heterogeneity" in all societies. That is, every society contains a huge mass of governed people and a small group of the governing elite. Marx considers this to be a fundamental but changeable distinction; Pareto considers it decisive and unalterable.

The Elite

Actually, Pareto defines an elite as "a class of the people who have the highest indices in their branch of activity" (Heller, 1969:35). These are the successful people in the society, business people, professionals, artists. However, such a definition is too broad and does not permit Pareto to deal with his real concern, which is power. Therefore, he divides the elite class into two classes: the nongoverning elite, or those who are successful in their occupations, and the governing elite, "comprising individuals who directly or indirectly play some considerable part in government" (Heller, 1969:35). Societies, then, have two strata: (1) a lower stratum, the nonelite, whose possible influence on government is not Pareto's concern; and (2) a higher stratum, the elite, which is divided into two groups: (a) a governing elite and (b) a nongoverning elite (Heller, 1969:35; see Fig. 2-3). Pareto's theory deals with the power relations between the nonelites and the governing elites, with the transference of power between the different kinds of governing elites, and to some extent, with the relations between the governing and the governed.

For Pareto, there are two kinds of *governing elites*—the *foxes* and the *lions*—who grasp and retain their power by using different methods. The foxes use stealth and cunning; the lions use brute strength and force. Yet history, according to Pareto, is "a grave-yard of aristocracies," because elites do not retain power for long, but rather the two groups alternate in a "circulation of elites." "The history of societies is the history of a succession of privileged minorities which appear, struggle, take power, enjoy that power, and fall into decadence, to be replaced by other minorities" (Aron, 1970:182). (See Fig. 2-3.)

Pareto explains why elites are unstable groups. One reason is that many of them are military elites and because they must con-stantly be in battle, their numbers are depleted rapidly by death. Second, the sons and grandsons of those in power often lose interest in retaining that power. They tire of remaining vigilant, lost interest in ruling, and turn instead to intellectual or artistic pursuits, abandoning their inherited power. Finally—and Pareto considers this the most important reason for the circulation of elites—sons frequently lack their fathers' natural endowments. Second and third generations often do not possess the vitality of the first generation, so that younger generations are less adept in the use of force or cunning than their ancestors. "The laws of heredity are such that it is never certain that the sons of those who were qualified to lead will themselves be so qualified" (Aron, 1970:183).

If this is so, how can stability in society be maintained? Pareto states that among the nonelites, there are always those few who are capable of joining the elites. The governing elite either can exterminate or exile them or permit them to enter the privileged class, thereby strengthening it. In this way, the elite in power may retain its authority for a longer period of time. Eventually, how-ever, it must become vulnerable and lose its control.

To review, Pareto's theory states that society contains only two groups: the ruled and the rulers. Thus all societies are unequal and will remain so. The governing elites obtain and maintain power using one of two methods: those whom Pareto calls the foxes use guile; those whom he calls the lions use brutality. Even-tually, for various reasons, the governing elite loses its power to another group and thus there is always a circulation of elites.

Critique of Pareto

Since Pareto is not taken as seriously by sociologists as he is by economists, there is little mention of him in the literature on

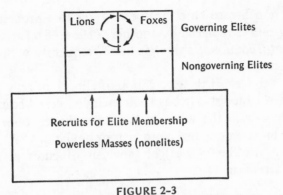

FIGURE 2-3
Graphic description of Pareto's theory of stratification. *(This diagram of a two-strata system with circulating elites courtesy of Clayton A. Hartjen.)*

stratification. One reason is that his writings are ponderous, ambiguous, difficult, and not quite within the orbit of sociological thought. American sociologists are disinclined to wade through his work.

A second reason for his exclusion is that for a while between World Wars I and II, Pareto was strongly suspected of being a fascist because he advocated an oligarchical system of government—masses governed by minority elites. Indeed, several Italian fascists did claim to be followers of Pareto and his argument that any attempt to abolish violence altogether can only lead to more violence was adopted by the Italian fascists, who distorted it to justify their assertion that governing elites had to be violent if they were to be effective.

Some sociologists find that Pareto's treatment of elites is too psychological (Aron, 1970:205). His descriptions of lions as violent and of foxes as cunning are psychological characterizations, antithetical to the sociological perspective. Furthermore, his treatment of the circulation of elites is an oversimplification. He may be correct in his premises that societies are inegalitarian and that elites rule by force or guile, but he ignores the deeper questions: "What is the relation between the privileged minority and the many? What are the principles of legitimacy invoked by the different elites? What are the methods by which elites stay in power? What possibilities exist for those who do not belong to the elite to gain admittance into it?" (Aron, 1970:206).

Bottomore criticizes Pareto on the grounds that he did not make explicit what he meant by the "circulation of elites." Does it refer to a process in which individuals move from elite to nonelite and from nonelite to elite; or does it refer to a process in which one elite group is replaced by another? (1964:48). Pareto uses the term in both contexts, although more frequently with the latter meaning.

Pareto's theory of the circulation of elites is of only peripheral interest to sociologists. It has been included here because it contrasts sharply with the work of Marx and Weber, both of whom are much more concerned with mass populations. While Pareto rarely mentions the masses, his analysis of elites in society is worthy of attention.

Bibliography

Aron, Raymond, *Main Currents in Sociological Thought*. Vol. I, translated by Richard Howard and Helen Weaver. Garden City, N.Y.: Doubleday Anchor Books, 1968.

——, *Main Currents in Sociological Thought*. Vol. II, translated by Richard Howard and Helen Weaver. Garden City, N.Y.: Doubleday, 1970.

Bottomore, T. B., *Classes in Modern Society*. New York: Vintage, 1966.

——, *Elites and Society*. Baltimore: Penguin, 1964.

Cox, Oliver C., "Max Weber on Social Stratification: A Critique." *American Sociological Review*, 15:2, 223-227, 1960.

Durkheim, Emil, *The Rules of Sociological Method*. New York: Free Press, 1938.

Gerth, H. H., and Mills, C. Wright, eds. and trans., *From Max Weber: Essays in Sociology*. New York: Oxford University Press, 1946.

Heller, Celia S., ed., *Structured Social Inequality*. New York: Macmillan, 1969.

Lichtheim, George, "Marx and the Asiatic Mode of Production." *Far Eastern Affairs*, 3. Carbondale, Ill., 1963.

Marx, Karl, *A Contribution to the Critique of Political Economy*. Translated by N. I. Stone. Chicago: Charles H. Kerr, 1859.

Pareto, Vilfredo, *The Mind and Society*. Translated by A. Bongiorno and A. Livingston. New York: Harcourt Brace, 1935.

Reissman, Leonard, *Class in American Society*. Glencoe, Ill.: Free Press, 1959.

Samuelson, Paul E., *Economics*. 9th ed., New York: McGraw-Hill, 1973.

Weber, Max, *The Theory of Social and Economic Organization*. Translated by A. M. Henderson and Talcott Parsons. New York: Free Press, 1947.

Wittfogel, Karl A., *Oriental Despotism: A Comparative Study of Total Power*. New Haven: Yale University Press, 1957.

chapter 3

Issues in
Social Inequality

Social Differentiation and Social Stratification

Perhaps the most basic problem facing students of inequality is the use of the terms *social differentiation* and *social stratification*.

Dennis Wrong equates social differentiation with a division of labor. "There is the existence of role differentiation, or division of labor itself, irrespective of whether or how the roles are ranked and their incumbents unequally rewarded" (1959:73).

Others argue that differentiation is more than a simple division of labor, and that it includes an evaluation and a ranking. Mayer put the matter succinctly:

> Social differentiation refers to the hierarchical ordering of social *position*. Evidently this is a universal characteristic of all societies since a division of specialized functions and roles is essential for their survival. Inherent in this functional differentiation of roles is a process of evaluation and ranking. Every society not only develops a division of labor, but also judges it and evaluates the importance of different functions and thereby ranks the positions in its social structure in importance (Mayer, reprinted in Stub, *op. cit.*, 1972:63).

Still other sociologists would claim that Mayer's definition of differentiation applies to stratification, and that evaluation and ranking are inherent in differentiation. Barber, for example, defines stratification as "a structure of regularized inequality in which men are ranked higher and lower according to the value accorded their various social roles and activities" (1957:7). These sociologists believe that as soon as one is faced with distinguishing between two or more people, positions, or objects, one will naturally evaluate and rank them.

However, social stratification is more than a division of labor and more than a ranking of different social positions. Focusing on *individuals* rather than on *position*, some theorists stress the important distinction between a system of differentiation and a system of stratification, in that the latter can be transmitted from generation to generation.

> Social stratification, on the other hand, refers to the fact that in many, though *not* in all, societies certain *collectivities of people* continue to occupy the same position through several generations. In other words, *if* societies are stratified there exist groupings of people, social strata, who manage to monopolize access to certain positions on a *hereditary*, *permanent* basis (Mayer, 1972:63; see also Buckley, 1958).

Stratification is thus a system based not only on a division of labor and on evaluating and ranking the statuses within the system, but also on family lineage and inheritance. Differentiation can develop without hierarchy; hierarchy cannot develop without differentiation. Differentiation is universal, whereas theoretically stratification may be entirely absent.

It seems that the most plausible distinction between the two concepts is that differentiation is simply a matter of a division of labor along any given criterion, while stratification is concerned with evaluating and ranking positions within the division of labor. It would seem to be going too far in today's rapidly changing society to say that class positions are fixed and continue for several generations. Often the first, second, and third generations of a family are in different strata of society. Power and privilege can be lost or gained. No family can be assured that it will continue at its present status level, especially with today's greatly increased educational and occupational opportunities. *Social differentiation* will be defined here as a universal process in which certain statuses and roles in society are observable and recognized. *Social stratification* is a process in which those positions and roles which have been differentiated are evaluated, ranked, and differentially rewarded by the members of the society on the basis of criteria which are considered important to the society's survival and continuance.

Structural-Functional Theory and Conflict Theory

In sociology today there are two major theoretical schools of thought which address the question of stratification. *Structural-functionalism* is generally agreed to be the more conservative school, while *conflict* theory is considered to be more radical. Both perspectives have made important, although contradictory, contributions to the study of inequality. Each of these theories is discussed briefly here, followed by an in-depth analysis of the specific stance each takes on the question of social inequality.

Functionalism

Sociology was in its infancy during the nineteenth century, a time when all sciences were influenced significantly by Darwinism. In *The Origin of the Species*, Charles Darwin demonstrated how, in the animal and plant worlds, evolution from lower to higher forms depended upon the survival of the fittest members of the species. Early sociologists, such as Herbert Spencer, were inspired to explain social order in similar biological terms and to describe societies as if they were living organisms. These sociologists termed certain classes, nations, or races superior or inferior on the basis of their relative ability to adapt to the conditions of life. Since the survival of the human species depended on the survival of its fittest members, it followed that such individuals should be given the best opportunities in life. However, almost all sociologists now agree that when applied to human beings, Darwin's theory is useless because it fails to account for a lack of equality of opportunity. Nevertheless, it was pervasive in the social sciences for a long time.

As functionalism developed under Durkheim, Malinowski, and

Radcliffe-Brown, the extremism of Spencer gradually diminished, but certain basic assumptions persisted. For example, societies were seen as self-regulating, self-maintaining systems having basic needs which, if met, would preserve their equilibrium. As a system, society was considered to have interrelated and interdependent parts, much as a living body has, all cooperating for the purpose of maintaining societal homeostasis. This perspective leads one to study the structure of the social system and its various parts as an entity. It also implies that sociology should define the conditions required for equilibrium so that members of a society can perform the functions necessary for the social balance of a healthy society. The underlying assumption is that the well-balanced society is a harmonious society.

Modern functionalism is represented by Talcott Parsons and Robert K. Merton, among others, who continue to describe social systems in terms of their needs for survival and the functional cooperation of the participating members. They postulate that there is a basic correlation between the needs of the social system and the individuals within it; that is, what is good for the whole is good for the parts. Thus a social system has a social structure, a pattern of interrelated statuses and roles, which together form a whole. The parts act together because they share common values, goals, and norms. For example, a family is a social system with parents and children forming a social structure in which each member acts in accordance with his or her status, and all members work for the good of the family unit because they share the same goals and values.

Conflict Theory

Conflict theory can be said to express ideas that are almost the opposite of functional theory, although it came into being at about the same time, in the early nineteenth century. It derives originally from the work of Marx and Georg Simmel. Marx, as already noted in Chapter II, contended that a class struggle, or class conflict, was inherent in any known type of society except communism. He wrote that class war between polarized classes was both inevitable and continuous. Like Marx, Simmel also viewed conflict as unavoidable in society (1956:23), in part because he felt that people have an instinct for hate as well as an instinct for love, making conflict inevitable since it arises from the human personality.

Instead of seeing conflict as destructive, however, Simmel

conflict

viewed it as a means of social continuity. "Conflict is thus designed to resolve dualisms; it is a way of achieving some kind of unity, even if it be through the annihilation of one of the conflicting parties" (1956:13). Conflict, in short, is functional in the classic sense.

Lewis Coser, whose theoretical orientation is basically that of functionalism, deals with the issue of the benefits of conflict, using the theories of Simmel. In the preface of *The Functions of Social Conflict*, Coser writes:

Our concern is mainly with the functions, rather than the dysfunctions, of social conflict, that is to say, with those consequences of social conflict which make for an increase rather than a decrease in the adaptation or adjustment of particular relationships or groups. Far from being only a "negative" factor which "tears apart," social conflict may fulfill a number of determinate functions in groups and other interpersonal relationships ... (1956:8).

In providing examples of the positive functions of conflict, Coser describes how it can lead to social change, release tension between competing groups, and promote cohesiveness among members of the "in-group."

In contrast to the functionalist view of society as a system with cooperative parts that operate to keep the system in balance because of shared values and interests, conflict theory stresses the struggles within societies which constantly threaten to destroy their equilibrium. Conflict theory is concerned with social disorder rather than with social order. The social system does not survive because of consensus and cooperation, but in spite of, and sometimes because of aggression and competition. Thus, conflict theorists reject the functional notion that there is harmony and order in society because everyone and everything works toward common goals. Instead, a society is a setting in which conflicts are played out; between those who want and those who have; the basis of social life is not consensus but dissension. Given these general outlines of the two theories, we will next examine how they view social inequality.

The Issue of Stratification: Two Points of View

Talcott Parsons, the leading exponent of functionalism, stresses the basic assumption that stratification is inevitable in all human interaction, whether in a group as small as a dyad or as large as a nation. People naturally evaluate, and they do so in a hierarchical fashion(1953). Ranks are determined by the members, who agree on what is or is not valuable. Thus, the stratification system is integrative because it reflects the values held in common by the members. Barber states Parsons's view this way: "when we say the stratification system is integrative, we mean, integration to the extent that it expresses a common and shared set of values" (1957).

Kingsley Davis and Wilbert E. Moore (1945) approached the problem of social inequality from the functionalist perspective by supplementing Parsons's outline. They claim that inequality in society is necessary and inevitable; its function is mainly as a device which enables societies to ensure that the most needed positions in society will be competently filled by the most qualified people. In other words, in societies there are jobs that must be performed which require hard work, long training periods, and entail great expense. Society must motivate its talented members to enter such occupations. Therefore, when one becomes, for example, a physician, one is rewarded with a high income, high status, and power. If society did not provide such incentives, Davis and Moore argue, few would endure the needed training and the years of deprivation.

The functionalists make it clear that they are speaking of positions, rather than of individuals. If social positions were "all equally pleasant to the human organism, all equally important to the societal survival, and all equally in need of the same ability or talent, it would make no difference who got into which positions, and the problem of social placement would be greatly reduced" (Davis and Moore, 1945). Thus, the functionalists hold that "stratification arises basically out of the needs of societies, not out of the needs or desires of individuals" (Lenski, 1966:15).

Conflict theory, on the other hand, rejects the notion that inequality is a permanent feature of social systems. It does not guarantee that the most highly qualified people will occupy the most important positions. Rather than stressing the needs of society, conflict theorists view stratification in terms of individuals and subgroups within a society.

Accordingly, this theory argues that inequality exists in society because there is always a shortage of available valued goods and services, and therefore there is always a struggle over who shall get what. Different groups with different needs and interests will battle to gain possession of those things which each group considers essential to its survival and continuance. Inequality results because desirable social positions are attained not by talent or ability, but by force, by accident of birth, by dominance, by exploitation, or by fraud and coercion.

According to conflict theory, the result is that the most able people are not necessarily in the most needed positions. Indeed, because of inequalities in the opportunity structure, many talented people never get the chance to put their abilities to work for themselves or the society. Furthermore, conflict theorists argue that the functionalists are incorrect when they claim that the greatest rewards accrue to the people in high status occupations. Some positions are highly rewarded which are only peripherally necessary, such as athletes or entertainment stars. Some are highly rewarded which are actually socially harmful, such as criminals. Other positions, such as those of minister, social worker, or professor, without which societies could not continue to develop, receive few material rewards, little prestige, and virtually no power. In short, the conflict theorists argue that stratification is dysfunctional for society. It limits opportunity, thereby depriving both society and the individual; it is divisive because it polarizes groups and creates hostility between them; and it is unnecessary because more equitable means of social placement are possible. This controversy, which has raged for over 20 years, can be summarized in the following questions: Is stratification integrative because it is based on a common, shared value system, as the functionalists say? Or is stratification coercive and nonintegrative because it is based on inequality or power, as the conflict theorists would have it? Is consensus or dissensus the basic element in society?

Synthesis of the Theories

Dahrendorf and Lenski
There have been a few attempts to integrate the two theories. Ralf Dahrendorf (1959) claims that the synthesis is inherent in both theories. The functionalists do not deny that different interests exist in society; nor do the conflict theorists deny that there is some agreement between social groups. The problem is that each theory claims its position most accurately reflects the basic condition of society; but this is questionable because "in a sociological context, neither of these models can be conceived as

exclusively valid or applicable. They constitute complementary, rather than alternative, aspects of the structure of total societies as well as every element of this structure. . . . We cannot conceive of society unless we realize the dialectics of stability and change, integration and conflict, function and motive force, consensus and coercion" (Dahrendorf, 1959:163). Society, then, to use Dahrendorf's phrase, is "Janus-headed"—it has two faces: integration and conflict. Dahrendorf contends that both schools are simply studying different aspects of society while ignoring the problems of how and why they coexist.

Seven years after Dahrendorf's book, *Class and Class Conflict in Industrial Society,* Gerhard Lenski (1966) made the claim that his own theory represented a further step toward a synthesis of functionalism and conflict theory in stratification.[1] Both theories, Lenski asserts, are normative because they address the question of morality and justice; the synthesis is analytical because it is concerned with relationships and causes, and employs empirical findings.

Lenski uses the dialectic method to correlate the theories. This method is intended to lead to a synthesis by integrating the postulates of the thesis and the antithesis, thus raising the question to a higher level. Lenski took what he considered the valid elements of functionalism and conflict theory, added other elements not found in either, and synthesized all of these into a more reasonable theory of stratification. By reformulating the concepts and breaking them down to their basic components, Lenski addressed himself primarily to two questions: (1) What is the nature of social stratification [which he defined as "the distributive process in human society—the process by which scarce values are distributed" (Lenski, 1966:x)]; and (2) What are the causes of its uniformities and variations? He was also concerned tangentially with the consequences of social stratification.

Lenski began by reviewing the basic differences between the two theories, noting that out of necessity he had to make generalizations which sometimes did not hold since there was disagreement among the members of each school. However, in general he states that for the functionalists, inequality is basically just, while

---

1. Lenski notes that several sociologists had already begun to synthesize the two theories. Among those he cites are: Dahrendorf, *op. cit.*; Pitirim Sorokin, *Social Mobility*; Stanislaw Ossowski, *Class Structure in the Social Consciousness*; and Pierre van den Berghe, "Dialectic and Functionalism: Toward a Theoretical Synthesis."

for the conflict theorists it is basically unjust. Functionalists argue that people are not "naturally" good and therefore require restraining institutions which maintain the common good; conflict theorists assert that human beings are good and that the institutions may not be trusted because they are used as tools of oppression by those in power. Functionalists describe society as a social system with needs that are satisfied through the cooperation of the members; conflict theorists portray society as a battleground on which subgroups constantly struggle against one another. Functionalists suggest that there is little overt coercion in society and that inequalities arise because people are differentially endowed and agree on the placement of the members of society into statuses; conflict theorists say that most institutions, especially stratification, could not exist unless the members were forced to obey imposed rules. Conflict theorists regard inequality as a cause of conflict; functionalists tend to deny this. The more radical school stresses force, fraud, and inheritance as the means by which individuals gain power and privilege; the conservatives emphasize talent, ability, and hard work.

Using these basic disagreements as a springboard, Lenski formulated his synthesis on the nature and causes of social stratification. He describes man as "a social being obligated by nature to live with others as a member of society" (Lenski, 1966:25). Functionalism and conflict theory agree on this point. Second, Lenski agrees with the functionalists, that "when men are confronted with important decisions where they are obliged to choose between their own, or their group's interests and the interests of others, they nearly always choose the former" (Lenski, 1966:30). Thus, people are not innately "good," but rather "altruistic action is most likely to occur in the minor events of daily life when little is at stake" (Lenski, 1966:30). Third, in consonance with the conflict theorists, Lenski believes that the things people strive for in society are always in short supply and, indeed, human beings are insatiable in their demand for scarce goods. Therefore, "a struggle for rewards will be present in every society" (Lenski, 1966:32). Finally, Lenski concedes the functionalists' view that people are not born equally intelligent, talented, physically endowed, and so on. However, while these inequalities alone could not be the primary source of stratification, they do encourage the functionalist notion that stratification is natural.

In his approach to the nature of society, Lenski again regards some aspects of each theory as valid. "Cooperation is certainly a pervasive feature of all human life and so, too, is conflict" (Lenski, 1966-33). Some human action is determined by the needs of society; some by the needs of subgroups and individuals. This means that Lenski cannot accept the functionalist concept of *social system* because of its tendency to imply that there is no variation in the degree of interdependence and interrelationships of the parts in different societies. "There is no such thing as a perfect human social system in which the actions of the parts are completely subordinated to the needs of the whole" (Lenski, 1966:34). Therefore, he admonishes us to cease postulating the existence of such a system and to stop trying to see all social action as utilitarian. It must be recognized that some behavior is antisocial, just as some is altruistic. Finally, Lenski points out that "we must learn to think of distributive systems as reflecting *simultaneously* system needs and unit needs, with each often subverting the other" (Lenski, 1966:34).

In summarizing his work, Lenski concludes that he has replaced the two older theories of stratification with a new synthesis. He explains the distributive process by asserting first that human beings are naturally self-seeking and live in societies which are far from perfect, cooperating systems. Cooperation *and* coercion exist in all societies, but cooperation is dominant in those which have small or large economic surplus; coercion tends to be more prevalent in developing societies (see Chapter I). This coercion leads to conflict between subgroups. As for the acquisition of power and privilege, "the importance of force varies greatly from one type of society to another. In the least advanced societies and in constitutionally advanced societies, force plays but a limited role" (Lenski, 1966:442). It plays a more powerful role in those societies, such as agrarian societies, which are neither primitive nor highly industrialized.

With respect to the oppressive nature of the state, Lenski contends that both kinds of thinkers are right, depending on the type of society. In advanced horticultural and agrarian societies law is frequently a tool of oppression and exploitation; in the two more primitive types, hunting and gathering societies and simple horticultural societies, government is beneficial to the masses of people and less valuable to the privileged group. Finally, Lenski sides with the functionalists when he says that inequality is inevitable, given human nature; but the degree of inequality can vary widely, depending again on the type of society.

Further Debate

In a further article in this seemingly endless debate, Wilbert Moore (1963) summed up the criticisms. Referring back to an early paper written with Kingsley Davis (1945), he conceded that originally they had given too much credit to the functions of stratification and had neglected the dysfunctions. He also conceded that their equation of unequal rewards with social stratification had been an error.

In the same issue of the *American Sociological Review*, Melvin Tumin, one of the first to disagree with the Davis-Moore position, stated that the entire problem is basically a semantic one (1963). He offered a typology of five sources of social inequality, all or some of which are found in all societies. The first, "role and attribute differentiation" refers to natural, nonevaluative distinctions attached to social positions, such as father or mother. The second, "rank ordering by intrinsic characteristics," means that people are compared on such things as height, intelligence, physical attractiveness, etc. The third source, Tumin states, is generic to social organization. He calls it "ranking by moral conformity," in which people are ranked according to how morally acceptable their behavior is.

The fourth type, "ranking by functional contribution," is analytically separable into two subcategories: (a) "ranking according to contribution or exemplification of 'ideals'," meaning people are unequal in terms of how much they conform or contribute to the values of the group; and (b) "ranking according to functional contribution to desired social goals," which entails the degree to which individuals contribute to the common welfare. The fifth source of inequality Tumin terms "diffusion of differentials in property, power, and prestige," by which he means that there is a tendency for any inequality to increase over time and to diffuse into other areas.

Tumin also asserts that any or none of these sources of inequality may become stratified, but no stratification is necessary for societal survival. "Most existing stratification, we insist, enjoys little or no consensus, has little to do with social integration, and is probably seriously dysfunctional for social productivity" (1969:25). More concisely, inequality exists of necessity; stratification can be eliminated from social life.

Jack L. Roach and his associates (1969:55) have compared the two opposing views of social stratification, as shown in Table 3-1.

It seems apparent that no one has yet won or is likely to win

TABLE 3-1
Two Views of Social Stratification

The Functional View	The Conflict View
(1) Stratification is universal, necessary, and inevitable.	(1) Stratification may be universal without being necessary or inevitable.
(2) Social organization (the social system) shapes the stratification system.	(2) The stratification system shapes social organization (the social system).
(3) Stratification arises from the societal need for integration, coordination, and cohesion.	(3) Stratification arises from group conquest, competition, and conflict.
(4) Stratification facilitates the optimal functioning of society and the individual.	(4) Stratification impedes the optimal functioning of society and the individual.
(5) Stratification is an expression of commonly shared social values.	(5) Stratification is an expression of the values of powerful groups.
(6) Power is usually legitimately distributed in society.	(6) Power is usually illegitimately distributed in society.
(7) Tasks and rewards are equitably allocated.	(7) Tasks and rewards are inequitably allocated.
(8) The economic dimension is subordinate to other dimensions of society.	(8) The economic dimension is paramount in society.
(9) Stratification systems generally change through evolutionary processes.	(9) Stratification systems often change through revolutionary processes.

this argument, and most sociologists conclude that there is wisdom on both sides. Society is "Janus-headed" in that both conflict and cooperation are present. Furthermore, in heterogeneous, complex industrial society, people cannot be equally endowed biologically and even if they were so endowed, equal opportunity and motivation could not be provided for each individual by any available means. Thus, inequality may be unjust, but it is also inevitable.

The Concept of Social Class

The most widely used term in the study of social stratification, perhaps in all sociology, has been *social class*, referred to less frequently as *socioeconomic status*. Almost no research is carried out in which people are not, in some manner, differentiated according to their positions in the hierarchy of social class placement. Hundreds of variables are analyzed in terms of social class. We find social class differences in childrearing practices, in marital relationships, in crime rates, in occupational and educational aspirations, in motivation levels, and even in sexual behavior. Terms like "middle class" and "working class" are part of every sociologist's vocabulary and, indeed, are quite familiar to the layman.

Yet, as was noted briefly in Chapter 1, there is an enormous amount of conceptual confusion surrounding the phrase "social class." Each researcher tends to use an idiosyncratic definition. Like "schizophrenia," "social class" has become a wastebasket term, with so many meanings that it has none at all. To the social realist, social classes are real, recognizable phenomena; to the social nominalist, they are an invention of the sociologist, convenient for summarizing observed inequalities.

There are those who hold that the term was useful when groups of people were readily assigned social class categories. There was no problem discriminating between the upper-class Lady Marjorie who lived "Upstairs" and her lower-class servant, Rose, who lived "Downstairs." Everything about them—accents, clothing, mannerisms, values, attitudes—was distinctly different. Today, in complex societies, the distinctions are disappearing. There are others who believe that the concept still serves a purpose, and that social classes are discernible in industrial as well as in preindustrial societies. The question is: Should the concept of class be retained as an analytic tool, thus also retaining a stress on economic differences in society; or should it be abandoned and replaced by an emphasis on other factors—such as status or inequality—as significant differentiating variables?

Theorists of Social Class

Harold Hodges
Harold Hodges suggests that:

A social class is much more than a convenient pigeonhole or merely arbitrary divisional unit—like minutes, ounces, I.Q. points, or inches—along a linear continuum. It is a distinct reality which embraces the fact that people live, eat, play, mate, dress, work, and think at contrasting and dissimilar levels. These levels—social classes—are the blended product of shared and analogous occupational orientations, educational backgrounds, economic wherewithal, and life experiences. . . . Social class in such terms as these refers to something more than single aggregates of individuals who occupy similar points on prestige, economic, or occupational scales (1964:13).

Furthermore, Hodges contends that "our positions in the social class structure are increasingly potent influences in determining our social behavior ... as the traditional statuses which have helped to determine our behavior—racial, ethnic, religious, regional, rural-urban, and even adolescent-adult and male-female— have declined in importance" (1964:14). In other words, Hodges asserts that various once powerful statuses are declining in differentiating power, so that the Polish-American is indistinguishable from the Italian-American, and middle-class blacks are more like middle-class whites in value orientations than they are like lower-class blacks.

Ralf Dahrendorf

Ralf Dahrendorf (1959) also chooses to retain the concept of social class, although his reasons differ from those of Hodges. Dahrendorf argues pragmatically that any category of people can be called by any name. Since sociologists have gotten used to the term "social class," there is no reason to confuse or distort by inventing new terms or using old ones in ambiguous ways. "The problem of the applicability of the concept of class is a purely terminological problem. . . . Logically, there is no reason why we should not call quasi-groups and interest groups classes or anything else" (1959:201).

However, Dahrendorf prefers to identify classes in terms of social conflict and power. "Classes are social conflict groups, the determinant of which can be found in the participation in or exclusion from the exercise of authority within any imperatively coordinated association. In this sense, classes differ from other conflict groups which rest on religious, ethnic, or legal differences" (1959:138). Therefore, when classes are defined in relation to authority, an "economic class" becomes merely one kind of class.

Methodologically, then, Dahrendorf accepts the concept of social class because any label is as good as any other and social class is already in wide use. Ideologically, he sees a social class, as Marx does, as a group in social conflict with other groups. However, he does not subscribe to Marx's two-class system. Rather, he says that there are as many classes in society as there are power hierarchies. Thus, all conflict groups are classes and all classes are conflict groups.

Gerhard Lenski

Gerhard Lenski suggests retention of the concept of social class, but insists that past usage has been too narrow. The term should be broadened and distinctions should be made between different kinds of classes. Thus, his definition of class is "an aggregation of persons in a society who stand in a similar position with respect to some form of power, privilege, or prestige" (1966:74–75). Moreover, people can be members of several different classes at the same time. One can be a member of an occupational class, a property class, a social-ethnic class, an educational class, an age class, and a sexual class (1966:80). A class, then, is any hierarchy arranged according to any criterion, and individual membership in any number of classes can be simultaneous, although classes are not of equal importance. For Lenski as for Dahrendorf, the most important class system is that which is ranked according to power. A power class is "an aggregation of persons in a society who stand in a similar position with respect to force or some specific form of institutionalized power" (1966:75). In addition, although they may be unaware of it, members of power classes share common interests; thus there is always potential hostility between classes, because members have a vested interest in protecting the power they have and in reducing the power of other classes. Like Dahrendorf, Lenski sees classes as conflict groups.

One final point Lenski makes is that classes are not discrete, clearly discernible entities. Instead they are on a continuum and lines of demarcation cannot readily be drawn. Therefore, regrettably, precise criteria cannot be used in defining classes; only broad groupings are possible, i.e., working class, middle class; or the classes may be subdivided into such groups as high ranking executives, middle ranking executives, and low ranking executives.

Dennis Wrong

Dennis Wrong (1964) is the most outspoken sociologist against the concept of social class. He takes the position that social classes are nothing more than convenient figments of the sociological imagination. He rejects all attempts to label social classes as "quasi-groups" or "interest groups" or any similar euphemistic term. A social class, he says, is a group whose "members are conscious of their unity and of the boundaries separating them from other classes" (in Stub, 1972:72). If such awareness of group identity does not exist, the concept of social class is meaningless. And in the United States, according to Wrong, there is surely an absence of class consciousness. In fact, by stressing social class, American sociologists have obscured the inequalities that actually do exist. "The emerging social structure of post-bourgeois industrial society can best be understood if . . . we abandon the concept of social class and re-define much of the work done under this label as a contribution to the sociology of equality and inequality" (in Stub, 1972:75).

In other words, Wrong is saying that while he believes there are no real classes (as he defines them) in the United States, inequality is more prevalent than ever. It is therefore necessary to find some other means to define social inequality, since social class requires class consciousness.

While the debate over the usefulness of "social class" continues it has taken a somewhat different and more meaningful direction in recent years. Instead of simply arguing over what to term a given group or whether to term it anything at all, some sociologists have advanced the notion that the discussion should be narrowed and focused on what to call, how to differentiate, and how to analyze what has been casually called the "middle class."

Holger Stub

Holger R. Stub has been responsible for some of the most insightful theorizing in this area (1972:92-107). He begins by reiterating the confusion surrounding the use of the terms "social class" and "social ranking." "The former refers to a hierarchy of groups established over time and possessing a 'class consciousness' or mutality of interest, and is often restricted to those possessing appropriate and valued characteristics" (1972:93). Social ranking, however, merely represents aggregates of people graded according to some social characteristics—wealth, occupation, prestige— but who are unaware of their similarities. The problem, says Stub, is that "most research considering social inequality as a factor involves the use of social ranking rather than social class analysis" (1972:4).

Stub's definition of class is based on Marx's notion of *Klasse für sich*—class-for-itself, as opposed to *Klasse an sich*—class-in-itself. An aggregate of people, ranked together, become a true class only when they have class consciousness. But Stub also finds that Marx's two-class system is inadequate because "the rapidly expanding middle levels of modern society cannot be accurately categorized as being either capitalist or proletariat. . . . neither dependent upon nor independent of the 'controllers' or the 'controlled'" (1972:94). Stub argues that clearly there are classes at the top and at the bottom of the stratification system, but the term is inapplicable to the myriad, heterogeneous groups in between. Therefore, when speaking of the groups in the middle, Stub utilizes Weber's concept of status group (see definition in Chapter 2). In preference to Marx's notion of a class as related to the means of production, or the notion of class consciousness alone, Stub opts for Weber's theory of community, which exists only when the members share common attitudes toward a situation which leads to shared action. He believes that the members of various occupational groups or professions in the middle levels of society have this kind of mutual orientation. Stub notes that Dennis Wrong (1964), Stanislaw Ossowski (1963), Don Martindale (1960), Joseph Bensman (1966), and Kurt Mayer (1963) all agree that the middle strata cannot be analyzed in terms of social class.

Stub also points to Edward Lauman's work (1966) on social distance, prestige, and intimate association among occupational groups, which indicates that intimate interaction frequently is limited to occupational groups.

Stub cites the work of Kurt B. Mayer (1963), who shows that the middle socioeconomic levels no longer form classes (which, according to Mayer, are based on family membership and inheritance). In this segment of the labor market, jobs provide unusual opportunity for rapid mobility, so that the old symbols of class membership are disappearing; there is increasing interclass marriage; traditional life styles are very mutable, social distances between classes are narrowing; and thus, "a general democratization of behavior patterns has destroyed the clear-cut status distinctions of an earlier time" (1972:97). He suggests that the concept of status community should be used "in dealing with the kind of collectivities that manifest similar life styles, adhere to somewhat specific status distinctions and symbols, and whose members feel they belong together" (1972:99). Status communities, then, represent a fusion of Weber's three dimensions of class, status, and power.

To summarize, Stub suggests that the term "social class" should be reserved for the upper and lower strata of American society, but the term "status community" should be used for the middle strata because "with the emergence of many new occupations annually, a society such as that of the United States can be characterized as consisting of a vast array of coexisting, cooperating, competing, and conflicting occupational or status communities. The effects will be a constant alignment and realignment of these communities in terms of class, status, and political influence" (1972:101).

Joseph Bensman

Joseph Bensman's (1972) study of musicians illustrates the notion that *status community* is a more useful and appropriate concept than *social class* when attention is directed to those groups between the clearly demarcated upper and lower classes. He defines a status community as a *consensual community*, in preference to Robert MacIver's definition of community in terms of territory (1932). In turn, MacIver states that a community is the smallest territorial unit within which a person lives his daily life. Bensman contends that a community transcends geography because its members probably are more at home with another member of the same community, even if they live thousands of miles apart, than they may be with a next-door neighbor of a different status group. Furthermore, a consensual community is voluntary inasmuch as one chooses one's occupation; and therefore, contrary to MacIver, community membership is voluntary. Thus, according to Bensman, a status community is one "in which the individual chooses to organize his major life interests within a framework of institutions, cultures, practices, and social relationships that are consistent with his adherences to a set of values" (1972:115).

An individual becomes a member of a status community if he or she possesses "those technical, social, and symbolic skills and loyalties upon which the status community bases itself" (1972:115). Once this is accomplished, the member uses the status community as the major vehicle for organizing his or her social life. Social relationships are primarily limited to other members of the status community. "Professional musicians, for example, will draw their friends mainly from among other professional musicians and devoted amateurs, will frequently marry musicians or music students, and will raise children who become seriously interested in music" (1972:116). According to Bensman, musicians have contact outside the music community only with family members and neighbors. Thus, in urban societies each status community is so specialized that members can live almost completely

to be a consequence of power rather than a determinant of it or a necessary component of it" (Bierstedt, 1950:731). For Bierstedt, then, when the two concepts are associated, it is an incidental but not a necessary relationship.

Power and Influence

"Influence is persuasive while power is coercive" (Bierstedt, 1950:731). People allow themselves to be influenced because they admire or respect the one who influences them, but one submits to power because one has no choice. Students have no alternative but to submit to the power of the teacher because the teacher has the right to evaluate their performance. On the other hand, a teacher gains influence over students if he or she displays qualities which the students value and which they might wish to emulate. Thus, influence and power also are independent variables which may or may not be associated. Karl Marx, for example, had a tremendous amount of influence, but he had no power. Stalin had influence, but only because he first had power. Bierstedt maintains that ideas, not people, are influential. "Influence attaches to an idea, a doctrine, or a creed, and has its locus in the ideological sphere. Power attaches to a person, a group, or an association, and has its locus in the sociological sphere" (1950:731–732).

Power and Dominance

Power is sociological in that it is located in groups and in intergroup relationships. Dominance is psychological because it is found in individual and interpersonal relationships. Power accrues to a person because he or she occupies a status within a formal organization; dominance is a personal trait and a function of personality, and thus there are dominant and submissive people in powerful and in powerless organizations. Indeed, some groups acquire great political power because so many of the members are submissive to the few dominant leader.

Power and Rights

"Rights" is a term that in itself is difficult to define. Nevertheless, a right must have some social support, although not necessarily legal support. Furthermore, rights are always attached to statuses, as are responsibilities, privileges, duties, and obligations. Generally, then, power supports rights which are claimed legitimately. On the other hand, one may have rights without having the power to exercise them. "A 'right,' like a privilege, is one of the perquisites of power and not power itself" (1950:733).

Power, Force, and Authority

Thus we see that power may be distinguished clearly from prestige, influence, dominance, and rights; but it is more closely related to both force and authority, although it is not synonymous with either one. In explaining power in terms of both force and authority, Bierstedt offers three definitions and examines their implications. (1) Power is latent force; (2) force is manifest power; (3) authority is institutionalized power (1950:733).

The first two definitions are circular; but force also can be defined independently. Force means the application of sanctions or the elimination of alternatives from one group or individual by another. "Surrender or die"; "Your money or your life"; "Publish or perish"—all are examples of the elimination of possibilities. This is force, then, or power made explicit. "Power itself is the predisposition or prior capacity which makes the application of force possible" (1950:733). Holding a gun to someone's head is power; shooting the gun is force. Power is thus merely the ability to use force and therefore it is always successful. When power is not successful, that is, when the gun jams, it is no longer power.

Power becomes authority within formal organizations. Those in authority have the legitimate right to exercise power and to use force, if necessary, because their rights are attached to their statuses. Institutionalized power, then, is attached to statuses, not to individuals, and authority is useless without power or force.

In summary, power can be understood using Bierstedt's interrelated definitions of power, force, and authority. Power is implied because when challenged, it becomes force; when legalized, it becomes authority. Therefore "power is always potential; that is, when it is used it becomes something else, either force or authority" (1950:736).

Sources of Power

Bierstedt also discusses the sources of power, locating them in (1) numbers of people, (2) social organization, and (3) resources.

The majority always possesses strength, and it can control a minority when it has at least some of each of the other two sources of power. The only reason majorities, especially economic and political ones, have not been in power through most of history is because they have lacked both organization and resources. The power of the majority can, of course, be seen in democratic countries where political candidates are elected but aside from these events, majorities are usually powerless without organizations and resources.

Organization, the second source of power, is essential if majorities are to have control. It is organization which permits the small cadre of policemen to overcome the mob. Yet this source must occur in conjunction with the third source of power, which is also essential. The mob gives in to the police because it knows the police have resources which it does not possess, that is, guns.

There are, of course, many kinds of resources: property, wealth, competence, knowledge, fraud, deceit, secrecy, etc. Powerful countries have natural resources, such as coal, iron, lumber, oil. Powerful churches have supernatural resources, such as gods and a belief in the hereafter.

In isolation, none of these three sources constitutes power; nor are any two sufficient. It is only when a group has all three—numbers, organization, and resources—that it has power. "There is one, and only one, kind of social situation in which the power of opposing groups is completely balanced. The numbers on each "side" are equal, their social organization is identical, and their resources are as nearly the same as possible" (Bierstedt, 1950:737–738).

To recapitulate, in order to have power, a group must be relatively large; it must be organized to behave in an orderly fashion; and it must have the resources to enforce its prescriptions.

Who Has the Power? Elitism versus Pluralism

Of all the classical debates in the area of social inequality, perhaps the essential one is the problem of who really has the power. Most sociologists (see Domhoff, 1967: Baltzell, 1958) would agree that there is a national upper class. The question is whether or not this class is also a "governing elite."

Those who maintain that it is are generally referred to as elitists: those who say it is not are called pluralists. Elitists claim that there is a small minority which controls societal power. Pluralists contend that no single unified group could do this in a complex society, and therefore the power is divided among a multitude of conflicting, sometimes cooperating interest groups. Elitism holds that power is centralized in the upper classes; pluralism holds that it is decentralized.

Veto Groups versus the Power Elite: David Riesman and C. Wright Mills

Two of the main protagonists in this debate are David Riesman (1961) and the late C. Wright Mills (1959). Riesman's book, *The Lonely Crowd*, supports the notion that power is divided among veto groups. He defines veto groups as:

> . . . a series of groups, each of which has struggled for and finally attained a power to stop things conceivably inimical to its interests and, within far narrower limits, to start things. . . . These veto groups are neither leader-groups nor led-groups. The only leaders of national scope left in the United States today are those who can placate the veto groups. The only followers left in the United States today are those unorganized and sometimes disorganized unfortunates who have not yet invented their group (1961:213).

Riesman holds that veto groups include corporate managers, organized farmers, organized labor, and other such groups, and are really defense groups rather than leadership groups. If they have any national power it is because of their mutual tolerance and willing cooperation. Thus, there is no "ruling class" in the United States. Rather, power is determined by issues; the one or two groups concerned with the issue will compromise in most cases so that neither really "wins" or "loses." This is the pluralists' view of power. Power is divided among many competing interest or veto groups, each of which is concerned only with acquiring power within its special sphere of interest. These groups constantly change in membership, so that ultimately the power structure in America has become amorphous in terms of composition, and balanced in that the groups effectively neutralize one other.

C. Wright Mills's (1959) theory of the power elite is almost diametrically opposed to Riesman's. Mills contends that there is an elite group in this country, and that it is composed of the leaders of big business, the men at the top of the military, and those in the upper echelons of government—a "power elite." The people in these upper-class positions constitute a governing elite, although one that is not based on aristocracy. They are people who know each other personally (or at least know of each other), belong to the same clubs, go to the same places for vacations, intermarry, and cooperate for mutual benefit. Below this group is a middle-level power group which is not well-organized and is therefore much less effective. At the bottom of the pyramid is the majority of people, who comprise a powerless mass. Thus for Mills power at the national level is controlled by a triumvirate of big government, big business, and the military.

Kornhauser's Analysis

William Kornhauser (1966:211) makes explicit the difference in these two points of view in the following diagrams (Fig. 3-1).

The top of Mills's pyramid of power is a unified elite comprised of those holding *the most important* positions in government, the armed services, and corporations. The middle level is composed of a plurality of interest groups with minimal power. The third level is the powerless mass which is controlled and dominated by the upper two groups. Riesman's pyramid eliminates the power elite altogether, with the upper layer containing diversified interest groups, and the lower level made up of the public from which the upper layer seeks cooperation in their competitive activities, but which is not under its control.

Kornhauser examined the controversy and concisely defined the areas of disagreement between the two theorists, comparing their views on power in the United States along five dimensions: the structure of power, changes in the structure of power, the operation of power, the bases of power, and the consequences of the structure of power. Kornhauser's analysis is helpful in clarifying the two positions.

The first dimension, the structure of power, has already been discussed (see pp. 67-69). Now we will turn to an examination of changes in that structure.

Mills and Riesman agree that the American power structure has gone through four major historical periods. The first era began when the Republic was established, and it ended in the 1830s.

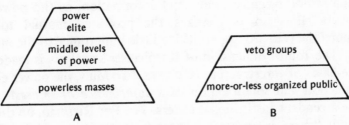

FIGURE 3-1
Two pyramids of power: A, Mills's pyramid; B, Riesman's pyramid.

Riesman claims that during this time America had a clearly demarcated ruling class composed of a landed aristocracy and a mercantile-money group. Mills contends that at this time social life, political life, economic life, and the military converged into a controlling group.

The second era extended from the 1830s to the Civil War. Mills and Riesman agree that power was more widely diffused during this period, and a ruling class could no longer be discerned. Riesman dates the third epoch from the Civil War to the end of the nineteenth century, while Mills extends it into the 1930s. They both agree, however, that pluralism diminished during this period when economic institutions dominated the sources of power. The fourth period lasted until World War II. Riesman believes the veto groups developed fully at this time; Mills allows this, but argues that there was a change in the middle of the Roosevelt administration when the power elite came into full control.

It is at this point, in their interpretation of the events of the period of the 1940s, that the divergence between the two theorists becomes explicit. Mills contends that World War II, because of its impact on American society, provided the conditions for the development of a true power elite. Riesman denies this, stating that the war caused a diversification of power.

The third dimension of their argument concerns the operation of power. Mills stresses the dominance of the power elite in all areas of social life, particularly in the making of foreign policy. Riesman maintains that the distribution of power depends on specific issues, and thus the number of power groups tends to equal the number of problematic areas. Both agree, however, that manipulation rather than persuasion or force is the way power is gained and used. Mills maintains there is secrecy behind the manipulation, especially in the way the mass media are used to suppress or magnify issues and information, as the power elite directs. Riesman emphasizes the professed mutual tolerance among the veto groups, attaching little importance to the media.

The fourth dimension of Kornhauser's analysis is made up of the bases of the structure of power. "To Mills, the power elite is a reflection and solidification of a *coincidence of interests* among the ascendant institutional orders. . . . For Riesman, on the other hand, "there is an amorphous power structure which reflects a *diversity of interests* among the major organized groups" (1966:213). Both agree that there is widespread apathy in the

United States, but Mills says it is primarily among the masses; Riesman claims it is found in all strata. In any event, power is left by default in the hands of either the power elite or the veto groups.

The consequences of the power structure are fourfold. (1) For Mills, the power elite gains its own ends *without consideration of the masses*, while for Riesman, no single group remains in power over others for any length of time. (2) Both maintain that people are losing interest in political issues, partly because they can no longer comprehend them, and partly because they do not believe they are directly affected by public policies. (3) Mills argues that Americans maintain the myth that power is in the hands of the people, and therefore they do not hold those who actually have the power accountable for their actions. Riesman agrees with this more or less, but asserts that responsibility cannot be localized because power is so widely dispersed. (4) Finally, Mills believes that "if power tends to be located in a small group which is not accountable for its power, and if politics no longer involves genuine public debate, then there will be a *severe weakening of democratic institutions*" (1966:214). Riesman says, "If, on the other hand, power tends to be dispersed among groups which are primarily concerned to protect and defend their interests, rather than to advance general policies and their own leadership, and if at the same time politics has declined as a sphere of duty and self-interest, then there will be a *severe weakening of leadership*" (1966:214).

Kornhauser concludes that despite their points of difference, there are fundamental areas of agreement between Mills and Riesman. Both point to an absence of effective political action and a decline in political participation in our society. Political institutions, including the Congress, the presidency, party leadership, and the public are inadequate, especially in terms of leadership in foreign affairs. *Mills fears democracy is dying*; *Riesman fears leadership is disappearing*. Thus, there is considerable danger in the United States because both strong government and diversified power are required for political health. Finally, Kornhauser states that the controversy cannot be resolved without empirical research, for until it can be shown which theorist is more correct in his diagnosis, very little can be done to correct the "political malaise."

Four Classic Studies of Elitism versus Pluralism
Those researchers who have tried to test the theories of Riesman and Mills have had difficulty, because any research on a

national scale is prohibitive in terms of both time and money. Indeed, such research can be considered as practically impossible because of its scope. Therefore, many sociologists have studied small communities in order to understand the underlying community power structure, in the hope that they will be able to generalize their findings to the national level. These studies generally focus on community decision-making, the important question being: Who has the biggest voice in decisions concerning the community and its problems?

Four such studies are considered classics. One was conducted by Robert S. and Helen M. Lynd (1937); another by Hollingshead (1949); a third by Floyd Hunter (1953); and a fourth by Arthur J. Viditch and Joseph Bensman (1960). The findings of each researcher revealed that a small power elite existed in each town, composed of a group of people who were closely acquainted. Each power elite comprised members from wealthy families, usually business people, lawyers, and bank executives. But wealth alone, while a prerequisite for entry into the elite, was not sufficient. In general, the individual had made a conscious choice to enter into the political life of the community.

The Lynds found that "Middletown" was controlled by one manufacturing family of five brothers. However, according to the Lynds, their dominance was not a result of deliberate manipulation, but was unplanned and informal, deriving from the family's high economic position and their desire to be politically active. An equally wealthy family in "Middletown," in contrast, exercised no political power.

Hunter's study of "Regional City" concluded that access to political power in this community was obtained only through closed associations and appointed advisory boards of business executives. Thus, there was an elite governing group composed of the society's top business and industrial leaders. However Hunter's "power elite," unlike Mills's, is confined to an economic dimension only.

Hollingshead's "Elmtown," like "Middletown," also was controlled by a few wealthy families, mostly farmers, business people, and professionals, who owned almost all of the real estate in the town. Public office was held only by those who obliged the controlling families with low taxes and limited public expenditures; the interests of the wealthy were paramount.

Viditch and Bensman, in their study of a small town in upstate

New York, found an "invisible government" dominated by four leaders: a businessman, two lawyers, and the editor of the local newspaper, who together made all the important decisions in the town. Elected government officials were without any actual policy-making power.

On the other side of the argument, Robert Dahl also conducted an important study of community power in New Haven (1961), in which he found a pluralistic city government with several veto groups having interests in different issues and with political power deriving from different sources.

John Walton (1966) summarized the results of 33 community power studies conducted between 1953 and 1965. He found that 18 of these communities had the kind of "pyramid" structure described by Mills, with power concentrated in the hands of a small power elite. Seventeen had "factional" structures, meaning that there were one, two, or three relatively permanent competing veto groups in control. Fourteen were classified by Walton as "coalitional," having several fluid interest groups. Five were unclassifiable, apparently lacking a discernible and consistent power structure. The diversity of the results of these studies leaves unresolved the question of who has the biggest voice in decision-making in small communities. The variations may be explained in part on the basis of the different methodologies used, which will be discussed later in this chapter. However, there is some suggestion that most small communities are controlled by power elites, usually composed of the economic interests of the town, which operate informally.

Unfortunately, the findings do not help to answer the problem of how power is distributed on a national level, so any generalization from community to national power studies is invalid. Thus, the Mills-Riesman controversy remains unresolved, and the question of national power is blurred and will continue to be so until more empirical evidence can be amassed.

Suzanne Keller is perhaps the only sociologist who has attempted to refute Mills's thesis without resorting to a criticism of his methods, or without questioning the validity of his evidence or of his rationale. She has, instead, broadened the pluralistic theory by contending that highly industrialized societies are characterized by many "strategic elites," defined as "minorities of individuals designated to serve a collectivity in a socially valued way" (1963:4). In addition to a political elite, an economic elite, and a military elite, Keller discusses cultural, moral, intellectual, scientific, religious, and diplomatic elites, among others. Keller's elites are really interest groups in the sense that they possess similar degrees of political power and are confined to specialized areas. She writes:

> In highly industrialized societies power . . . is increasingly shared among various groups and institutions. The differentiation of elites into specialized and partly autonomous entities has shattered the image of a single, homogeneous power center. . . . Today no single strategic elite has absolute power or priority (1963:277).

Keller may indeed be correct, but until more data are gathered the question of whether national power is in the control of a power elite or veto groups remains moot. In any case, it is probable that in American society, contrary to popular myth, "the people" neither possess nor dispense power.

Problems of Measurement

Continuum versus Category

Another controversy in sociology revolves around the question of whether classes are on a continuum (i.e., there is no exact point at which one can say that a class begins or ends), or whether they can be divided into separate and distinct categories. One is called the "class structure" hypothesis, the other the "status continuum" hypothesis. Until recently, most sociologists (Lynd and Lynd, 1929; Warner and Lunt, 1941; Hollingshead, 1949; and Gordon, 1963) preferred the latter notion because they considered social classes to be real groups which share common life styles and have "consciousness of kind."

John Cuber and William Kenkel (1954) represent those sociologists who prefer to think of social classes as continuous, or without any sharp demarcations between them. The following arguments presented by Cuber and Kenkel are based on research by Lenski, 1952; Hetzler, 1953; and Kenkel, 1954.

1. If social classes were distinct entities, there would be agreement on how many exist. Instead, some sociologists use a two-class system, some a four-class system, some six classes, and some as many as nine. (This point will be discussed in somewhat more detail further on.)

2. No matter what criteria are used to define social classes, there are always some people who are unclassifiable.
3. The "category" notion is too rigid. Actually whole classes can move upward or downward, and in fact, the entire stratification system is constantly in flux.
4. The criteria frequently used are not well-correlated with each other. For example, those who have high incomes often do not have high prestige or power, and vice versa.
5. Actually, and regardless of which variables are used, data always reveal a continuum.

Milton Gordon (1963) partially refutes this argement, claiming that all variables, such as income, education, or occupation, can readily be broken down into distinct categories. However, Gordon concludes that "the concept of the American status structure as a status continuum is a model which lies at one end of a scale of possibilities, the other end of which is represented by a series of sharply delineated status groups. . . . We suggest that the empirical answer as to the nature of the American status order lies somewhere between these two extremes" (1963:188).

Number of Classes

The issue of whether classes are continuous or distinct is important, because each conceptualization results in different consequences; but it is less vital than the question of the number of classes in American society. Apparently there are almost as many conceptions of the class structure as there are researchers who study it, and there is little consensus on how many classes there are, how large each class is, or which variables best discriminate between class groups. There are those, usually Marxist in orientation, who admit to only two classes: the rich and the poor. Many more tend to think in terms of three classes: the upper, middle, and lower. Some sociologists use a nine-part scheme of upper-upper, middle-upper, lower-upper; upper-middle, middle-middle, lower-middle; and upper-lower, middle-lower, and lower-lower. These distinctions presumably are useful when dealing with an enormous sample of people. Lloyd Warner's system of six classes tends to be used very widely (1941):

1. The upper-upper class, comprising about 1.5 percent of the population, is composed of families who have been wealthy for two or more generations.

2. The lower-upper class contains about the same percentage of people, but its members have newly acquired wealth.
3. About 10 percent of the population is in the upper-middle class, which is comprised of successful business and professional people.
4. The lower-middle class contains about 28 percent of the population, and generally is composed of white-collar workers and some foremen.
5. The largest class is the upper-lower class, representing about 33 percent of the population. These are blue-collar workers.
6. Twenty-five percent of the population is in the lower-lower class, including derelicts and the unemployable, or the "dregs" of society.

Warner's scheme, especially its distribution, represents an old New England town shortly after the Great Depression of the 1930s and for this reason we can view the percentages with some skepticism. Joseph Kahl's scheme is perhaps more useful and realistic because it was devised during a more stable period in American history. Kahl divides the population into five classes: the upper class (1 percent), the upper-middle class (9 percent), the lower-middle class (40 percent), the working class (40 percent), and the lower class (10 percent) (1957:187).

Kahl notes that there is little agreement on the number of classes to be found in the United States, and his decision to use five classes is a purely arbitrary one because "the answers are not really contradictory, for the basic outlines are agreed upon, and it is mainly the question of precise divisions between the levels that causes argument" (1957:186).

As discussed earlier, there are those who maintain that there are really only two distinct classes in America: the upper and the lower. "Status communities" lie between these two extremes, and there is no way of counting how many of these there may be (see pp. 60–64).

Criteria for Class Placement

There are two different kinds of issues in the area of class placement: the first concerns the location of those who hold the power in the community; the second deals with methods for individual placement. Should people be placed in class categories because that is where they believe they belong? This is the subjective view. Or should people be placed in class categories because the researcher has used objective variables to classify them, such as income, education, or occupation? If one uses the objective method, which variables are the most accurate indicators of social class?

Positional, Reputational, and Decisional Methods

The positional stance assumes that those holding the key positions in a community, such as elected and appointed officials, leaders of voluntary organizations, business executives, etc., will occupy decision-making statuses. Using this method, researchers list the formal statuses, and those who hold the greatest number of them are assumed to be the ones who set the community policies. "Viewed in this manner, power is a structural property and the power of an individual is directly related to the position he occupies in the structure" (Bonjean and Grimes, 1974:378). Hawley (1963) has made a slight variation in this approach by attempting to see which sectors of the community have more or less power than others, thus increasing concern with structure, since Hawley addresses himself to the status rather than to the individual occupying it.

Hunter (1953) challenged the positional approach on the ground that its basic assumption is incorrect. How can we be sure that those in official or influential statuses necessarily make the key decisions? Officials may be mere puppets; those in influential positions may be disinterested. Therefore, Hunter used a new technique to discover the power-holders: the reputational approach. He asked some residents of Atlanta to identify the people in the city whom they believed had community control, and from their responses, he compiled a list of those who were most often named.

The reputational approach has not escaped criticism. For one thing, it is said to measure the reputation of power, not power per se. Two, the method assumes a power structure to be monolithic and therefore is incapable of uncovering a pluralistic power structure. Three, Hunter is said to have generalized beyond the scope of his data, assuming that his list of leaders acted in concert, when they actually may have been acting independently or even in opposition to one another (Bonjean and Grimes, 1974:379).

The third approach in community power studies is called decisional or "issue analysis." Robert Dahl (1961), for example, selected community issues and then attempted to determine the process through which they were resolved. Unlike either the positional method, which focuses on structures, and the reputational method, which focuses on individuals, the decisional method focuses on the decision-making process itself. Dahl looked at several issues, discovering by reconstruction who started the process, who tried to carry it through, who opposed it, and finally who made the decision.

In this fashion it is possible to identify the individuals who hold the real power and the processes through which power is wielded. However, one problem with the method is that it over-stresses direct observation, which may obscure any covert activities and another is that revealing issues may be quashed before they actually become controversial. Also, as a nonmember of the community, the observer may be studying decisions that are not really representative or important ones, and thus may be unable to identify the real decisionmakers (Bonjean and Grimes, 1974:379).

An examination of these methods leads us to conclude that no one method is adequate alone, since each has built-in bias. The reputational method is likely to reveal a "power elite" type structure, resulting in a relationship between findings and approach. The debate, however, has ended, since no sociologist today studying community power would opt for any one method; instead, most seek a combination of at least two.

Subjective versus Objective Classification

The subjective view of class position is related to *perceived* notions of inequality that people hold. It is based on an assumption that individuals are aware of their status in the class hierarchy, and if membership in a given class is claimed, the self-evaluation can be accepted and is in agreement with objective criteria. The objective view of class position is related to actual inequalities between people. Therefore, those who use objective methods consider classes as distinct entities that can be categorized by observation, regardless of whether the members of a class are aware of their membership. The subjective approach, then, is concerned with class consciousness and the interpretation and evaluation members of a society put on their own and others' classes. The objective approach is concerned with the external, real inequalities that actually exist in the social structure.

Subjective View

Richard Centers has done the most provocative work on the subjective aspect of social class. He defines a class as "no less than what people collectively think it is . . . It is a psychological structuring . . ." (1949:78). Centers's study was carried out in response to a poll conducted by *Fortune* magazine in which 80 percent of those polled claimed middle-class status. This finding led *Fortune* to conclude that America is truly a "middle-class" nation and most of its citizens are class-conscious. Centers took exception to this interpretation, claiming that the *Fortune* results appeared this way because respondents were given only three choices and were forced to select one. That is, when offered a choice between "upper," "middle," and "lower," most respondents selected "middle" rather than "upper" which might appear to be boasting, or rather than "lower," which is pejorative. Using a national, random sample of over 1,000 adult white men, Centers added a fourth choice: "working class". Approximately 50 percent placed themselves in this category. Centers maintains that his respondents' answers correspond to reality. Seventy-five percent of the white-collar, professional, and business people accurately defined themselves as middle class; and about 80 percent of the blue-collar workers correctly placed themselves in the working or lower class. Thus, according to Centers, there is class consciousness in the United States.

His subsequent studies supported his original findings, and Centers concluded that the *Fortune* study merely showed an American distaste for the term "lower class," rather than a belief that America is a middle-class country (1950, 1951). Nevertheless, Centers can be criticized on the ground that he overgeneralized from his data by not giving enough attention to the fact that a substantial part of his sample misranked themselves. For example, about one-fifth of the blue-collar workers ranked themselves as middle class, and about one-third of the white-collar workers placed themselves in the working class. Furthermore, people showed a tendency to raise their own level by including higher ranking groups within their own.

Joseph Kahl and James Davis (1953) have argued that questions which demand forced choices between class labels are not sufficient to establish whether people possess awareness of class identification. Respondents should also be asked open-ended questions which can be categorized later. These two researchers presented a series of such questions to about 200 white men in Massachusetts. They found that 12 percent had no concept of a stratification system; 6 percent denied that one existed in the

United States; and 5 percent admitted there was such a thing but disapproved so strongly that they refused to talk about it. The remaining 77 percent gave a reasonably accurate description of their own and other strata. Kahl and Davis also asked the same forced-choice question Centers had asked: "To what social class do you consider you belong?" Comparing the answers to the two types of questions and comparing their work to that of Centers, Kahl concluded:

> Therefore it appears that we have a hard core of the business and professional plus some of the white-collar persons who call themselves middle class, no matter how you ask the question. And we have a hard core of manual workers who are working class, regardless of the form of the question. But we may have two intermediate groups who are not sure of themselves. One consists of some low-level white-collar people and some manual workers; they sometimes see themselves as middle, sometimes as working class. The form of the question determines the answer. The other intermediate group consists of the people who are the least class-conscious; they say there is no class system—but on second thought, if they have to choose, they will tend toward working class (1957:170).

Centers and others also attempted to find a correlation between socioeconomic class and political attitudes. Centers showed that class self-placement was predictive of ideological orientations. Thirty-five percent of the middle class and 12 percent of the working class were ultraconservative; 33 percent and 23 percent, respectively, were in the conservative group; 7 percent of the middle class and 19 percent of the working class were radical; 4 percent and 13 percent, respectively, were ultraradical; and 21 percent of the middle class and 33 percent of the working class were middle-of-the-roaders.

Holding occupations constant, however, produced a variation in the replies. For example, professionals and white-collar workers were on the whole more conservative; but those who ranked themselves as middle class were more conservative than those who considered themselves working class. Centers held that this confirms the veto group theory, because people who correctly classified themselves had attitudes more typical of that class than the ones who—using occupation as the objective criterion for comparison—misranked themselves.

Joseph Kahl does not completely accept Centers's cause and

effect relationship between occupation, class consciousness, and ideological beliefs. "A cautious interpretation of the data would suggest that both class consciousness and ideology tend to be consequents of occupational position, but the sequence of causation between class consciousness and ideology is not clear" (Kahl, 1957:166). For Kahl, then, predicting political ideology on the basis of class identification rather than on the basis of occupation yields more reliable results.

Arthur Kornhauser analyzed the work of Centers and others, and concluded that opinions on politico-economic issues tend to be based on self-ranked class positions rather than on occupation. In addition, he rejects Centers's conservative-radical scale because it does not hold up on such issues as religion, race relations, and foreign policy questions. Instead, Kornhauser postulates that the differences between the middle and working classes "are in directions to be expected if people's opinions coincide with their own interest as they perceive it and the means to advance it. Be it noted, however, that there are great numbers of exceptions—substantial minorities who do not go along with their fellows who are similarly situated" (1955:334).

In an overall view, we may say that the subjective technique suffers from several weaknesses. One is a lack of consistency in the way researchers approach the problem; for the most part the "lawyers lead the witnesses" by framing their questions in ways which influence the answers. Second, Kahl claims that academic researchers who utilize the subjective approach create concepts and then "endow their concepts with connotations that derive from the researchers' own general philosophy" (1957:176). Third, this approach does not firmly establish that there is a relationship between class self-identification, occupation, and ideology. Fourth, self-identification is not based on occupation alone. As Elizabeth Bott notes:

When an individual talks about class he is trying to say something, in a symbolic form, about his experiences of power and privilege in his actual membership groups both past and present. . . . the psychological situation for the individual, therefore, is one of belonging to a number of segregated, un-connected groups, each with its own system of prestige and power. When he is comparing himself with other people or placing himself in the widest social context, he manufactures a notion of his general social position out of these segregated group memberships" (1954:262).

Objective View

According to Weber, inequality has three dimensions: class, status, and power. Sociologists who utilize the objective approach usually try to determine inequality on one or more of these dimensions. Inequality of power has already been dealt with (pp. 64–74), and therefore this section will be confined to class and status. Class is an economic dimension and will be discussed in terms of income distribution. Status is a prestige dimension and will be reviewed in terms of occupational honor.

Class Inequality

In general, sociologists have neglected the area of economic inequality because they have considered it the province of the economists. Until recently, there have been a great many difficulties in the interpretation of income statistics. "We can now quantify with some degree of certainty the annual changes in the distribution of income among families (using several different definitions of income and family), changes in the composition of lower and upper income groups, and the amount and direction of income changes among occupations and industries" (Miller, 1972:376–377).

Most studies focus on earned income, not because the researchers are unaware of other kinds of monetary resources, but because this kind of data is most accessible and most easily measured. Many people, in addition to salaries, receive housing and automobiles from employers. Others have income from sources outside employment, such as interest on capital and investments. Even the control of money can be an indirect source of income. University presidents, professors with research grants, and business executives have the use of money which is indirectly beneficial to them. Despite these exceptions—and they are numerous and significant—sociological research centers on "before-taxes" as opposed to "after-taxes" income, received in return for services and goods.

The question that concerns most of these studies is the equalization of income in the United States. No one disputes the fact that real incomes have risen almost continuously over the decades; the question is whether or not wealth is more or less equitably distributed. Is the gap between the rich and the poor widening or narrowing over time?

Estimates of income distribution based on income tax returns for the top 1 percent and the top 5 percent of the population were made by Simon Kuznets for the years 1913 to 1948 (1953). He found that distribution was relatively stable from 1913 to 1929, with the top 1 percent getting about 15 percent of the total wealth of the nation, and the top 5 percent receiving about 25 percent. Between 1930 and 1948, however, these two segments received a smaller share of the pie. The top 1 percent got 10.6 percent, and the top 5 percent got 20.7 percent. Thus, during the Great Depression of the 1930s and during World War II, the top 6 percent of the population received a smaller share of the total income (Glenn, 1974).

Glenn contends that this redistribution was partly the result of a "decline in the difference between the earnings of workers in some of the more highly rewarded occupations and the earnings of unskilled and semi-skilled workers" (1974:393). He felt that this decline resulted from increased strength of the labor unions, a labor shortage during World War II, and a loss of prestige among some skilled workers.

Since 1948, there appears to be almost no change in the income distribution. For example, the top 5 percent of the population got 21 percent of the total income in 1944 and 20 percent in 1962. The lowest one-fifth received 5 percent in 1944 and again in 1962. "These figures hardly support the view held by many Americans that incomes in our society are becoming more evenly distributed" (Miller, 1972:378). Glenn's data, which extend to 1972, support Miller's claim (1974:396). Furthermore, both researchers agree that although "one might suspect that there has been a greater redistribution of after-tax income than before-tax income" (Glenn, 1974:397), because of the so-called progressive rate schedules, this is not the case.

Table 3-2 shows the income distribution for American families in 1971.

The table clearly shows enormous inequalities in income in America. One-half of all families are below the median income of $10,285. (The mode is about $9600.) Samuelson calculates that if all incomes were to be distributed exactly evenly, each family would get $11,583 (1973:83).

Samuelson used the latest figures available from the Department of Commerce. He suggested that if one wished to know what the figures would be for the mid-1970s, the money incomes

TABLE 3-2
Distribution of Incomes of American Families, 1971*

Income Class	Percentage of All Families in This Class	Percentage of Total Income Received by Families in This Class
Under $2500	6	1
$2500–4999	12	4
5000–7499	14	8
7500–9999	15	11
10,000–12,999	15	16
12,500–14,999	12	14
15,000–24,999	20	30
25,000 and up	6	16

*Adapted from Samuelson, P. A., 1973:83. His source: U.S. Department of Commerce.

should be increased by 20 percent. Note, however, that this merely shows a general income rise, with no accompanying change in the income distribution. The top 6 percent of the population would still control 16 percent of the wealth, and the lowest 6 percent would continue to get only 1 percent of the total national income. Obviously, income inequality in the United States is widespread, despite any subjective feelings by Americans that this is a nation of middle-class people.

Status Inequality

In direct contrast to the relatively small number of sociological studies on economic inequality, the area of status inequality has not lacked attention. The first to systematically study status inequality was W. Lloyd Warner and his associates, in "Yankee City." Most of their findings are summarized in *Social Class in America*. Although Warner purports to be analyzing social class, he is really discussing status as revealed in his definition of class as "two or more orders of people who are believed to be, and are accordingly ranked by all members of the community in socially superior or inferior positions" (1949:159).

Warner used the reputational method (pp. 77–78), asking members of the community to place other people in the community in one of six strata. He claimed that people were ranked in high strata not only on the basis of wealth, but also through the use of such criteria as "taste," "good living," family background and others. Heller contends that regardless of Warner's interpretation, his data show that wealth is the basis of prestige, and "in order to be at the top of the status hierarchy one must either have old money or 'translate new money' into socially approved behavior and possessions" (1969:116).

Nevertheless, the reputational method remains the one most commonly used to ascertain occupational prestige. In 1947, the National Opinion Research Center (NORC) at the University of Chicago ranked 90 occupations on the basis of 2920 people's opinions. Each respondent was asked to assign a rank to each occupation in relation to the others. The results showed remarkable consistency among people across the nation, as seen in the following list, presented in the order of ranking:

U. S. Supreme Court justice
Physician
State governor
Cabinet member in the federal government
Diplomat in the U. S. Foreign Service
Mayor of a large city
College professor
Scientist
United States representative in Congress
Banker
Government scientist
County judge
Head of a department in a state government
Minister
Architect
Chemist
Dentist
Lawyer
Member of the board of directors of a large corporation
Nuclear physicist
Priest
Psychologist
Civil engineer
Airline Pilot
Artist who paints pictures that are exhibited in galleries
Owner of factory that employs about 100 people
Sociologist
Accountant for a large business

Biologist
Musician in a symphony orchestra
Author of novels
Captain in the regular army
Building contractor
Economist
Instructor in the public schools
Public school teacher
County agricultural agent
Railroad engineer
Farm owner and operator
Official of an international labor union
Radio announcer
Newspaper columnist
Owner-operator of a printing shop
Electrician
Trained machinist
Welfare worker for a city government
Undertaker
Reporter on a daily newspaper
Manager of a small store in a city
Bookkeeper
Insurance agent
Tenant farmer who owns livestock and machinery and manages
     farm
Traveling salesman for a wholesale concern
Playground director
Policeman
Railroad conductor
Mail carrier
Carpenter
Automobile repairman
Plumber
Garage mechanic
Local official of a labor union
Owner-operator of a lunch stand
Corporal in the regular army
Machine operator in a factory
Barber
Clerk in a store
Fisherman who owns his own boat

Streetcar motorman
Milk routeman
Restaurant cook
Truck driver
Lumberjack
Filling station attendant
Singer in a nightclub
Farmhand
Coal miner
Taxi driver
Railroad section hand
Restaurant waiter
Dock worker
Night watchman
Clothes presser in a laundry
Soda fountain clerk
Bartender
Janitor
Sharecropper
Garbage collector
Street sweeper
Shoeshiner

In order to test the correlation between this reputational evaluation of occupational status and objective variables, other researchers found that educational and income levels had a great
deal to do with the prestige of an occupation (Reiss, Duncan,
Hatt, and North, 1961:195). Thus there appears to be a close
relationship between the three variables: education, occupation,
and income. By obtaining a certain level of education, people
qualify for certain occupations and receive a certain income; education is a "cause" of occupation and income is the "effect" of
that occupation.

There are, of course, other ways of classifying social status.
One of the most important is the Index of Status Characteristics.
Warner and his associates (1949) used four status characteristics:
occupation, source of income, house type, and dwelling area, each
rated on a seven-point scale. The seven occupational categories
(professionals, proprietors and managers, businessmen, clerks and
kindred workers, manual workers, service workers, and farmers)
were ranked according to skill and prestige assigned by respon-

dents. Occupation was found to be most highly correlated with social status by Warner and by others who tested the ISC (Haer, 1955 and 1957; Kahl and Davis, 1955; Hetzler, 1953).

There is no question that members of society rank occupations according to prestige. One problem, however, is the multitude of occupations; another is the fact that they may be ranked on the basis of several different criteria. In an effort to solve this problem, Paul Hatt (1950) attempted to construct categories of occupations which would include the various dimensions, using eight categories: political, professional, business, recreation and esthetics, agriculture, manual work, military, and service. These categories appear to be on a single-dimensional continuum.

Richard Morris and Raymond Murphy devised a similar typology of 10 unidimensional categories, each judged to be of equal value to the society. Nonetheless, people tend to rank them unequally (1959). For example, a group of manual workers ranked the categories in the following order: education and research, extraction of raw materials, legal authority, health and welfare, commerce, building and maintenance, transportation, finance, entertainment, and manufacturing.

In conclusion, there seems to be no doubt that there is a stratification system in the United States in terms of both class (income) and status (occupation). While the objective approach to studying these phenomena can be validated with comparative ease, the subjective approach cannot be ignored (see section on class and political behavior in Chapter 6). If people *feel* they are poor or if they *feel* the work they do is inconsequential, then for all practical purposes, their subjective evaluation is true and they will live their lives accordingly. Once again W. I. Thomas's famous remark is applicable: "If men define situations as real, they are real in their consequences."

Bibliography

Baltzell, E. Digby, *Philadelphia Gentlemen*. Glencoe, Ill.: Free Press, 1958.

Barber, Bernard, *Social Stratification*. New York: Harcourt, Brace, and World, 1957.

Bensman, Joseph, "Status Communities in an Urban Society: The Musical Community." *In* Stub, Holger R., ed., *Status Communities in Modern Society*. Hinsdale, Ill.: Dryden Press, 1972, 92-107.

Bendix, Reinhard, and Lipset, Seymour Martin, *Class, Status, and Power.* 2nd ed. New York: Free Press, 1966.

Bierstedt, Robert, "An Analysis of Social Power." *American Sociological Review*, 15:6, 730–738, 1950.

Bonjean, Charles M., and Grimes, Michael D., "Community Power: Issues and Findings." *In* Lopreato, Joseph, and Lewis, Lionel S., eds., *Social Stratification: A Reader.* New York: Harper & Row, 1974, 376–90.

Bott, Elizabeth, "The Concept of Class as a Reference Group." *Human Relations*, 7:259–286, 1954.

Bottomore, T. B., *Classes in Modern Society.* New York: Vintage Books, 1966.

Buckley, Walter, "Social Stratification and the Functional Theory of Social Differentiation." *American Sociological Review*, 23:369–375, 1958. Reprinted in Roach, Jack L., Gross, Llewellyn, and Gusslin, Orville R., eds., *Social Stratification in the United States.* Englewood Cliffs, N. J.: Prentice-Hall, 1969, 23–32.

Centers, Richard, *The Psychology of Social Classes.* Princeton, N. J.: University of Princeton Press, 1949.

——, "Toward an Articulation of Two Approaches to Social Class Phenomena, Parts I and II." *International Journal of Opinion and Attitude Research*, 4:Win., 499–514, 1950–51; 5:Sum., 159–178, 1951.

Coser, Lewis, *The Functions of Social Conflict.* New York: Free Press, 1956.

Cuber, John C., and Kenkel, William F., *Social Stratification in the United States.* New York: Appleton-Century-Crofts, 1954.

Dahl, Robert A., *Who Governs?* New Haven: Yale University Press, 1961.

Dahrendorf, Ralf, *Class and Class Conflict in Industrial Society.* Stanford, Calif.: Stanford University Press, 1951.

Davis, Kingsley, and Moore, Wilbert E., "Some Principles of Stratification." *American Sociological Review*, 10:2, 242–249, 1945.

Domhoff, G. Willism, *Who Rules America?* Englewood Cliffs, N. J.: Prentice-Hall, 1967.

Glenn, Norval D., "Income Inequality in the United States." *In* Lopreato, Joseph, and Lewis, Lionel S., eds., *Social Stratification: A Reader.* New York: Harper & Row, 1974, 391–398.

Gordon, Milton M., *Social Class in American Sociology.* New York: McGraw-Hill, 1963, chapters VI–VIII.

Haer, John L., "A Test of the Unidimensionality of the Index of Status Characteristics." *Social Forces*, 34:56–58, 1955.

——, "Predictive Utility of Five Indices of Social Stratification." *American Sociological Review*, 22:541–546, 1957.

Hatt, Paul, "Occupation and Social Stratification." *American Journal of Sociology*, 55:533–543, 1950.

Hawley, Amos, "Community Power and Urban Renewal Success." *American Journal of Sociology*, 68:422–431, 1963.

Heller, Celia S., *Structured Social Inequality*. New York: Macmillan, 1969.

Hetzler, Stanley A., "An Investigation of the Distinctiveness of Social Class." *American Sociological Review, 28*:493–497, 1953.

Hodges, Harold M., Jr., *Social Stratification*. Cambridge, Mass.: Schenkman, 1964.

Hollingshead, August B., *Elmtown's Youth*. New York: Wiley, 1949.

Hunter, Floyd, *Community Power Structure*. Chapel Hill, N. C.: University of North Carolina Press, 1953.

Kahl, Joseph A., *The American Class Structure*. New York: Holt, Rinehart and Winston, 1957.

——, and Davis, James A., "A Comparison of Indexes of Socio-Economic Status." *American Sociological Review, 20*:317–325, 1955.

Kavaler, Lucy, *The Private World of High Society*. New York: David McKay, 1960.

Keller, Suzanne, *Beyond the Ruling Class*. New York: Random House, 1963.

Kenkel, William F., "Social Stratification in Columbus, Ohio." *In* Cuber, John C., and Kenkel, William F., eds., *Social Stratification in the United States*. New York: Appleton-Century-Crofts, 1954.

Kornhauser, Arthur, "Public Opinion and Social Class." *American Journal of Sociology, 55*:333–345, 1955.

Kornhauser, William, "'Power Elite' or 'Veto Group'?" *In* Bendix, Reinhard, and Lipset, Seymour Martin, eds., *Class, Status, and Power*. 2nd ed., New York: Free Press, 1966, 210–218.

Kuznets, Simon, *Share of Upper Income Groups in Income and Savings*. New York: National Bureau of Economic Research, 1953.

Lauman, Edward, *Prestige and Association in an Urban Community*. New York: Bobbs-Merrill, 1966.

Lenski, Garard E., "American Social Classes: Statistical Strata of Social Groups?" *American Journal of Sociology, 58*:139–144, 1952.

——, *Power and Privileges*. New York: McGraw-Hill, 1966.

Lynd, Robert S., and Lynd, Helen M., *Middletown*. New York: Harcourt, Brace, 1929.

MacIver, Robert M., *Society: Its Structure and Changes*. New York: Ray Long and Richard R. Smith, 1932.

Martindale, Don, *American Social Structure*. New York: Appleton-Century-Crofts, 1960.

Mayer, Kurt B., "The Changing Shape of the American Class Structure." *Social Research, 30*:458–468, 1963. Reprinted in Stub, Holger R., ed., *Status Communities in Modern Societies*. Hinsdale, Ill.: Dryden Press, 1972, 62–69.

Mayer, Kurt B., and Buckley, Walter, *Class and Society*. 3rd ed., New York: Random House, 1970.

Miller, Herman P., "Recent Trends in Family Income." *In* Thielbar, Gerald

W., and Feldman, Saul D., eds., *Issues in Social Inequality*. Boston: Little, Brown, 1972, 375–405.

Mills, C. Wright, *The Power Elite*. New York: Oxford University Press, 1959.

Moore, Wilbert, "But Some are More Equal than Others." *American Sociological Review*, 28:13–18, 1963.

Morris, Richard T., and Murphy, Raymond J., "The Situs Dimension in Occupational Structure." *American Sociological Review*, 24:231–239, 1959.

National Opinion Research Center, "Jobs and Occupation: A Population Evaluation." *Opinion News*, 9:3–13, 1947.

Ossowski, Stanislaw, *Class Structure in the Social Consciousness*. Translated by Sheila Paterson. New York: Free Press, 1963.

Parker, Richard, *The Myth of the Middle Class*. New York: Harper & Row, 1972.

Parsons, Talcott, "A Revised Analytical Approach to the Theory of Social Stratification." *In* Bendix, Reinhard, and Lipset, Seymour Martin, eds., *Class, Status and Power*. Glencoe, Ill.: Free Press, 1953, 92–128.

Reiss, Albert J., Jr., Duncan, Otis Dudley, Hatt, Paul K., and North, Cecil C., *Occupation and Social Status*. New York: Free Press, 1961.

Riesman, David, *The Lonely Crowd*. New Haven: Yale University Press, 1961.

Riessman, Leonard. *Class in American Society*. Glencoe, Ill.: Free Press, 1959.

Roach, Jack L., Gross, Llewellyn, and Gusslin, Orville R., eds., *Social Stratification in the United States*. Englewood Cliffs, N.J.: Prentice-Hall, 1969.

Samuelson, Paul A., *Economics*. 9th ed., New York: McGraw-Hill, 1973.

Simmel, Georg, *Conflict and the Web of Group Affiliation*. Translated by Kurt H. Wolff. Glencoe, Ill.: Free Press, 1956.

Sorokin, Pitirim, *Social Mobility*. New York: Harper & Row, 1927.

Stub, Holger R., "The Concept of Status Community." *In* Stub, Holger R., ed., *Status Communities in Modern Society*. Hinsdale, Ill.: Dreyden Press, 1972, 92–107.

Tumin, Melvin, "On Social Inequality." *American Sociological Review*, 28:19–26, 1963.

van den Berghe, Pierre, "Dialectic and Functionalism: Toward a Theoretical Synthesis." *American Sociological Review*, 28:695–705, 1962.

Viditch, Arthur J., and Bensman, Joseph, *Small Town in Mass Society*. Garden City, N. Y.: Doubleday, 1958.

Walton, John, "Discipline, Method, and Community Power: A Note on the Sociology of Knowledge," *American Sociological Review*, 31:684–689, 1966.

Warner, W. Loyd, and Lunt, Paul S., *The Social Life of a Modern Community*. New Haven: Yale University Press, 1941.

—— et al., *Social Class in America*. New York: Harper Books, 1949.

Weber, Max, "Class, Status, and Party." *In* Bendix, Reinhard, and Lipset, Seymour Martin, eds., *Class, Status, and Power*. 2nd ed., New York: Free Press, 1966, 21–8.

Wrong, Dennis H., "The Functional Theory of Stratification: Some Neglected Consideration." *American Sociological Review*, 24:772–782, 1959.

——, "Social Inequality Without Social Stratification." *Canadian Review of Sociology and Anthropology*, 1:1, 1964. Reprinted in Stub, Holger R., ed., *Status Communities in Modern Society*. Hinsdale, Ill.: Dryden Press, 1972.

chapter 4

Social Mobility

Definitions of Social Mobility

Social mobility can be defined as the movement of an individual or a group from one social stratum to another. Pitirim Sorokin wrote the first book on social mobility (1927), in which he noted that no society, even one with a caste system such as India, is absolutely without social mobility, that is, is completely closed. On the other hand, Sorokin also observed that no society is ever completely open, in the sense that everyone can move freely up or down in the stratification system. Finally, Sorokin pointed out that no two societies are exactly alike in the amount of movement permitted or encouraged. Indeed, not only are societies different in this respect, but individual societies differ over time as their technology and institutions change.

Sorokin was responsible for increasing sociological interest in social mobility, and he coined several terms that are still in current usage. For example, he identified two different types of mobility: *vertical* and *horizontal*. *Vertical mobility* refers to movement up or down the class ladder, such as the movement of an individual from a salesman or saleswoman, to a sales manager, or from the vice presidency of a company to the presidency. *Horizontal mobility* refers to movement within the same stratum, such as the movement of an individual from selling shoes to selling clothing, or from truck driver for Company A to truck driver for Company B; no change in economic class or status group takes place. Although there is a tendency to think of vertical mobility as upward, it can also be downward. In every society movement is in both directions: some rise in the stratification system, and some fall back. These social mobility rates are of great interest to sociologists, primarily because any fluctuation in them is an indicator of social change, as we shall see later in this chapter.

Regardless of how open or closed its stratification system, not everyone in a society is equally mobile. There are several reasons for this, such as differences in individual intelligence and motivation. The most important differentiating factor, however, is one's starting point, for it is clearly more advantageous, for example, to be born into a wealthy family than a poor family. Thus, two terms are important for this discussion: *ascription* and *achievement*.

Ascribed and Achieved Statuses

Ralph Linton, the anthropologist made the classical distinction between the terms *ascribed status* and *achieved status* (1936). *Ascribed statuses* are those acquired at birth. As soon as an infant is born he or she—with rare exception—enters at least three inescapable statuses: sex, race, and age. A fourth status ascribed at birth is social class, but this is alterable. *Achieved statuses* are those which are earned during one's lifetime, and are presumed to be statuses over which one has control. If one achieves high status, it is merited or earned.

While ascribed and achieved statuses are analytically independent, much of what people achieve depends upon their ascribed statuses. In general, sociologists treat the two terms as if they were alternatives. "Technically, any role is said to be achieved if it is not ascribed" (Johnson, 1960:140). However, there are those who take exception to this assumption. Thielbar and Feldman prefer the word "attainment" to "achievement" because it does not only imply that an increase or decrease in social standing is merited, but also includes things that happen to a person which are beyond his or her control, such as being drafted into the service or inheriting money (1972:540). However, it is not easy to persuade sociologists to reword a concept with which they are familiar and in agreement, despite the usefulness of the Thielbar-Feldman distinction.

A more important objection is that Linton's usage does not stress how often achieved statuses are dependent on ascribed ones. A professional's son[1] can more easily become a professional himself than a laborer's son can, because the former's father is more likely to be in a position to help his son to attain his goal. As Kingsley Davis notes:

Accomplishments, however, are already partial products of statuses ascribed at birth, so that differences of achievement can never be interpreted purely as differences of inherent capacity. Ascribed statuses, coming first in life, lay the framework within which the transmission of the cultural heritage is to take place. They determine the general goals (e.g., the adult statuses) toward which training shall aim and the initial persons who shall carry it out. When, accordingly, we know the child's sex, age, age relations, and the class, religion, region, community, and nation of his parents, we know fairly well what his socialization—indeed, his life—will be (1948:116).

John Finley Scott (1972) also takes issue with the notion that achievement is only earned or merited, noting that too little attention is given to the effect of the family on the stratification system. Scott points out "that all the members of any one family occupy the same status on all dimensions of status which are not necessarily differentiated within it because of reproductive functions" (1972:584). Thus the family has the function of status placement because it reaches the child first and has the greatest influence on his or her aspirations, motivations, and early training. Furthermore, the community tends to identify the child with the family from which he or she comes, and therefore is likely to offer each child differential opportunity for achievement.

[1]Masculine gender is used in this chapter because almost all studies of social mobility have used male subjects. No sexism is intended by the present author.

In brief, ascribed statuses and achieved statuses are theoretically independent. However, what one achieves frequently flows from one's ascribed statuses at birth, though there is not a one-to-one relationship in all cases. Many people born into lower-class families achieve a great deal in their lifetimes. In contrast, some individuals born into high-status families may move downward in the stratification system. Thus ascription does not guarantee class rigidity, nor does achievement guarantee class mobility.

Intragenerational and Intergenerational Mobility

Rates of mobility generally are studied in two ways. *Intragenerational mobility*, also referred to as *career mobility*, is the study of one person's occupational progress through a lifetime, and is unrelated to former generations. In other words, the researcher concerned with career mobility might follow a worker as he progresses from office boy, to salesman, to regional manager, to vice president. The variable most often used is occupation.

Intergenerational mobility is defined as a vertical change from one social stratum to another from one generation to another. Most researchers study occupational status, assuming that occupational achievement is a measure of social worth. Thus, upward mobility occurs when the child rises to a higher occupational level than the parent. This type of study is more common than intragenerational analysis.

Measuring Social Mobility

Sorokin has suggested that there is a need for an overall index of social mobility which would combine the amount of distance crossed (movement from one class to another) with the numbers of individuals moving either downward or upward. This index has not yet been successfully devised, for several reasons. One, researchers generally interview living people who have not completed their careers. Two, comparisons between fathers and sons are difficult to make because, for example, the son's occupation may be more prestigious but may generate a lower income. Three, time has a way of changing meanings, so that what was a prestigious occupation in 1920 may not be a highly valued occupation in 1970; or a 1920 occupation may have disappeared altogether by 1970; or a 1920 occupation cannot be compared usefully with a 1970 occupation that did not exist a decade earlier.

Cross-Cultural Comparisons

This leads directly into another, very important methodological problem—one of cross-cultural comparisons. Obviously a study of social mobility in one society is more meaningful when it can be compared with a study of another society's mobility. Most sociologists who discuss this problem point to four areas which make cross-cultural studies of social mobility difficult: (1) the occupational categories must have the same meanings in terms of prestige rating, monetary returns, and proportional representation; (2) it must be possible to compare opportunities for upward mobility; (3) samples must not vary in age distributions; and (4) there must be comparable data-gathering efficiency and techniques (Tumin, 1967:88; Heller, 1969:312; Broom and Jones, 1969). There is, therefore, a dearth of cross-cultural studies of social mobility.

The Social Distance Mobility Ratio

Natalie Rogoff has devised a social distance mobility ratio which has been utilized widely and which is generally considered valuable. The ratio is defined as "the ratio between actual mobility and the amount of mobility we would expect were there no relation between the son's occupational class and the occupational class of his father. The expected mobility values represent the amount of movement that would occur if social distance factors did not operate, in other words, if only availability factors influenced occupational movement" (1953:31–32).

This model has drawn many criticisms. Tumin, for example, feels that it ignores several issues: (1) changes in the occupational structure within two generations may not affect power, prestige, and property distributions; (2) the difference in subjective comparisons a son may make when comparing himself to his peers and to his father; (3) mobility in the highest and lowest strata; and (4) differential mobility among the sons of the same father (1967:90).

Occupational Status

Several problems arise when comparing a man's occupational status with that of his father as a measure of social mobility. Colin Bell, for instance, declares that such comparisons assume that occupations indicate social status, which may or may not be true.

Furthermore, when standard occupational classifications are used, the unemployed, housewives, the young, the aged, and students are excluded. Finally, when occupations are grouped according to what is assumed to be equal ranks, the result is an occupational class, so that social mobility becomes movement on an occupational scale in which ascriptive criteria are ignored. Bell contends that most studies do not conceptualize social mobility as a process, but rather as a structural framework within which mobility operates. Bell also claims that structural analysis is static because it only identifies the elements of a social system and the formal relations which tie one status to another. Process analysis, on the other hand, actually describes what occurs during human interaction, an aspect of social mobility that has been neglected (1968:9 and 21).

Permeability

A related problem concerns the interpretation of permeability, defined by Kaare Svalastoga as "the degree to which positions are filled without respect to social origins or other characteristics determined at birth" (1965:70). Such a definition implies that the permeability of a society can be placed on a continuum of uncertainty-predictability. Given a man's social origin—his father's occupation—how predictable is his social status, or his own occupation? When social status can be attained without regard to origin, uncertainty is high; when sons follow fathers' occupations, predictability is high. Svalastoga predicts that "permeability is inversely related to the absolute value of the correlation coefficient relating paternal and filial status" (1965:40). In other words, if there is a high correlation between the father's and the son's occupations, it is unlikely that the societal positions will be filled without regard to social origin.

Svalastoga's procedure has been found objectionable, given the kind of data to which it pertains, because the correlation coefficient describes the joint distribution of two variables (McFarland, 1969). In calculating approximate correlations, Svalastoga had to assume that occupational status is unidimensional, and he also had to guess at the shape of the underlying distribution of the social status values. Furthermore, he was obliged to assume the distribution would be constant over time and place and that categories were ordered from high to low before he could assign a range of numerical values to the occupations within each category. McFarland contends that this method places every occupation at the median point of each category, so that ultimately the assigned values must deviate from the assumed distribution.

Conceptualization in Social Mobility

There are also conceptual issues in the study of social mobility. Kahl, for example, equated the period between 1920 and 1950 with intergenerational mobility, assuming that sons completely replaced fathers in the job market over a 30-year period (1961). Instead, there is a great overlap. Broom and Jones (1969) warn that it must not be assumed that fathers represent a previously existing labor force; nor can it be assumed that fathers and sons each represent a generation. Any sample of workers contains overlapping generations and it is also necessary to take into account fathers and sons who may be only 20 years apart and fathers and sons who may be 40 years apart.

Defining a Generation

Lipset and Bendix (1959) also note the problem of defining a generation. They argue that the conventional method of comparing sons' present occupation with fathers' major occupation and calling the difference "social mobility" is conceptually weak because, for one thing, the comparison is not age-specific; for another, the stages in careers are not the same. The father may be at the peak of his career, while the son may be just beginning. Or the father may be at the end of his career, while the son is at his peak. Lipset and Bendix suggest that the question should be reformulated to ascertain the father's occupation when he was his son's present age. Furthermore, these sociologists claim that it is not possible to say that any period in a career is representative of a whole occupational status. However, they do not think it would be possible to get information on the complete career histories of both generations, although this would be ideal.

Motivational Factors

Another conceptual issue concerns the assumption that all those in the lower strata of a society desire to attain upward mobility. John Porter has criticized this assumption rather sharply, noting that motivation for upward mobility is acquired during socialization and is not inherent, as many sociologists seem to assume. Porter cites several studies (Rodman, 1963; Perralla and Waldman, 1966), showing that "the notion of common values about mobility has serious implications when social policies assume . . . that by providing certain opportunities where they do not previously exist, latent mobility aspirations and achievement motives will be triggered and the previously deprived will be brought into the mainstream of an upwardly mobile and achievement-oriented society" (1968:13 see also Kerckhoff, 1972).

Indicators of Mobility

Social mobility studies have been restricted almost exclusively to the analysis of occupational mobility. However, one can be mobile without being occupationally mobile. Miller, for example, mentions that "the resort to concentration on occupational prestige as *the* indicator of mobility is a choice largely based on the relative simplicity of the procedures involved. . . . On the grounds of economy, if not always of sensitivity, occupational prestige likely merits its premier place in the study of social mobility. The danger lies in believing that occupational prestige has the only place" (1960:4–5). Since occupational mobility occurs in a broad context, it can be qualitatively as well as quantitatively measured and be related to other types of changes because mobility phenomena, like geographic mobility and job shifts, often interact. Furthermore, geographic mobility must be included with occupational mobility in order to conceptualize social mobility. A job change, frequently involving movement to a new location, means that new social groups are encountered. These groups may well have different values from groups known in the past, so that an individual's social status changes. Further, one's social status might change independently of one's occupational status because occupational prestige may be differentially evaluated by different groups in different parts of the world. Hence both occupational mobility and geographic mobility structure social relationships (Bell 1968:170).

Kurt Mayer and Walter Buckley point out that status mobility also has been given too little attention. Although a rise in occupational level is frequently accompanied by a rise in status level, the "two processes are by no means identical" (1970:143). Mayer and Buckley describe a study by Leila Deasy (1953) which illustrates how occupation and prestige are distinct from each other. Deasy showed that the most upwardly mobile people in a small city in New York State were newcomers to the area. Apparently in this city it was difficult for long-time occupants of lower social standing to win acceptance from the highest status group if they had been born outside the group, even when considerable occupational success had been achieved. Thus, according to Mayer and Buckley, "the finding that newcomers to town encounter less resistance to social acceptability than long-time local residents confirms the widespread popular belief that individuals who were born 'on the wrong side of the tracks' if socially ambitious, should move to different communities where their 'lowly' social antecedents are not so well known" (1970:144).

To review, there are several methodological and conceptual problems in social mobility studies. One, there is a need for an overall index of social mobility which includes measurement on several dimensions. Two, international studies are hampered by lack of comparable categories of occupations, occupational opportunities, age categories, and data collection techniques. Three, means must be found for ascertaining differences in subjective comparisons between different reference models. Four, preconceived notions that people are motivated equally to move upward in the class system must be dismissed. Finally, intergenerational social mobility msut be reconceptualized to include indices other than occupation, such as geographic and status mobility.

Social Mobility of Cross-Cultural Comparisons

As stated previously, the question of cross-cultural mobility has always been of interest to sociologists, although it has invariably been difficult to study. The major question remains: Does the United States have a more open class system than other industrialized nations?

Fox and Miller (1965) attempted to make comparisons between the social mobility rates of four countries: Great Britain, Japan, the Netherlands, and the United States. They began by acknowledging all the problems inherent in such studies that have been noted in this chapter, and pointed out that their findings should be considered only as approximations. Using the conventional dichotomy between manual and nonmanual workers, Fox and Miller compared the inflow mobility (passage into) and the outflow mobility (passage out of) rates of the four countries. Manual inflow and nonmanual outflow reflect downward mobility for sons of nonmanual origins; manual outflow and nonmanual inflow reflect upward mobility of sons of manual origins into the nonmanual strata. Table 4-1 shows these rates of inflow and outflow for the four countries under consideration.

The table shows that in Great Britain, Japan, and the Nether-

TABLE 4-1
Comparative Manual and Nonmanual Inflow and
Outflow Mobility (in Percentages)*

Nation	Manual Mobility		Nonmanual Mobility	
	Inflow	Outflow	Inflow	Outflow
Great Britain	24.83	24.73	42.01	42.14
Japan	12.43	23.70	48.00	29.66
Netherlands	18.73	19.77	44.84	43.20
United States	18.06	30.38	32.49	19.55

*From Fox, T. and Miller, S. M.: In Bendix, R., and Lipset, S. M., eds., Class, Status, and Power. 2nd ed., New York: Free Press, 1966:575.

lands, the rate of outflow is higher for nonmanual workers than for manual workers. Thus, downward mobility in these countries exceeds upward mobility. In the United States the opposite obtains: the number of people who leave the manual worker category exceeds the number who leave the nonmanual worker category.

Fix and Miller claim that downward mobility is a better indicator of social fluidity than is upward mobility. They note that industrialization is associated with a decline in the number of people in manual work, thus facilitating upward intergenerational mobility. Downward mobility, however, indicates that sons do not automatically inherit their fathers' social class positions. They must rise because of talent or ability or be replaced by someone from the lower strata. "If this argument is valid, then the social structure of Great Britain and the Netherlands is less congealed in some respect than in the United States and Japan—contrary to popular opinion" (1966:575-576).

Table 4-2 shows the results when Fox and Miller broke the nonmanual category into elite and middle class groupings. The

TABLE 4-2
Outflow of Sons of Elite and Middle Class Origins
into Manual Status (in Percentages)*

Social Origins	Great Britain	Japan	Netherlands	U.S.
Elite	17.92	26.92	24.26	14.81
Middle Class	47.62	31.62	49.16	20.75

*From Fox, T., and Miller, S. M.: In Bendix, R., and Lipset, S. M., eds., Class, Status, and Power. 2nd ed., New York: Free Press, 1966:578.

United States and Great Britain have the lowest rates of elite out-flow, indicating greater occupational inheritance, while in Japan elite inheritance is lowest. In the middle class, once more the United States shows the lowest rate of outflow, which again indicates the rigidity of the mobility pattern.

Fox and Miller's study indicates that sons of elite fathers are most likely to become elites themselves in the United States and least likely to do so in Japan. In the United States, middle-class sons and skilled sons are more likely to become elites than the same groups in the other three countries. Furthermore, American sons of semiskilled workers are more likely to inherit their fathers' statuses than are their counterparts in Japan and Great Britain while sons of unskilled American workers show a greater probability of leaving this stratum than unskilled sons in any of the other three countries.

Thus, the United States has the highest probability of inheriting high status and the most opportunity for obtaining high status. This sustains *and* demolishes the myth about American mobility, in that the American stratification system is *both* rigid (for the elite groups) and flexible (for the nonelite groups). In addition, it does not differ greatly in the broadest sense from other industrialized nations.

Peter Blau and Otis Dudley Duncan's study (1967) largely substantiates the Fox and Miller findings. Their data revealed that in the United States there is somewhat more opportunity for advancement than in several other countries. Nevertheless, the differences are not great. Blau and Duncan showed that in the United States 37 percent of those men in white-collar occupations had fathers who were in blue-collar occupations. When compared with surveys in other industrialized countries such as Great Britain, Japan, Sweden, France, and Denmark, the mobility rates are remarkably similar (Lipset and Bendix, 1959; Miller, 1960; Fox and Miller, 1965; and Lenski, 1966).

This similarity is explained by Lipset and Bendix as follows: Inherent in all industrialized societies are the same structural factors which tend to encourage the same degrees of mobility. Furthermore, individual ambition is not limited to the American character and when there is opportunity, people of any nationality will seek upward social mobility. Blau and Duncan, however, claim that there is more movement of manual workers' children into the professions in the United States because American working-class children have better access to college education than do children in other parts of the world (1959:434).

Bendix and Lipset draw the following conclusions from their analysis of varying amounts, causes, and consequences of social mobility in different countries:

1. There is relatively little difference in rates of social mobility as measured by the shift across the manual-nonmanual line.
2. There is considerable national variation in the social origins of those in professional work.
3. There is national variation in the social origins of high-ranking civil servants.
4. There is relatively little difference in the backgrounds of high-level business leaders in Sweden, Great Britain, Switzerland, the Netherlands, and the United States.
5. Opportunity to enter the political elite through the electoral path is greater in Europe than in America.
6. The similarities in rates of mass mobility (manual to non-manual) among countries with such diverse social structures suggest that a propensity for mobility cannot be correlated with national cultural patterns, since some cultures encourage and others discourage social mobility.
7. Mobility patterns in Western industrialized societies are determined by the occupational structure (1959:72-73).

In conclusion, although the studies are somewhat contradictory in their findings, in part because measurement techniques vary, some generalizations can be made. Apparently there is more opportunity in the United States than in other countries for sons of lower strata fathers to rise in the occupational hierarchy. At the same time, there is greater probability that American sons of upper-class parents will inherit the elite positions in society than the sons in other industrialized countries. However, it also seems that as industrialization increases in any nation, the ability of elite sons to inherit decreases. Thus, throughout the world there is a probability that talent and ability will more and more take precedence over ascription.

Social Mobility within the United States

America has so often been called the "land of opportunity" that it has become a folk legend that this is the most fluid society

in the world and always has been so. In the United States, supposedly, the common man can rise to the top if he works hard
and diligently. However, it has also been observed that in the past
the American class structure was more open, and that it has become increasingly rigid in recent times.

Historical Studies

One problem in studying social mobility and changes in social
mobility rates in the United States is the paucity of historical data.
In one of the few studies carried out, Stephen Thernstrom (1966)
examined the career patterns of working-class men in a nineteenth-
century New England town. He found that most of the fathers
remained unskilled laborers all of their lives while three out of
four of their sons moved out of this social stratum. However, most
moved only one step higher, into the semiskilled category, and
very few became skilled workers. Furthermore, those who did skip
a category were sons of native-born fathers, not sons of first-
generation Americans. Table 4–3 illustrates Thernstrom's findings.

Thernstrom concludes from the table that "the cross-tabulation
provides no positive support for the belief that exceptionally
mobile workmen imparted exceptionally high mobility aspiration
to their children, nor for the hypothesis that a mobile father was
able to ease his son's entry into a higher status occupation"
(1966:607).

Furthermore, social mobility has always been present in the
United States, but the class structure has never been as open as
myth would have it. In the nineteenth century, "few of these men

TABLE 4–3
Occupational Status Attained by Laborers' Sons According
to the Highest Occupation of Their Fathers*

Son's Occupation at the Last Census on Which He Was Listed in the 1850–1880 Period	Father's Highest Occupation in the 1850–1880 Period			
	Unskilled	Semiskilled	Skilled	Nonmanual
Number in Sample	234	38	23	24
Unskilled	26%	3%	9%	29%
Semiskilled	54	63	70	29
Skilled	13	24	17	8
Nonmanual	8	10	4	23

*From Thernstrom, S.: In Bendix, R., and Lipset, S. M., eds., Class, Status, and Power.
2nd ed., New York: Free Press, 1966:607.

and few of their children rose very far on the social scale; most of the upward occupational shifts they made left them manual workmen still" (1966:615). . . . Chances to rise from the very bottom of the social ladder in the United States have not declined visibly since the nineteenth century; they seem, in fact, to have increased moderately in recent decades" (1966:614).

Other historical studies of social mobility support Thernstrom's findings. Lipset and Bendix claim that it has always been difficult for a person from a working-class background to move to a high occupation. These researchers studied the background of business executives born between 1770 and 1920, and found that about 70 percent of them over the entire period had come from upper classes, 20 percent had middle-class backgrounds, and only 10 percent came from working-class homes.

> The evidence cited so far points strongly to the favored social and economic background of a great majority of those whose later careers placed them in the American business elite. And since the proportion of business leaders coming from middle class and working class families has not changed greatly with time, our overall finding is that the recruitment of the American business elite has remained reasonably stable. . . . Our data allow us, therefore, to question the validity of the doctrine that the successful businessman had proved himself to be the fittest in the struggle for survival (1959:127).

In a similar study of engineers during three periods (1911–1930, 1931–1940, and 1941–1950) Robert Perrucci (1961) confirmed Lipset and Bendix. In this study the sons of fathers in high occupational categories were over-represented in the high-status positions and the sons of fathers in low occupational categories were under-represented in the high-status positions in each period of time; but the relationship strengthened for the successive periods. Thus Perrucci found a direct relationship between class origin and class position, and also observed that the relationship was increasing over time. Contrary to Thernstrom, this investigator concluded that there is a trend toward a more closed class system in the American opportunity structure.

On the other hand, Erwin O. Smigel compared the percentage of partners listed in *Who's Who in America* and *The Social Register* in prestigious law firms for the years 1957 and 1968 (1969:372–373). He found a 6 percent drop in the number listed in *Who's Who* and an 8 percent drop in the number listed in *The*

Social Register. These findings seem to indicate that the class system is opening, as Thernstrom suggests, rather than closing, as Perrucci suggests.

The most complete work on social mobility was done by Peter Blau and Otis Dudley Duncan (1967), who collected data from 20,000 males concerning their own educational and occupational backgrounds and those of their fathers, thus analyzing simultaneously intergenerational and intragenerational mobility.

The Blau and Duncan model of the process of stratification traces the interdependence of four determinants of occupational achievement. Two of these, father's education and father's occupation, refer to social origins. Two others, education and first position, refer to the individual's own training and experience. These researchers concluded that although social origin exerts an extremely important influence on occupational success, a person's own training and experience are even more significant, with education having the strongest direct effect. Furthermore, the study revealed that: (1) occupational inheritance is very high; (2) social mobility is pervasive; (3) upward mobility is more prevalent than downward mobility; and (4) short-distance movement is more likely to occur than long-distance movement. Thus, this study confirms some of the findings of all of the studies discussed previously. Table 4–4 illustrates these patterns.

Blau and Duncan offer the following explanation of the social-structural features relating to upward mobility. First, the most important feature is development in the American economy, causing long-term changes in the occupational structure and leading to continuous expansion at the higher levels and contraction at the lower levels. Second, classes have different fertility rates, with the upper classes having lower birth rates than the lower classes. This means that the upper classes fail to supply the personnel needed for the expanding number of jobs at the higher ranks, thus permitting people from the lower strata to move upward to fill this demand. Third, the immigration of unskilled labor from other countries and the movement of unskilled labor from rural areas within the United States into urban areas tends to push groups which are already urbanized into higher levels.

Hauser and Featherman reported on the trends in occupational mobility for the years from 1962 to 1970. They found that there were net shifts in the male occupational distribution during this period away from self-employment, laborers, and farm work, and

TABLE 4-4
Mobility from Father's Occupation to Son's First Occupation
for U.S. Males 25 to 64 Years Old (Percentages)*

| | Son's First Occupation | | | | | |
Father's Occupation	Higher White Collar	Lower White Collar	Higher Manual	Mid Manual	Lower Manual	Farm
Higher White-Collar (professionals, managers, proprietors)	28.6	28.2	9.8	22.6	8.5	2.4
Lower White-Collar (sales and clerical)	21.1	33.3	7.9	25.1	9.6	3.0
Higher Manual (craftsmen and foremen)	7.4	20.5	17.4	36.0	14.0	4.6
Mid Manual (operatives and service workers)	6.6	17.3	9.6	47.5	14.8	4.1
Low Manual (laborers)	4.6	13.6	6.8	37.2	30.3	7.6
Farm	4.1	6.7	5.8	21.0	12.0	50.3

*From Kerckhoff, A. C.: *Socialization and Social Class.* Englewood Cliffs, N.J.: Prentice-Hall, 1972:9, adapted from Blau and Duncan (1967), Table J2.2. (The entry in each cell is the percentage of sons whose fathers were in the occupational category listed at left and whose first job was in the category listed at top. E.g., 28.2 percent of the sons whose fathers were in the higher white collar occupations were first employed in lower white collar occupations.)

toward employment as salaried professionals, managers, craftsmen, and foremen. This means a generalized shift in the occupational structure from manual to nonmanual and from lower to higher status within both groups. Most of the change is accounted for by changing patterns of intragenerational mobility.

The patterns, however, do not seem to be uniform or inevitable. "For example, there appears to have been more change in occupational mobility patterns in 1962–1970 than in 1952–1962, but less than in 1942–1952" (1973:309). The authors contend that the lack of continuity is the result of the depletion of certain occupations, such as service workers, farmers, and laborers, which in the past were sources of recruitment into higher status occupations.

Effects of Intergenerational Mobility

Some sociologists have attempted to assess the effects of social mobility on individuals. Melvin Tumin lists several consequences of upward mobility. Movement from a lower to a middle class is likely to result in political overconformity and conservatism, feelings of familial rejection, diminished family cohesiveness, and a belief that the United States is an open class society. Downward mobility also usually leads to political conservatism, an acceptance of the stratification system, and low family integration. Tumin concludes that:

... the mobility experience in a status-minded society is likely to have some disruptive consequences, either because of the status orientation or anxiety of the mobile individual, or because of his inability to adjust successfully to the new groups into which he moves, whether up or down (1967:97).

Other sociologists (Blau, 1956; and Lipset and Bendix, 1959) agree with Tumin that mobility frequently results in anxiety, adjustment problems, tension, and a general social and psychological disruption of the individual.

A more recent examination (Kessin, 1971) of these assumptions indicates that while upwardly mobile people do interact less with their families, it is stretching a point to say that they experience family disorganization. However, for the downwardly mobile, family disorganization is somewhat more apparent. Nevertheless, Kessin claims that simply because there is less family interaction, one cannot infer that the quality of the relationship is poor, nor can it be concluded that mobile people are detached or isolated from their families.

In terms of mental health, Kessin reports that the upwardly mobile display higher levels of anxiety and psychosomatic illness than those who do not move up or down, and downwardly mobile people show higher levels of more serious emotional disturbances. In other words, upward mobility can lead to neurosis, while downward mobility can lead to psychosis.

Further, Kessin found that contrary to earlier studies, downward mobility does not necessarily mean that interaction in the strata of origin or arrival is stressful. In fact, downward mobility tends to lead to high levels of interaction, perhaps, according to Kessin, because such people "seek to compensate for loss of rank by increasing their participation in solidary groups" (1971:15).

Kessin concludes that most of the earlier findings are generally correct, with the exception of the assertion that downward mobility is associated with low group participation. Mobility is more likely to be disruptive in a traditional society when anticipatory socialization is absent, when mobility is rare, when a person crosses more than one stratum, and when movement is highly visible. In light of this, Kessin anticipates that minority groups that are currently upwardly mobile in the United States will experience personal and social disruption.

Female Social Mobility

Although the entire question of the position of women in the American stratification system will be discussed in detail in Chapter 7, it seems appropriate to discuss female occupational mobility briefly in this chapter.

Cynthia Epstein has commented on the special limitations placed on female mobility within the professions (1970). Epstein notes that in recent decades women have entered several upper-level occupations which were once almost the exclusive province of men. That does not mean, however, that women have risen to the top of these professions. The sex-linked boundaries continue to exist, embedded in the structure of the professions themselves, making sex status more salient than occupational status.

One impediment to female upward mobility in the professions is the sex-typing of occupations. People in occupations defined as "male" regard women who attempt to enter them as deviant and place obstacles in their paths. Even if women successfully bypass the entry blocks, their acceptance by colleagues and clients is limited.

A second impediment relates to social characteristics of professions. Members of a profession tend to be socially homogeneous; they share attitudes and norms, and they interact frequently on an informal, "buddy" level. In predominantly male professions, women, just because they are women, often fail to become integrated into the informal professional networks, and because of this they are denied access to many important exchanges between colleagues which may help to advance their careers.

Related to the informal colleague system just described is the protégé system, in which an established professional sponsors and teaches a neophyte. According to Epstein, males are reluctant to accept females as apprentices because they cannot envision them as their successors, or because they do not believe in their commitment to their careers. Furthermore, a relationship of this sort between a man and a woman may arouse feelings of jealousy and suspicion from both of their other role partners. The result of this lack of sponsorship often deprives the female professional of the kind of help in entering the "inner circle" that the male beginner takes for granted.

Within professions, performance is judged largely by one's peers by standards that are not pertinent to this discussion. In addition to formalized guidelines, there are always informal social controls to ensure conformity among members. Such rules are learned during socialization into the profession and interaction with one's peers, and "women professionals are not involved in the collegial networks to the extent that men are" (Epstein, 1970:972). This means that women often are not able to learn the rules, thus precluding fair judgment of their performance. In addition, women tend to be less visible in their professions, which in itself hinders performance evaluation by peers.

Women, then, do not fit easily into a professional structure. They are not as well-socialized; they interact less with colleagues; they feel self-conscious in the presence of their male counterparts; they try to attract attention by purposely maintaining a low profile; they overcompensate for their professional insecurity by being too willing to please and placate; and they accept the evaluation of themselves that they encounter as accurate. For all these reasons, female upward mobility in the professions has been limited.

In a more general study of female mobility, Peter DeJong and his associates reported that female intergenerational mobility patterns are essentially the same as those for males in the American occupational structure. These investigators claim that female occupational inheritance is similar to that of males: women are as mobile as men and upward mobility is more common than downward mobility among them, just as it is for men; short-distance mobility is more frequent than long-distance mobility; and the same major barriers exist for women as for men—between manual and nonmanual work, and between blue-collar and farm occupations. They conclude that "there are no major differences in the patterns for males and females. Generalizations about occupational mobility which have been made for males apply to females" (1971:1040).

Since these findings contradict all other theoretical formulations and empirical explanations, DeJong contends that prior theory may be at fault. Female role conflict may be exaggerated or it may be decreasing. The belief that women derive their social status from men may be erroneous. In other words, theorists and researchers have been wrong to claim that men have more access to occupational attainment and mobility than women.

Havens and Tully have taken strong exception to DeJong's findings (1972). Basing their criticisms primarily on methodological errors, these researchers claim that DeJong's conclusions do not follow logically from his findings. In addition, they accuse DeJong of ignoring documented evidence of discrepancies in occupational distributions and income differentials between the sexes. Citing Blau and Duncan, Havens and Tully point out that mobility ratios cannot be used as a basis of comparison, because the two populations do not have the same marginals and are therefore not comparable. Finally, DeJong is criticized for ranking occupational categories appropriate for men, but inappropriate for women.

Tyree and Treas also have presented counterarguments to DeJong. They compared women's occupational mobility with their "marital mobility," defining the latter as movement through marriage. Marital mobility for a woman is a change in occupational status from her father's to her husband's occupation (1974:297). Tyree and Treas found that women's occupational mobility and their marital mobility patterns resembled each other more than women's and men's occupational mobility patterns did. In other words, women have two possible kinds of mobility: occupational and marital. Marital mobility is more similar to the occupational mobility of men than it is to the occupational mobility of women.

Undoubtedly there will be many more studies of female social mobility in the future as the feminist movement gains greater momentum; but for the present, it is necessary to conclude that social mobility is greater for men than it is for women, the statements of DeJong and his associates notwithstanding.

Conclusion

While there are contradictory findings, it appears that, in general, most investigators of social mobility agree that the class structure in the United States is not as open as is popularly believed, despite the tremendous amount of short-distance movement. At the ends of the class structure continuum—the highest and lowest classes—social origin is especially significant in determining an individual's social class position. Also, the notion that there is more opportunity for economic and social advancement in the United States than in other industrialized countries does not appear to be true. Finally, it would seem that for a century the American class structure has remained relatively unchanged in terms of being more open or more closed, although it is probably slightly more open today.

Bibliography

Bell, Colin, *Middle Class Families*. London: Routledge & Kegan Paul, 1968.

Blau, Peter M., "Social Mobility and Interpersonal Relations." *American Sociological Review, 21*:290–295, 1956.

———, and Duncan, Otis Dudley, *The American Occupational Structure*. New York: John Wiley, 1967.

Broom, Leonard, and Jones, F. Lancaster, "Father-To-Son Mobility: Australia in Comparative Perspective." *American Journal of Sociology, 74*:4, 333–342, 1969.

Davis, Kingsley, *Human Society*. New York: Macmillan, 1948.

Deasy, Leila Calhoun, "Social Mobility in Northtown." Ph.D. dissertation, Cornell University, 1953.

DeJong, Peter Y., Brawer, Milton J., and Robin, Stanley S., "Patterns of Female Intergenerational Occupational Mobility: A Comparison with Male Patterns of Intergenerational Occupational Mobility." *American Sociological Review, 36*:6, 1033–1042, 1971.

Epstein, Cynthia F., "Encountering the Male Establishment: Sex-Status Limits on Women's Careers in the Professions." *American Journal of Sociology, 75*:6, 965–982, 1970.

Fox, Thomas, and Miller, S. M., "Intra-Country Variations: Occupational Stratification and Mobility." *Studies in Comparative International Development, 1*:1, 1965. Reprinted in Bendix, Reinhard, and Lipset, Seymour Martin, eds., *Class, Status, and Power*. 2nd ed., New York: Free Press, 1966, 574–581.

Hauser, Robert M., and Featherman, David L., "Trends in the Occupational Mobility of U.S. Men, 1962-1970." *American Sociological Review, 38*:3, 302–310, 1973.

Havens, Elizabeth M., and Tully, Judy Corder, "Female Intergenerational Occupational Mobility: Comparisons of Patterns?" *American Sociological Review, 37*:6, 774–777, 1972.

Heller, Celia S., ed., *Structured Social Inequality*. New York: Macmillan, 1969.

Janowitz, Morris, "Some Consequences of Social Mobility in the United States." *In Transactions of the Third World Congress of Sociology*. London: International Sociological Association, 1956.

Johnson, Harry, *Sociology: A Systematic Introduction*. New York: Harcourt, Brace, 1960.

Kahl, Joseph, *The American Class Structure*. New York: Holt, Rinehart and Winston, 1961.

Kerckhoff, Alan C., *Socialization and Social Class*. Englewood Cliffs, N.J.: Prentice-Hall, 1972.

Kessin, Kenneth, "Social and Psychological Consequences of Intergenerational Occupational Mobility." *American Journal of Sociology*, 77:1, 1–18, 1971.

Lenski, Gerhard, *Power and Privilege*. New York: McGraw-Hill, 1966.

Linton, Ralph, *The Study of Man*. New York: Appleton-Century, 1936.

Lipset, S. M., and Bendix, Reinhard, *Social Mobility in Industrial Society*. Berkeley: University of California Press, 1967.

Mayer, Kurt B. and Buckley, Walter, *Class and Society*. 3rd ed. New York: Random House, 1970.

McFarland, David D., "Measuring the Permeability of Occupational Structure: An Information-Theoretic Approach." *American Journal of Sociology*, 75:1, 41–61, 1969.

Miller, S. M., "Comparative Social Mobility." *Current Sociology*, 9:1960.

Perralla, Vera C., and Waldman, Elizabeth, "Out of School Youth—Two Years Later." *Monthly Labor Review, 89*: August, 860–866, 1966.

Perrucci, Robert, "The Significance of Intra-Occupational Mobility: Some Methodological and Theoretical Notes, Together With a Case Study of Engineers." *American Sociological Review*, 26:874–883, 1961.

Porter, John, "The Future of Upward Mobility." *American Sociological Review, 33*:1, 5–19, 1968.

Rodman, Hyman, "The Lower-Class Value Stretch." *Social Forces*, 42:1963.

Rogoff, Natalie, *Recent Trends in Occupational Mobility*. Glencoe, Ill.: Free Press, 1953.

Scott, John Finley, "Ascription and Mobility." *In* Thielbar, Gerald W., and Feldman, Saul D., eds., *Issues in Social Inequality*. Boston: Little, Brown, 1972, 580–597.

Smigel, Erwin O., *The Wall Street Lawyer*. Bloomington, Ind.: Indiana University Press, 1969.

Sorokin, Pitirim, *Social Mobility*. New York: Harper & Brothers, 1927.

Svalastoga, Kaare, *Social Differentiation*. New York: David McKay, 1965.

Thernstrom, Stephen, "Class and Mobility in a Nineteenth Century City." *In* Bendix, Reinhard, and Lipset, Seymour Martin, (eds.), *Class, Status, and Power*. 2nd ed., New York: Free Press, 1966, 602–615.

Thielbar, Gerald W., and Feldman, Saul D., eds. *Issues in Social Inequality*. Boston: Little, Brown, 1972.

Tuman, Melvin, *Social Stratification*. Englewood Cliffs, N.J.: Prentice-Hall, 1967.

Tyree, Andrea, and Treas, Judith, "The Occupational and Marital Mobility of Women." *American Sociological Review*, 39:3, 293–302, 1974.

chapter 5

Social Class
Differences in
Life Styles

Social Class as a Descriptive Term

As discussed in Chapter 3, sociologists are not
in agreement as to the meaning and use of the
term "social class." Social classes can be regarded
as discrete categories or as on a continuum. They
may be perceived as "real" or as figments of the
sociologist's imagination. They can be considered as economic entities only, or as self-aware
entities. One can view them as unavoidably
stratified or as merely "different." One can
accept that there are only two true classes—(the
upper and the lowest)—with status communities
in the middle, or one can regard the middle class
(or classes) as true classes also. However classes
may be perceived, it is clear that generalizations

115

can be made about broadly defined social strata. In industrialized societies there are subgroups comprised of people who, because of their different types of occupations, levels of education, and income, are similar in their life styles. They have distinctive characteristics; they strive toward different goals because they have different values, motivations, and aspirations; and they are accorded differing degrees of prestige from the society. We can construct ideal type profiles of social classes as relatively discrete and separate groups.

Social Class Differences in Early Childhood Socialization

Orville Brim defines socialization as "the process by which individuals acquire the knowledge, skills, and disposition that enables them to participate as more or less effective members of groups and the society" (1966:3). This definition implies that socialization is a lifetime process and that individuals are continuously being prepared to enter new statuses. In other words, socialization is necessary if one is to become a college student, a member of a profession, a spouse, a parent, an old person, or even a member of an athletic team. While Brim's definition is useful and its implications correct, the focus in this chapter will be on early childhood socialization, during which the child is prepared, primarily by the family, to enter the society.

Socialization occurs in all societies because all children must learn the values, norms, attitudes, and beliefs of the group to which they will some day belong as members. The process is carried out differently by different societies. The emphasis here, however, will be on the American process of socialization and how the differences between social classes affect the child's future status in the stratification system; the values he or she will hold; the behaviors they will engage in; and the kind of personality that will develop.

Compared to nonindustrialized societies, socialization is a lengthy process in the United States because American children do not become "adult" as early in life as do children in nonindustrialized societies. Americans generally consider a person adult when he or she marries or enters the labor force. Less technological societies usually define adulthood in terms of physical and sexual maturity. Furthermore, adulthood is not consistently defined in the United States. For example, social classes consider individuals to be adult at different ages because the age at marriage and the age at which one enters the labor market differ according to class. The society cannot seem to reach a consensus as to when a person reaches maturity. Americans may drive a car at one age, drink at a bar at another, marry, get drafted, or vote at other ages, depending on the state in which an individual resides. Thus, the American socialization process is neither uniform, consistent, nor clear in its definition of adulthood.

The process of childhood socialization accomplishes two things: Individuals develop a sense of self—a personality, and also develop into participating members of their society.

In the nuclear family, consisting of the mother, father, and children, the infant's contacts with society outside of the family are limited. Parents, particularly mothers, play the most important role in the young child's life. This family is called a *primary group.*

By primary group I mean those characterized by intimate face-to-face association and cooperation. They are primary in several senses, but chiefly in that they are fundamental in forming the social nature and ideals of the individual. The result of intimate association . . . is a fusion of individualities in a common whole, so that one's very self, for many purposes at least, is the common life and purpose of the group (Cooley, 1909:25).

George Herbert Mead described how the process of socialization works in the primary group (1934). First of all, a child must be within normal physical and mental limits. Second, no one can become human except by interacting with other human beings. People, then, are the products of both the hereditary and the social systems. Thus, *whether or not* a person learns is predetermined by his or her biological inheritance; *what* is learned is determined by the social system. Since our concern here is the social development of the individual, we will assume that the biological equipment is operative and normal.

Socialization begins, in a sense, even before a child is born. The parents have already been socialized. Most parents have met, courted, married, and performed the sexual act in socially accepted ways and they are already predisposed to socialize their children in approved ways. Thus, at birth, the background is already firmly prepared, and the direct socialization which follows birth leads to the emergence of a self through communication and interaction with others.

One important way in which the child develops is by *role-*

taking, a process during which the child puts his or herself in the place of the "other" in order to understand and anticipate the others' reactions. Furthermore, during role-taking the child learns what his or her own self is like. "Significant others" (the influential people in one's life) have a view of the child which is reflected back. Children observe how others treat them and develop a general concept of themselves. Cooley called this "the looking-glass self," meaning that a person's self-image is a reflection of what that person thinks others think of him. The self, then, is only one's *opinion* of others' opinions, because we can never be sure of what others really think of us.

Thus, through the process of role-taking with other human beings, especially those in the primary group, children become conscious of their own selves, adopting the attitudes and evaluations of significant others and behaving in accordance with them. Gradually children learn about their social world, how to live in it effectively, how to behave in order to gain acceptance, and how to control their lives. Clearly, the social class standing of the significant others in one's life influences the kind of values the child accepts as his or her own, and the ways in which those values are transmitted. A note of caution: The descriptions of socialization patterns in different classes are extemely broad. As discussed in Chapter 3, there are no definite boundaries between classes and much of the behavior described is overlapping.

Middle-Class and Working-Class Socialization Patterns

Bronfenbrenner (1958) has reviewed several studies of parental behavior during the early socialization period. He found that there were clearly discernible social class differences, although there had been important changes in such behavior between the 1930s and the late 1950s. For example, between 1930 and 1945, working-class mothers tended to be more permissive with their children than middle-class mothers. They were more apt to breast-feed their babies, to feed them on demand rather than on schedule, to wean them later, and to toilet train them later. After World War I, however, the middle-class mothers became more permissive in their attitudes and behaviors than the working-class mothers. Middle-class mothers also have been found to have higher expectations for their children. They expect their children to be more responsible for themselves and to do well in school. Furthermore, in terms of discipline, the middle-class parent is more likely to use reasoning, to appeal to the child's sense of guilt, and to threaten to withhold love. The working-class parent more often may resort to direct physical punishment. In general, Bronfenbrenner reported that the studies consistently showed middle-class families to be more accepting and egalitarian, and working-class families to be more interested in maintaining obedience and conformity.

The question then becomes: Why do parents in different social classes use different childrearing techniques? Duvall (1946) contended that there were two distinct value orientations which predisposed parents to behave in different ways toward their children. The *traditional value orientation* stresses order, authority, cleanliness, obedience, and respect, and is more often the orientation of working-class families. The *developmental value orientation*, found more frequently among middle-class families, stresses motivation, self-control, the development of initiative and curiosity, and reasoning and consideration.

M. L. Kohn (1963) claims that socialization techniques are related to the values and attitudes that are endemic to certain kinds of occupations. Middle-class occupations differ from working-class occupations in three significant ways. First, middle-class occupations require skill in handling ideas and personal relationships; working-class occupations require skill in handling objects rather than ideas, and require little skill in interpersonal interactions. Second, middle-class occupations permit self-direction; working-class occupations are usually much more closely supervised and are more routinized. Third, middle-class occupations are individual-oriented; working-class occupations are group-oriented. These differences in types of work are reflected in shared class value systems, and during socialization the values are passed on to the children. This explains why middle-class parents, who value independence, initiative, and individuality, tend to teach their children to be responsible, self-reliant, and striving; and why working-class parents, who value security and order, teach their children to be conforming and obedient.

Kohn's later research (1969) refers to these two different value orientations as "conformity" and "self-direction." The conforming working-class parent relates to the child in terms of externality, and behavior is judged by its consequences. Middle-class parents, on the other hand, relate to their children in terms of internality, and behavior is evaluated on the basis of motives and underlying attitudes. Kohn stresses that parents relate to their children in terms of those attributes that are viable in their own lives. Working-class life requires conformity, authority, and rigidity, while middle-class life demands initiative, self-expression, and independence.

Table 5-1 summarizes the differences in the methods used and the values transmitted in socialization practices between middle-class and working-class parents.

Up to this point we have compared only two social classes—middle and working—because more research has been done with families in these strata. Because of the limited data available, much less can be said about children's socialization in the upper and lower classes.

Upper-Class Socialization Patterns

According to Cavan (1969), children in the upper class are considered less as members of the nuclear family than as members of the kin group. Like children in the ancient Chinese family, upper-class children are regarded as links in family generations. They are trained and educated to think this way of themselves, that is, to remember who they are and to behave according to prescribed high standards that will enhance the family name and honor.

TABLE 5-1
Childrearing Attitudes and Behavior Among
Middle-Class and Working-Class Parents

Differences in Methods	
Middle Class	Working Class
continuous warmth and affection	sporadic warmth and affection
supportive father	uninvolved father
reasoning and discussing	commanding
interest in what behavior means	interest in what behavior results in
guilt-provoking and withholding love	physical punishment
aggression permitted	aggression suppressed

Differences in Values	
responsibility for self	obedience to others
people can manipulate their world	people must submit to Fate
people should have individual goals	people should have group goals
the world is good	the world is cruel
there is pleasure in variety	there is safety in sameness
people should develop competitive skills, intellect, initiative, and curiosity	people should develop physical toughness, conformity, and acceptance

Furthermore, children in the upper class are less closely tied to their parents than children in the two classes discussed earlier. They are likely to be brought up by "nannies" or governesses, and to be sent to private schools and summer camps. There is less interaction between parents and children, because children often become emotionally attached to the parent substitute, and because they are taught that their primary loyalty is to their extended kin. This lack of closeness to the parent results in a weakening of parent-child ties, which not only means less emotional intensity, but also more friendliness. Others, such as grandparents and paid teachers impose the rules, making for a more amicable relationship with the parents.

Children of the upper class are constantly being reminded of family history and famous ancestors, and are expected to carry out family traditions. They are made aware that the college they will attend and the occupations they will enter may be decided for them. During their socialization they are taught the family rituals, the sense of what is correct, the hierarchal structure of the family, and the importance of family solidarity. "In other words, they [the family] both control and restrict behavior, and at the same time incorporate each member firmly into the family" (Cavan, 1969:96).

Upper-class extended families tend to be unified and their contacts (except for servants and teachers) frequently are limited to other families in the same stratum. Because of this the child generally develops a great sense of personal and social security. Upper-class children understand at a very young age that they have high status, which nurtures self-confidence and a feeling of self-worth. Everything in their environment is geared to supporting this sense of superiority—the deference of servants, cultural advantages, the sophistication that is perceived in adult company.

Cavan notes, however, that not all upper-class children feel this sense of security (1969:98–99). Although there are few outside pressures, there are many from within the family. Such close conformity to moral standards is demanded that some children feel they cannot respond adequately. Furthermore, upper-class children often are insulated from the shocks of the world, and when they do encounter emotional or social stress, they may be less well-prepared to cope with it. Upper-class young people may have more privilege and more material comforts than their middle- and working-class counterparts, but they also have less freedom in such things as choice of a college, an occupation, and a marriage partner.

In sum, upper-class children are likely to be reared by parental substitutes. They therefore generally are more distant from their parents and more involved emotionally with kindred. They are imbued with the importance of the past, tradition, and ritual, and tend to be secure and self-confident because their lives are free from financial concerns. At the same time, they may have less free choice and fewer options than children from lower strata, and be less prepared to cope with a variety of real-life situations.

Cavan also briefly described lower-upper class children who are socialized in a fashion similar to children in the very highest stratum, but to a lesser degree. In these families also there is a tendency for parent surrogates to have the primary responsibility for rearing the children, but there is more parent-child contact. Furthermore, while there is some stress on the extended family, the nuclear family is somewhat more cohesive. Again, there is similar sense of security and a similar restriction of options, but to a lesser extent (1969:106).

Lower-Class Socialization Patterns

The families of lower class children tend to be larger than those of any other social class. Table 5–2 shows the difference in the number of children born to American women, according to educational level.

Studies show that lower-class parents say they prefer to have

TABLE 5–2
Average Number of Children Ever Born per Woman,
Aged 45 and Over, Who Have Ever Been Married,
by Education of Woman, 1964*

Education of Woman	Average Number of Children
Total population	2.7
4 or more years of college	1.7
1 to 3 years of college	2.0
4 years of high school	2.0
1 to 3 years of high school	2.5
8 years	2.8
Less than 8 years	3.6

*From *Statistical Abstracts of the United States 1967*. Washington, D.C.: Government Printing Office, 1967:52.

three or four children, and those who have more do so because they use less effective means of contraception, or use them less conscientiously (Cavan, 1969:147). One study revealed that only one-third of all the lower-class parents studied used proper contraception. The respondents were either ignorant of contraceptive devices or feared them. Many of the women questioned said they would not use a diaphragm because it could "get lost" in their bodies, while the men did not like using condoms because they reduced pleasure. Even when effective means of contraception such as the pill were used by lower-class individuals, they tended to be careless (Rainwater and Weinstein, 1960). It should be noted that Catholics are over-represented in the lower classes, and since many adhere to the Catholic Church's edict against using birth control devices, the result often is large families. Also, a certain level of sophistication, self-control, and a notion of planning ahead are necessary for the efficient use of modern contraceptives, and these characteristics frequently are absent in the lower class.

Several other factors contribute to the size of lower-class families. Children in the lower classes are more frequently regarded as assets because they leave school early and earn money, helping to support the family. Then, lower-class parents do not spend as much money on their children as upper-middle and working-class families. Such things as routine visits to the pediatrician or the dentist, special lessons in art, dancing, or music, and even college are considered unnecessary. Also, girls marry at a younger age in the lower class, and therefore there is a longer span of childbearing years. Finally, lower-class parents, especially mothers, tend to think of children as a "natural" result of marriage, and if a woman's relationship with her husband is not satisfying, she will often turn to her children for love and companionship.

The lower-class child is socialized more by peers than by family members, because generally the mother is working and frequently the father is absent or completely uninvolved in child-rearing. These children are often "street-wise," and know their way around the city much better than the more closely supervised children in the other classes. This freedom also leads to toughness and an ability to protect oneself physically at a young age. At the same time, the very poor child fears the outside world and tends to stay within the safe, immediate neighborhood where there is less likelihood of encountering strangers.

The lower-class mother is less concerned with rearing her children "by the book." She often praises, loves, or rejects them in response to her own needs and moods instead of to what she is told she "should" do. Further, lower-class children occupy a much more subordinate status in the family, since they are not given as much special attention as other children get, and are not regarded as important until they begin to earn money.

Perhaps the most outstanding difference between the lower-class family and families in other classes is the more frequent absence of a male father figure. E. Franklin Frazier described the "maternal family" among blacks in the rural south (1939). He contended that this form of the family contributed to the poverty and dependency of the poor black family. Oscar Lewis (1965) likewise found that the poor Puerto Rican family was "mother-centered" as a result of movement to urban areas.

Andrew and Amy Billingsley (1966) have described three types of matriarchal families among poor blacks. The first is one in which no father or husband has ever been present, and the mother either lives alone with her children or with her own mother. The second type has a temporary "father" or a series of temporary "fathers." In such situations the mother and her children either live with the current "husband" or with the mother's mother. The third kind of matriarchal family contains a father, but the mother is the more powerful person because the father, given his unstable position in the labor force, is unable or unwilling to exercise parental authority.

This last type is most common in the slum areas, and the consequences are serious for children, who both fear and have contempt for the male parent. Often such a father, because he is frustrated in his attempts to play the traditional role of bread-winner, will be violent and physically abusive. There is no other way in which he can assert his manhood. Puerto Ricans and Mexicans refer to this as *machismo*, the superior male, but the phenomenon is evident also among poor blacks and whites. "There may be differences in the degree and expression of the sex war and the cult of masculine superiority among Negroes and Whites on the lowest socioeconomic level. Nevertheless, the similarities are striking" (Herzog, 1964:400).

There is rarely a permanent male in the lower-class family, and therefore lower-class children are socialized primarily by women (mother or grandmother, or both) and by their peers. When males are present, there may be a great deal of argument, physical abuse, and general unpleasantness. Childrearing is unplanned, usually characterized by little more than attempts to keep children out of serious trouble. There is little or no guidance or planning for the future and children thus are treated as liabilities or nuisances until they begin to bring money into the home.

To summarize, the role of social class in the socialization process is a serious one for the whole of an individual's life. It is fundamental in determining the social context within which the child is reared. It is probably true that as children grow older and move into the larger world, social-class origins become less significant, but they continue to serve as reference points in people's views of themselves and in the perceptions others have of them.

Social Class Differences in Marriage and Family Life

In the United States most marriages are endogamous. *Endogamy* is the requirement that one marry within certain of one's social groups. Thus, most Americans marry people in the same age group, religious group, ethnic group, racial group, and in the same social class. It is not difficult to understand why this occurs so frequently. In all of these groupings there is a feeling of "we-ness." That is, "we Jews" as opposed to "those gentiles"; "we blacks" as opposed to "those whites"; and "we Irish" as opposed to "those Italians." People with the same social identities tend to feel like an "in-group" and to treat others as a suspicious "out-group." Members of the same group often share similar values, goals, attitudes, values, and sentiments which nurture understanding and close feeling. Obviously they have reason to prefer each other as marriage partners. Most often, blacks marry blacks, Catholics marry Catholics, Italians marry Italians, and members of particular social classes marry people from similar social-class backgrounds.

Social classes, however, differ in the way they select mates and in the ways they treat their spouses.

The Lower Class

Elliot Liebow's study of street corner men (1967) is very revealing of the attitudes of lower-class men toward women and marriage, in which a clear distinction is made between legal marriage and consensual union. A marriage is recognized as having public, clearly defined, known rights and obligations which are absent in the consensual union. Furthermore, marriage is regarded as a superior kind of relationship because it carries higher status and more respectability.

> But as the man on the street corner looks at the reality of marriage as it is experienced day in and day out by husbands and wives, his universe tells him that marriage does not work. He knows that it did not for his own mother and father and for the parents of most of his contemporaries (Liebow, 1967, reprinted in Lejeune, 1973:141).

Therefore, although the lower-class man puts a high premium on marriage, acknowledging its advantages, he is cynical, disenchanted, and bitter about it. He is aware that his failure to succeed in the work force is sure to adversely affect his relationship with a wife and children. Frequently, of course, the lower-class male does marry, but he is likely to see himself as having been coerced into the union by the woman. Liebow says that this notion of being forced into marriage is only partially true.

> Thus the presumption of coercion in marriage is, in part at least, a public fiction. Beneath the pose of the put-upon male, and obscured by it, is a generalized readiness to get married, a readiness based principally on the recognition of marriage as a rite through which one passes into man's estate (Liebow in Lejeune, 1973:143).

Thus, in spite of protestations, the lower-class man usually marries at least one time. However, the relationship between husband and wife who live below the poverty line is not the same as it is in other social strata.

The bonds between women in this class are very strong. The young wife regards her female relatives, especially her mother, as the only truly stable people in her world. She may go to her mother for assistance in everything from advice on how to handle her children to money for the necessities of survival. Women are the only security the lower-class wife knows, because all of her life she has seen men come and go. She worries that her husband will leave her, and very frequently her worries are well-founded.

Generally the young couple lives with the girl's mother because they cannot afford their own apartment, or they live very close by because the wife does not want to leave her mother. The females form a closed group in which men are merely tolerated, a situation which often leads to marital friction. If the mother-in-law helps the wife too much, the husband may think his wife is not performing her proper role. If the wife confides in her mother too much, the husband may resent her violation of confidence (Komarovsky, 1962).

In lower-class marriage, then, there is a vicious circle. The husband and wife expect to be emotionally and socially isolated from each other, and this expectation forces the wife to turn to her mother, which in turn arouses the husband's resentment and further estranges the couple.

Arthur Besner (1966) explains that the separateness between lower-class conjugal couples derives from generalized feelings of helplessness and apathy among poor people.

The central assumption of the lower-class value system is that the situation is hopeless. Because he [the lower class person] has to struggle merely to stay alive, because he knows that respectable people sneer at him as "no good," because he lacks the technical and social skills necessary for success, the lower-class person gives up (Kahl, 1967:213).

There is thus a tendency for the lower-class couple to feel that they never had a choice about marriage in the first place. Marriage "just happened" to them. They do not expect success or happiness because they do not have it in other areas of life and they do not see it in other marriages, and their shared expectation of discontent and separateness often brings about the reality.

In the intact lower-class family the father is patriarchal, an attitude which may take the form of physical abuse of his wife and his children. Furthermore, there is a strict division of labor: the husband is the breadwinner (when and if he can find work) and the wife is the homemaker (even though she often earns as much or more than her husband). The conjugal relationship is sexual, and only rarely companionable.

Jack Roach's case study of the Crawfords graphically illustrates lower-class marriage (1969). The Crawford family consists of a 30 year old husband, a 27 year old wife, and 6 children between the ages of 11 years and 4 months. All are in need of dental and medical care. After five moves within ten years, they now live in a reconverted garage in a slum area. Mr. Crawford has a work record of short-term, unskilled jobs, interspersed with long periods of unemployment. If he had a choice, he says he would like to be a night watchman because, although the pay is low, the work is steady.

In response to questions about her children, Mrs. Crawford said all she hoped was that they would stay out of trouble. But the school had already warned her about the oldest boy. "They can't stand him. Well, I can't stand him either. He even started to hit me back last week. . . . The others are bad enough. I can lock them in a room or something when they get on my nerves."

When asked about their marriage, Mrs. Crawford said: "I get disgusted with things a lot but I guess we're gettin' by. Anyways we have stood it for 10 years now." And Mr. Crawford: "She's gotta put up with me, who else is she gonna find to put up with her and her temper like I do? . . . All I know is the wife's still the same. Still crab, crab, crab."

The replies of the Crawfords to Roach's question concerning the future are typical of the lower-class orientation to the present. Mrs. Crawford: "I have enough trouble with things now without thinking about 10 years from now. Besides the Bible says take no thought for tomorrow. . . . I'll be a wreck when I'm 40 if I ain't already that. Things can't be no worse, I know that." Mr. Crawford: "I don't believe in that day-dreamin' business. . . . Who knows anyways about the future? I don't know and I don't care. . . . I suppose I see myself as a bum in 10 years. They say I'm a bum now, so what's the difference?"

Obviously, marriage for people below the poverty line is not very happy or hopeful. Husbands and wives may be sexual partners, but they are rarely lovers or friends. They cannot control their children and generally they do not even try. Men cannot fulfill their masculine roles in the job market and are therefore without real authority in their homes, even though they may use their fists to create an image of control or mastery. Women often work at demeaning jobs while also having full responsibility for children and the home. For security and love a woman turns away from her husband and toward her mother, who represents stability and safety.

The Working Class

It has been said that for the young woman from a working-class background the most important time of life is just before marriage. This is a period of romantic dreams: becoming a movie star, meeting a rich, handsome man, living in a mansion with a swimming pool and servants. But everything seems to conspire against such fantasies.

Socialization among young people in the working class leads to sex-segregation, very much the way it does in the lower class.

Girls spend their time helping their mothers and boys are discouraged from engaging in any activity which could remotely be considered as "sissy." The sexes belong to same-sex clubs and groups, and young people are dependent on same-sex friends and relatives for support, admiration, and companionship. Even during the period of courtship, the sexes tend to intermingle in groups in public places. The custom of formal dating is rare in this class, and even sexual behavior is sex-segregated in some sense. Young men tend to sexually exploit young women because they can prove their masculinity by relating their adventures to their friends. Young women, on the other hand, avoid sexual intimacy unless they believe it will lead to marriage. Thus, socialization and courtship practices among working-class people portend the lack of communication which will persist in marriage.

Shostak (1969) distinguished between two types of working-class families: the traditional and the modern. Traditional working-class families are poorer, less well-educated, have fewer skills, and are less mobile than the modern working-class family.

Lee Rainwater presents a picture of "traditional" women who are passive, prudish, submissive, and isolated. Apart from husbands and children, there is little contact with the world, except for female relatives and neighbors and the television set. Most live with a precarious sense of security and in constant fear of upsetting the delicate equilibrium. These women are rarely members of social organizations, partly because of fear that they will not be accepted and partly because they cannot afford dues or baby-sitters. The working-class wife, then, is preoccupied with housework, children, and husband.

The working class wife's daily life is centered upon the tasks of homemaking, child-rearing, and husband-servicing. When these women describe a "typical day" they devote most of their reportorial attention to three aspects of the day: their housework, their children, and their husbands (Rainwater et al., 1959, reprinted in Blumberg, 1972:441).

Rainwater and his associates claim that their respondents characterized their "typical days" as "busy," "crowded," "a mess," "humdrum," and "dull, just dull." Weekend days are little different from week days; summer and winter bring no change. However, a woman in this stratum believes that she is just like all other women, "except those society leaders you read about in the newspapers," so that she does not feel her lot in life is worse than others. Comparing working- and middle-class wives, Rainwater reports that:

> Overall, it appears that the lives of working class wives are relatively more constricted to the triangle of the home, children, and husband than is the case with the middle-class families. Many satisfactions are found within this triangle which often expands to include the whole circle of relatives and the family clan. However, they also respond to the life lived within this triangle by feeling it does not provide them with as much variety or relief from monotony as they might like. They see themselves as "hard working" women. They feel "tied down to the house" by their small children. They are solaced in their sometimes unhappy reaction by the recognition that their "dull" lot in life is shared by many American housewives, including most of the women they know (Rainwater, 1959, reprinted in Blumberg, (1972:451–452).

The traditional working-class family is clearly patriarchal. Both sexes accept an ideology of male supremacy, although in reality the woman often may have more power because the man is held in low occupational esteem and because generally he is not involved in household matters.

Mirra Komarovsky (1962) also asked a group of working-class female respondents to describe a "typical day." Her findings are similar to Rainwater's inasmuch as she found that most of the women's hours are filled with home and child-related activities. However, Komarovsky also asked how much the husbands participated in domestic tasks and found that husbands in this stratum of society do almost none of the specifically feminine jobs. Only 4 percent "frequently" helped with the cooking, laundry, and cleaning. Thirty-six percent "frequently" helped with the care of infants, but this rose to 56 percent when the children grew older. Apparently, sharing household tasks is not even an issue for working-class families.

> Division of labor in the home presents few problems because not only the men but the women accept the traditional segregation of masculine and feminine tasks. The wives do not normally expect assistance from their husbands (Komarovsky, 1962:52).

Clearly, the wife in the traditional type working-class family suffers from economic deprivation, emotional starvation, narrow interests, and lack of husbandly attention, companionship, and sharing. Yet she compensates by investing much of herself in caring for her husband, her home, and her children, and in this way she finds some measure of satisfaction and feelings of self-worth.

Shostak contends that in the modern version of the working-class family both the husband and wife are likely to be high school graduates. Gender roles take on a different meaning because "the occupational success, greater earning power, and heightened self-esteem that frequently accompany educational attainment play a large part, as do also the improved powers of personal reasoning and the improved ability to communicate that hopefully go along with a high school or junior college diploma" (1969:133).

Furthermore, this type of working-class family is more likely to live in the suburbs and is thus geographically distant from the extended family. Elizabeth Bott (1971) found a correlation between closeness to extended family and separateness between husband and wife. A move to the suburbs segregates the couple from this traditional network and forces them into a closer relationship with each other and with people outside of the long-familiar circle.

Handel and Rainwater summarized the differences between the traditional and the modern working-class marriage:

In the traditional working class family, the wife thinks of herself in terms of what she does *for* her family. Her self-conception as a wife and mother centers around those situations in which she is separated from the other family members—cooking, doing the laundry, cleaning the house. The traditional wife considers the kitchen the most important room in her house.

The modern working class wife thinks of herself in terms of what she does *with* her family. Her self-conception is broadened from that of servant to the family's needs to that of sharer in family affairs. She considers the living room the most important room in her home because that is the room in which the family relaxes together (1964:40).

Life in the modern working-class family thus is more egalitarian than in the traditional type. Husbands and wives are more likely to share domestic chores; recreational, decision-making, and child-rearing activities, while wives are more often employed outside their homes and therefore experience the wider world more extensively.

Even sexual relations may show some change for the better. In the traditional family, sex is a man's pleasure and a woman's obligation. Fifty-four percent of Rainwater's traditional working men's wives reported that they actively disliked sexual activities. In contrast, only 31 percent of the modern working-class wives disliked marital sex (1964:457). This difference is partly owing to the fact that the moden wife has access to and knowledge of birth control devices, and partly because improved communication between husband and wife permits the woman to express her sexual preferences.

Thus it is possible to conclude that although the image of the working-class family has been one of routine, alienation, dullness and boredom, according to Shostack (1972), change is occurring. Contraception has freed the woman from unwanted pregnancies; isolation from kindred has encouraged closeness between the marital dyad; and television and new neighbors have suggested new ways of interaction. While the number of traditional working-class families is still greater than the number of modern working-class families, there is a distinct possibility that the proportion will change and that family life in the working class will more closely resemble family life in the middle class in the future.

The Lower-Middle Class

Joseph Kahl claims that the lower-middle class can be characterized by its stress on respectability (1967:202–205). This class comprises the people in semiprofessions, paraoccupations, and petty jobs. They are on the ladders that may lead upward, compared to the working class who are not on ladders at all. These are the white-collar workers who belong somewhere above the blue-collar workers and somewhere below the upper-middle class.

> Lower-middle-class people are those on the fence; they are more conscious of being in between than are any other group. They cannot cling too strongly to career as the focus of their lives, for their jobs do not lead continuously upward. Instead, they tend to emphasize the respectability of their jobs and their styles of life, for it is respectability that makes them superior to shiftless workers (Kahl, 1967:203).

Like the wife in the modern working-class family, the lower-middle-class wife is likely to have a job outside of her home. Nevertheless, she does not envision this job as a career, but rather as a means of helping her husband increase the family income. Her "real" job is the home, though more domestic activities are shared with the husband in this group than in any of the strata discussed thus far, because the lower-middle-class man has less need to "prove" his masculinity by avoidance of any task that appears even remotely feminine. In addition, lower-middle-class families are even more segregated from their kin networks than the modern working-class families, and this further encourages closeness between the married couple.

A woman in this social class occupies a position of "junior partner" to her husband. She has sufficient freedom from financial worry and sufficient education to become involved in community organizations and to engage in leisure-time hobbies. She is less home-and child-bound and more companionable with her husband.

Among the lower-middle class, family ties are strong. Because they are concerned with respectability, this class values those things which are associated with it. Most are at least high school graduates, and many complete junior college or special training schools. They are proud of their education and urge their sons and daughters to go to college, often at great sacrifice to themselves. Lower-middle-class couples are generally regular church members, because they perceive religion as another sign of respectability. Strong religiosity usually is accompanied by strong moralistic views. Therefore promiscuity, gambling, drinking, and divorce are disapproved of. Owning one's own home is also respectable, because it demonstrates family stability and solidarity. A great deal of time, effort, and money are expended to keep the house and grounds attractive, although furniture is conventional and standardized because lower-middle-class people are conformists who fear anything that might make them appear "different." Indeed, this need to conform, which extends even into sexual relations, can cause rigidity and restriction of self-expression. The lower-middle-class person often tries too hard to be respectable, and the price can be high in loss of innovativeness and spontaneity. Nevertheless, as Kahl writes:

For many the lower-middle-class way of life is quietly satisfying; it connotes the accomplishment of moderate education and moderate occupational achievement; it means successful Americanization from not-too-distant ethnic roots; it brings a strong, stable, family-centered life; especially in the smaller towns and cities, it brings a degree of public recognition as solid citizens. This way of life may be dull, but it is not necessarily stultifying (1967:205).

The Upper-Middle Class

Upper-middle-class people are the business people, the trained professionals, the specialists in American society. Although there are other types of upper-middle-class families, the corporate family is most generally representative of this stratum, and will be described here as an ideal type. They "do not have jobs, but occupy positions; they do not work, they pursue careers" (Kahl, 1967:193). Almost all are white and American born; most have college degrees and many have advanced degrees. They are aware of their importance to society and are active participants, not only in their professions, but in community affairs as well.

> The central value orientation for the upper middle class is "career." Their whole way of life—their consumption patterns, their sense of accomplishment and respectability, the source of much of their prestige with others—depends upon success in a career. The husband's career becomes the central social factor for all the family (Kahl, 1967:194).

Gail Fullerton has titled the chapter on this social stratum in her book "Man, Wife, and Corporation" (1972:210), correctly implying that marriage in the upper-middle-class contains a third active partner—the organization in which the man works. Fullerton claims that "there is little *individual* achievement in our society any more" (1972:212), and "many American men are beginning to identify with their corporate employer rather than with a profession" (1972:211–212). Since most American wives derive their social identities from their husbands, they also come to think of themselves as team members: corporate wives, faculty wives, etc.

> If the husband's sense of personal worth is derived from the accomplishments of his "team," and the wife's self-esteem and social status are derived from her husband's accomplishments, clearly she, too, has a stake in the success of the "team." She often comes to think of herself as part of the "corporate family," an identification with her husband's employer that some corporations try to encourage (1972:212–213).

William H. Whyte (1951) contends that corporate wives are important appendages to their husbands. They must be, first of all, acceptable to the corporation, conform to the official image, and behave in ways that reflect favorably on the corporation. They must be cooperative and not compete with the company for their husbands' time or attentions. The corporate wife is expected to be friendly with the "right" people (but not "too" friendly); to be adaptable because frequently the family must move to new locations on short notice; and to be self-effacing because her husband needs tranquility, peace, and a "sounding board" when he comes home from a demanding work day.

A corporate wife, then, plays a large part in her husband's career and contributes substantially to his success or failure. Her importance is reflected in her home, which must serve as a background for her husband's personality. It must be available for unexpected entertaining, and the wife is expected to be a superb housekeeper and hostess. The home also must be a resting place and an oasis for rejuvenation. A corporate wife's importance is also reflected in her appearance, in that she must be attractive and dressed in the latest fashion. Intelligence is desirable so long as it does not outshine her husband and his associates.

The rewards for fulfilling these requirements may vary, but one thing is certain, the corporate wife will receive all possible material comforts. She will also have a full (perhaps *too* full) social life and plenty of leisure time to pursue her own interests. However, she may find that her husband becomes tired of her and outgrows her, because his world constantly widens while hers tends to remain no more than a satellite to his star.

In brief, the upper-middle-class family revolves around the husband and his career. The wife is an important part of that career and, in order to play her part successfully, she frequently must modify her own personality and her own personal interests to satisfy the corporate image. At the same time her life can be relatively rewarding, since she has financial security, freedom within certain boundaries, and social prestige, although secondarily derived.

The Upper Class

The upper class which, according to Kahl, comprises one percent of the population, is characterized by "graceful living" (1967:187-193). The men in this social class come from families that have been wealthy for several generations. They serve on the boards of directors of universities, banks, and huge corporations, and their names are listed in *The Social Register* and *Who's Who in America*. They are graduates of Harvard, Yale, Princeton and other Ivy League schools, and they send their sons to the same schools and their daughters to Wellesley, Radcliffe, and Vassar.

Members of the upper class are international in the sense that they travel extensively, often have homes in two or more countries, and interact with people of several nationalities.

The stress in this class is on tradition and family lineage. There is an ever-present sense, instilled from birth, that one belongs to an exclusive group and must behave in ways that will bring honor to the family name and preserve the family fortunes. Unlike the classes below them, the very rich keep the memory of past generations alive because they serve as reminders of their own superiority. People in the upper-middle class, in contrast, often prefer to forget their more humble ancestry.

> A man of the old elite may have accomplishments, but they are embellishments upon those of his ancestors. . . . The family is solidary through the generations; a grandmother may be a matriarch to whom all pay homage; old people have power and knowledge and connections that are useful to the young ones. The family members all realize that their positions depend upon the behavior of the whole group and that they cannot go off to lead their own lives (Kahl, 1967:190).

Therefore, although the very rich have financial security and are permitted, within limits, to appear "eccentric," there are definite boundaries beyond which they may not venture. There must be no scandal in upper-class families. Control is maintained through the oldest living member, preferably a patriarch, but frequently a matriarch because women tend to outlive men.

Continuity is very important, and sons are expected to follow their fathers' occupations. Wives, especially if they marry into families that are more illustrious than their own, are expected to merge their identities with their husbands'. Upper-class men prefer wives who do not have serious careers of their own and who therefore will not develop separate identities (Baltzell, 1958).

In order to protect itself from would-be social climbers, the upper-class family maintains strong parental control over mate selection. Young people tend to obey their parents' wishes in this respect because they are aware of the financial risk involved in defiance, and because they lack opportunities to meet and associate with people in the classes below them. This rule of social-class endogamy is especially stringent for young women; some latitude is permitted to young men. (*Hypergamy*, referring to the custom of women marrying men in higher social classes than their own, is more acceptable throughout the United States than *hypogamy*, which refers to the marriage of a woman to a man in a lower social class.) For upper-class young women, then, the pool of eligible husbands is a rather shallow one. Yet marriage is the most desirable career for the rich young woman, and the highest rewards go to those who make "proper" marriages.

Although love is considered an acceptable reason to marry, the true purposes of marriage are to preserve the family line and to unite one wealthy family with another. Marriage is the means to a merger rather than a personal relationship. There is much less stress on the conjugal pair than on the extended family, with the result that family obligations outweigh nuclear demands.

The upper-class family system is truly a patriarchal one. Baltzell notes that the college attended by the upper-class woman is not even mentioned in *The Social Register* (1958:27). Education, in a formal sense, is not particularly useful to these young women because they are not expected to seek careers. If they display proper manners and understand the art of graceful living, no more is expected of them. Even a man's occupation is not tremendously important because, unlike the striving upper-middle class male, his ego is not dependent on what he *does*, but on who he *is*.

The division of labor in the upper-class family is clear. A wife remains completely apart from her husband's business life. Her domestic role is more symbolic than real, since she rarely engages directly in household chores or in childrearing activity. Thus, although the man has greater marital power, the woman is free to travel with her husband and to share fully in his social activities.

The ties between husbands and wives in the upper class are not as close as they are in some of the other classes. This probably stems from the stress placed on the kin group, and on the fact that they can satisfy their ego needs outside of their personal relationship. "The upper class has the money and the knowledge of many areas of interest to enable them to pursue a way of life that makes them less dependent on the marriage relationship" (Bell, 1971:67). This independence from each other extends into the sexual area.

With a minimum of difficulty some in the upper class can and do seek sexual satisfaction outside of marriage. An extramarital relationship, carried out with discretion, is not usually a reason for ending an upper-class marriage because the exclusiveness of the marriage relationship was not the prime reason for entering or maintaining the marriage (Bell, 1971:67).

To summarize, there are tensions in upper-class life for both males and females. Men have freedom from striving to get ahead, and opportunities for adventure but they must always keep uppermost in their minds that their demeanor reflects on their family name. Women have freedom from household drudgery, but they suffer from loss of personal identity and from lack of opportunities to validate their self-worth apart from their husbands and kin groups.

Table 5-3 summarizes some of the class differences in sex, marriage, family life, and childrearing patterns.

Class Differences in Culture in Everyday Life

Robert Bierstedt defines culture as "the complex whole that consists of all the ways we think and do and everything we have as members of society" (1974:128). Culture includes those behaviors, ideas, and possessions which are available in a society. They are socially acquired traits, and are wholly separate from biological considerations. No one is born believing in God, knowing how to serve steak, or desiring to own a Cadillac. Culture is learned by interaction with others—sometimes through imitation, sometimes through direct instruction—transmitted through the generations. "Each generation contributes something to this stream, but in each generation, too, something is left behind, some 'sediment' drops to the bottom and is lost to society" (Bierstedt, 1974:130).

In all societies, of course, there are formal, written, enforced laws that govern most behavior. But there are other kinds of culturally determined behaviors which are informal, unwritten, and carried on during day-to-day living. They are called *folkways* and *mores*. *Folkways* are social norms, traditional patterns of behavior considered proper by a given social group. They are based on custom, usually obeyed automatically, and enforced, not by law, but by informal social coercion. *Mores* are similar to folkways, except that they have a moral significance and are considered more obligatory than folkways.

Clearly there are cultural differences between societies and over time. In America one could not aspire to become a headhunter; in Nepal one could not plan to become a Jewish rabbi. In the United States beef is part of our diet; for Hindus in India, eating beef is repugnant. In America, men generally wear trousers and jackets; in India men wear *dhotis*.

Just as there are cultural differences *between* nations, there are cultural differences *within* nations, especially nations as heterogeneous as the United States. Culture is acquired through interac-

TABLE 5-3
Sex, Marriage, and Social Class*

	Highbrow	Upper Middlebrow	Lower Middlebrow	Lowbrow
How girl meets boy	He was an usher at her best friend's wedding	At college in the psychology lab	In the office by the water cooler	On the block
The proposal	In his room during the Harvard-Princeton game	In the back seat of a Volkswagen	After three drinks in an apartment he borrowed	In her home one night when mom and dad were at the movies
The wedding	In her living room performed by a federal judge	College chapel, non-denominational	City Hall	Neighborhood church
The honeymoon	Mediterranean	Bahamas	Any Hilton hotel	Disneyland
Marriage manual	*Kama Sutra*	*Sexual Efficiency in Marriage*, vols. I and II	Van de Velde	None
Sex novels she reads	Jane Austen	*Lady Chatterley's Lover*	*Myra Breckenridge* and any novel by Harold Robbins	*Valley of the Dolls*
Sleeping arrangements	Double bed; orgasmic; female-dominated	King-size bed or twin beds with one headboard; affectional-sexual	Twin beds with matching nighttables; affectional-sexual	Double bed; for male's pleasure; reproductive
Sleeping attire	Both nothing	He: red turtleneck nightshirt She: gown with matching peignoir	Both pajamas	He: underwear She: nightgown
Background music	Ravi Shankar or the Beatles	Wagner	Dr. Zhivago	Jackie Gleason and the Silver Strings

*From Simon, W., and Gagnon, John: In Feldman, Saul D., and Thielbar, Gerald W., eds., *Life Styles: Diversity in American Society*. Boston: Little, Brown, 1972, 86–87. ©Dr. William Simon, Director, Urban Studies Institute, University of Houston. *(continued)*

TABLE 5-3 (continued)

	Highbrow	Upper Middlebrow	Lower Middlebrow	Lowbrow
Turn-ons	Pot	Champagne and oysters	Manhattans and whiskey sours	Beer
The schedule	Spontaneously, on an average of 2.5 weekly. That means 2 times one week and 3 times another	Twice a week and when the kids go to the Sunday matinee	Twice a week and when the kids go to Sunday school	Twice on Saturday night
Number of children	One each by a previous marriage; one together	2.4	3	As many as God provides
Anniversary celebration	A weekend in Mexico	He gives her a new dishwasher and she gives him a power lawnmower	Corsage and dinner out	Whitman sampler and dinner at Howard Johnson's
Quarrels	I don't care what your analyst says	I don't care if he is your brother	What do you think I'm made of?	Drop dead!
If the marriage needs help	He consults her analyst; she consults his	They go either to a marriage counselor or to a minister	He talks to his successful brother; she to her best friend	He talks to the bartender; she to her mother
The affair	But I assumed you knew	It was basically a problem in communication	It was bigger than both of us	Some things a woman shouldn't have to put up with
Financial arrangements	Separate trust funds	Joint checking account	She gives him a weekly allowance	He gives her household money

Family structure	Individualistic, remarried couple, marriage for better only	Democratic, once-married couple, for better only	Democratic, for better or for worse, once-married	Hierarchal, for better or for worse, once-married
Husband and wife roles	Independent	Equal	Wife-dominated	Husband-dominated
Child role	Autonomous	Team member	Reflection of parents	Independent
Grandparent	Banished	Tolerated	Accepted	Needed
Goal	Personal happiness and independence	Happiness and getting ahead; service to the community	Conforming	Staying even
Divorce	Desirable if there is no personal happiness and sexual pleasure	Meaningful alternative	Tolerated	Sinful
Sex education	Ask the doctor, dear, when you see him tomorrow	Well, you see, daddy has something called a penis and mommy and daddy love each other very much	Daddy puts the seed in mommy's tummy	We got you in the hospital
Vacations	Europe in May. She takes the children to Cape Cod, he commutes weekends	Europe in July. Family camping in Yosemite	He hunts or fishes. She visits mother with the children	They visit brother Charlie in Des Moines
Who raises the children	English nanny, boarding school, analyst	Mommy and daddy, Cub Scouts, Dr. Freud	Mom and dad, the Little League, Dr. Spock	Mom, the gang, Ann Landers, good luck

tion. Since social classes are frequently subcultures in a society like our own, members of each social class acquire different ways of thinking, doing, and having and they transmit these ways from generation to generation. Several of these different ways of behavior will be described in the following sections.

Language and Speech

The use of language and the patterned ways in which people communicate with each other are excellent indicators of social class. In Germany, for example, the upper classes speak *Hoch Deutsch* or high German; the lower classes speak *Platt Deutsch* or low German. An upper-class Englishman is easily distinguishable from his cockney countryman. In England especially there are levels of dialect that distinguish different classes (Pear, 1955:86–87). In America, a few sociologists question the notion that speech is an indicator of social class.

> Regional differences in accent and diction are probably greater than differences of social class position. All social classes speak roughly the same except that the better-educated upper and middle classes have better diction and grammar. This is a product of their superior education (Barber, 1957:151).

Most sociologists tend to disagree with Barber. Harold Wentworth and Stuart Flexner have explained why different social classes use different speech. At the time when the middle classes were coming into their own in the United States, books on correct language usage also were appearing. Neither upper- nor lower-class people are aware of learning to speak the argot of their classes but the middle class is aware of its precarious position and makes great use of books that will help to avoid speech identification with those beneath them. For the upper-class individual, speech is something taken for granted; for the lower-class individual, speech is functional—if it produces the desired result, it has served its purpose. But for the middle-class individual speech causes anxiety because it is deemed important to speak "correctly" (1960:xiv).

John Kenneth Morland also demonstrated differential speech patterns. The lower-class people he studied typically used the double negative and the past participle instead of the correct verb form, and frequently mispronounced words. Upper and lower classes had different terms for the same object. For example, upper-class "mantel" is lower-class "fireboard." Pronunciation of the same word often differs: upper-class "deaf" becomes lower-class "deef" (1958:192, 277).

Leonard Schatzman and Anselm Strauss studied differences in modes of communication between middle-and lower-class people (1955). Modes of communication have to do with how many perspectives an individual can manage, the use of abstract terms, and the ability to listen. The investigators found that middle-class people use more abstract terms and richer imagery; they organize sentences around classifications and are not conscious of doing so.

Clifton Fadiman (1956:6 ff) listed nine characteristics of upper-class speech which contrast with nonupper-class speech.

1. They avoid jargon and slang, except for upper-class sports and colleges.
2. They use fewer words to express the same thought.
3. They prefer direct, simple words and avoid euphemisms.
4. They avoid dramatic or striking language.
5. They have a tendency to use words derived from French.
6. They accent the last syllable of many words (ice cream or weekend, for example) which are accented on the first syllable by those in classes below them.
7. They use Anglo-Saxon monosyllables.
8. They have a neatness of enunciation.
9. The pitch and tone of upper-class speech differs from that of the speech of others.

Several sociologists have shown that auditory cues are more salient to the observer than visual cues (Dusenbury and Knower, 1938; Ellis, 1964). Thus, Americans from all sections of the United States can readily recognize social class speech patterns.

Two studies of social class identification which used the method of having subjects listen to taped speech showed that subjects could listen to content-free language and correctly determine the social class of the speaker without hesitation (Putnam and O'Hern, 1955; Harms, 1961). This is an important finding because speech is part of the way individuals present themselves to the world. According to Ellis, this raises two questions: "(1) is this label a handicap to lower-status persons; and (2) if it is a handicap, how difficult is it to change one's speech?" (1967, reprinted in Stub, 1972:250).

Ellis reports that his own study and that of Harms indicate that speech can label and handicap an individual. Subjects have been found to give less credence to remarks made by people using lower-class speech than to those using upper-class speech. This implies that in an employment interview situation, a person speaking in a lower-class manner would be at a disadvantage. Apparently interviewers are as frequently influenced by an interviewee's manner as by his or her qualifications for the position (Bellows and Estep, 1954). Furthermore, the social class origins of a person can be detected by interviewers even if the interviewees are college graduates, so that hiring practices will be influenced by speech even when all applicants have been educated at the same level (Perrucci, 1959; Ellis, 1964). It seems clear that unacceptable speech and language use can be sources of discrimination.

According to at least one study, changing one's speech habits is difficult, if not impossible.

> It is known that speech habits are not easily altered. . . . Persons who grow to adulthood as members of an underprivileged social group may carry a mark of their origin through life and suffer from the various forms of discrimination which society imposes on members of the lower socio-economic classes (Putnam and O'Hern, 1955:23).

The British sociologist, Peter Trudgill, reports that in measurements of differences in speech patterns in England, the greatest differences are found between the manual and the nonmanual worker (1974:45). This supports the findings on social mobility discussed in chapter IV. The most difficult occupational line to cross is between working and middle class. Apparently this is also true in speech patterns. Harms (1961) and Ellis (1964) disagree with this point of view. They claim that time, education, and environmental change can alter speech patterns and conceal lower-status origins. However, both of these authors feel that current research is insufficient to allow a definitive answer to the question. The difficulty is that speech is only one indicator of social class, and if changes in speech are not accompanied by changes in values as well, the person involved may become an outsider in both social groups. Lasswell concludes that "the evidence for the existence of cultural social classes is unmistakable, at least insofar as language is an index of culture" (1965:224).

Commensality

There are clear differences among social classes in terms of what, when, where and how they eat and drink. Pear's description of such patterns in England indicates that they cross national boundaries (1955:107). One influence, of course, is cost. Poorer people simply cannot afford some of the foods richer people prefer; but more important, because members in each social class eat and drink differently from the time of their childhood, they eventually acquire different tastes and preferences.

Upper-class people usually eat either very elaborate or very simple meals, and they avoid prepared or frozen foods, and TV dinners." Upper-class people also dine on terraces or in dining rooms; middle-class families have "dinettes"; lower-class families eat in the kitchen. Upper-class people eat at a later hour than the classes below them. Dinner is frequently as late as eight o'clock; middle-class people tend to eat at about six in the evening; lower-class families have their evening meal as early as five o'clock because many lower-class men work on shifts that end at four in the afternoon. Furthermore, the social classes have different names for the same meal. "Upper- and middle-class persons have breakfast in the morning, lunch at midday, dinner in the evening, and supper at night. Lower-class persons have breakfast on arising, dinner at midday, and supper in the evening" (Lasswell, 1965:249).

Children in the upper class do not generally take their meals with their parents; middle-class children eat with their parents and are expected to display good manners and join in the conversation; lower-class children also eat with their families, but are expected to be quiet and attentive only to their food.

There have also been studies on drinking patterns in different social classes (Dollard, 1945). Among upper-class people, drinking per se is rarely a moral issue; the focus is on the kind of behavior that follows drinking. Good manners are expected whatever the state of one's sobriety. In the middle class, women drink less frequently than men. Most middle-class drinking is done at cocktail parties or at all-male gatherings such as business meetings or conventions. Lower-class people drink in same sex groups, usually in taverns or other public places.

Even the kinds of alcoholic beverages consumed are class-differentiated. Beer and sweet domestic wine are associated with the lower class; bourbon, scotch, and moderately priced foreign wines with the middle class; and cognac, champagne, sherry, and vintage wines with the upper class (Gottlieb, 1957).

Class Differences in Sexual Behavior

Popular literature generally portrays the upper class as sexually immoral and decadent; the middle class as sexually repressed and constrained; and the lower class as behaving like "animals." How much of this is true? Most data on sexual behavior and attitudes show that while men in all social classes express similar opinions about sex, there is actually a great deal of variation in their behavior. In contrast, women in different social classes express varying attitudes toward sex, but in practice there is little difference among them (Lasswell, 1965:254).

Lasswell's contention that there are social class differences in male but not in female sexual practices is supported by the findings of Abraham Stone (1955) and Clark E. Vincent (1961). Indeed, the Vincent study and a study by Gebhard (1958) reveal that race is a much more differentiating factor in female sexual behavior than class.

Kinsey used occupational and educational levels to define social classes. He found that:

> ... each group has sexual mores which are, to a degree, distinct from those of all other levels. ... The close identities of the sexual records thus independently arrived at constitute some of the best evidence yet available that social categories are realities in our Anglo-American culture (1948:334-335).

Kinsey reported that upper-class males tend to avoid premarital sex, but are willing to indulge in most other forms of sexual activities. This willingness to innovate is also seen in marital sex among the upper class (1948:571-582). Lower-class males, on the other hand, avoid petting or foreplay and prefer conventional sexual intercourse (1948:379). Lasswell speculates that these findings mean that the upper-class man seeks:

> ... complete sexual release under the most pleasurable conditions without lowering the status of his female partner in any way, and without risk of making her pregnant. ... Upper level males tend to have a greater respect for the personal dignity of other individuals *of their own social status.* ... it may appear that the lower-class male is more interested in going directly to the most

complete and pleasurable form of sexual gratification, with the attitude that females involved must look out for their own dignity and welfare (1965:255).

According to Kinsey, homosexuality is most prevalent in the middle classes, despite the fact that this is the class most likely to deprecate the practice. More male homosexuals are found at the top level of society than at the bottom level; but neither group shows as much anxiety over the practice as does the middle group (Kinsey, 1948:384).

To summarize, most studies indicate that in contrast to males, females display few, if any, social class differences in sexual behavior. Both upper- and lower-class males are less inhibited than the middle class, and the upper class is more innovative and experimental in their sexual activities than either of the other two strata. Upper-class young men are relaxed about masturbation, heavy petting, and even homosexuality. Middle-class males are anxious about all forms of sexuality. Lower-class men are relaxed about sexual intercourse, but anxious about masturbation, petting, and homosexuality.

Recreation and Leisure

The Greeks conceived of work as menial and necessary, but as without intrinsic value. Leisure, on the other hand, was the only proper activity for free men to engage in, for leisure was an opportunity for contemplation, a time for the cultivation of the self and the study of values. By the time of the Puritans, work had become the highest good and leisure was to be used for restoring and refreshing oneself in order to be ready to return to the only truly honorable activity—work.

In modern society, there has been a reluctant return to a modified version of the Greek meaning of leisure. While it is no longer regarded as a time for contemplation, it is also no longer considered as only a time for restoration of the self. Leisure is "choosing time." Clawson defines it as "discretionary time" (1964:1), and Catton says it is "all time beyond what is used for the direct tasks of existing and subsisting" (1972:520). The activities pursued during choosing time must be ends in themselves, intrinsically rewarding. Leisure time must be time free from fear, urgent interests, strong passions, and social and economic pressures. Leisure time must offer an opportunity for self-expression.

William Catton estimates that the typical American has from three to six hours of free time each day out of 240 work days per year. Furthermore, he or she has about 12 leisure hours during each of the 100 weekend days per year. The manner in which this enormous amount of time is used has received very little attention from sociologists. Catton contends that this neglect is because of the persistence of the Puritanical attitude in the United States—the conviction that leisure is wasteful and that even free time should be productive. This attitude, however, is changing in response to the conditions brought about by urbanization and industrialization: shorter work hours, the proximity of places in which to enjoy recreation, early retirement, increased money for luxuries, and improved health. Thus, it is appropriate to investigate more thoroughly what Americans do with this vast block of time at their disposal (1972:521).

What one does with one's leisure time is within socially defined limits, and many of these limits are set by membership in a social stratum (White, 1955; Dulles, 1965; Lasswell, 1965). People are socialized within a society and within a subgroup of that society, and will seek to fulfill themselves within the acceptable limits imposed by that group.

A study by Alfred Clarke (1956) demonstrated different leisure patterns on five occupational levels. At the highest level (professional), most leisure hours were devoted to theater, concerts, lectures, art galleries, formal organizational meetings, home visiting and entertaining, playing bridge, and reading for pleasure. At the second level (managers, proprietors, and officials) people attended football games, went visiting out-of-town, and went to parties. Third-level men (sales, white-collar, and clerical workers) spent most of their time playing golf. Skilled craftsmen at the fourth level worked on their cars during leisure hours. Men at the fifth level (semiskilled and unskilled laborers) watched television, fished, drove around for pleasure, played with their children, drank in taverns, and went to baseball games. It is interesting to note that the greatest number of activities occurred at the highest and the lowest levels.

Joel Gerstl asked 25 dentists, 25 admen, and 25 college professors what they would do with one or two extra hours a day. The dentists were not interested in spending the time on work-related activities and said they preferred just to relax. The admen favored hobbies and recreation with the family, or doing chores around the house. Only the college professors said they would use the time for work or work-related reading and were not interested in relaxing. Apparently there is a relationship between professionalism and leisure-time activities. People at the highest levels are least likely to separate work and leisure; people at lower levels are more likely to turn as far away from work as possible in their leisure time.

If work-related leisure activities are a sign of membership in higher professions, then television viewing can be considered a sign of membership in the lower strata. Table 5-4 clearly shows the relationship between social class and watching television.

Hodges claims that there are not only class differences in the amount of time spent in television viewing, but class preferences in type of program as well. For example, the lower classes clearly prefer westerns, detective stories, and quiz shows; the upper classes clearly prefer plays, panel discussions, and news analyses.

There is also a direct relationship between reading habits and social class. More reading and the most serious reading is done by upper-class members. When asked if they had read one book in the preceding three-month period, 48 percent of the upper-middle class, 26 percent of the lower-middle class, 10 percent of the upper-lower class, and 2 percent of the lower-lower class said yes. Furthermore, the higher the class, the greater the probability of selecting nonfiction as preferred reading (Hodges, 1964:163).

Participating in sports and attending sports events or watching them on television are also distinguishable by social class level. "The evidence relating to social class differences in the passive-activist sphere is fairly emphatic. It amounts, in essence, to this: the higher an American's social class position, the likelier he is to be a sports 'doer' than a sports 'viewer' (Hodges, 1964:166).

TABLE 5–4
Social Class Level and Television Viewing*

Class Level	Minutes Watch TV per Night	Percentage Who Never Watch
Upper class	16	33
Upper-middle class	31	30
Lower-middle class	63	18
Upper-lower class	100	9
Lower-lower class	180	6

*From Hodges, Harold M., Jr.: *Social Stratification*. Cambridge, Mass.: Schenkman, 1964, 161.

From the little evidence that is available, it seems that there is a difference among social classes in terms of how they spend their leisure time. It is unclear, however, why this is so. Catton's explanation is provocative:

> Perhaps there is some tendency for a division of play to arise from the universal human tendency toward ethnocentrism. A population might be subdivided into more or less discrete in-groups by their members' tendencies to regard leisure behavior that differs from their own as necessarily inferior. And the pleasure of an activity may be reduced if one is aware of its being done by some negative reference group (1972:536).

Job Satisfaction

In the discussion on leisure, it was noted that Puritan values still have some influence in this country. Part of the Puritan ethic defines work as the only acceptable means of gratification. Work is still seen as a means of self-identity, as a way of relating to society, and as a justification for occupying social space. Work is that activity in which human beings engage for the primary purpose of monetary compensation. Work is neither "good," as the Puritans would have it, nor "fit only for slaves," as the Greeks would have it. It is necessary for the maintenance and advancement of individuals and their society. Work is that which gives structure to the day and a feeling of personal adequacy. Work is necessary for one's image of oneself.

In a unpublished paper (1969) the author constructed five ideal types of attitudes toward work for five occupational categories. For members of the highest professions, work satisfies the central life interest (Dubin, 1963). Its intrinsic value lies in its service as a symbol of personality, of authority, of ability to contribute to society, and as a source of self-expression, independence, security, and self-pride. The professional's work is a mark of personal identity and his or her prime social status. It provides psychic fulfillment, mental stimulation, and meaning to life. It is pleasure through achievement, and therefore an end in itself.

The work of the semiprofessional also satisfies these same needs: it provides a central life interest, justifies the occupation of social space, gives psychic appreciation of one's own worth, self-pride, independence, and security. However, because the semiprofessional is on a lower rung of the status ladder, there is less likelihood that he or she can derive these benefits from work to the high degree that the professional does.

The white-collar worker is likely to view work through the telescope of the Protestant Ethic. Work serves to justify a relationship to society, and is an economic and emotional necessity. It gives one a sense of responsibility and adulthood; its loss would cause shame and self-deprecation. For the white-collar worker, then, work does not have an intrinsic value; it is rather a means to an end.

The blue-collar worker also views work as emotionally necessary, as giving structure to life. However, there is less satisfaction and feeling of self-worth derived from work for the blue-collar worker than for the categories already mentioned. Blue-collar work in no way satisfies a need for a central life interest. It is frequently mechanical, boring, monotonous, and something from which to escape as soon as possible.

The unskilled laborer works only to maintain life. The work satisfies no psychic, physical, or mental need, and lacks intrinsic value, being completely and absolutely utilitarian. The unskilled worker brings little or no effort, interest, or motivation to labor, and derives nothing from it beyond the means of subsistence. There is total disengagement or alienation from work.

In order to test the hypothesis that satisfaction with work varies directly with social class, 140 people were asked how important work was in their lives. Because of the small number of the sample, the occupational categories were collapsed. Professionals and semiprofessionals were combined into one category of "professional"; white-collar workers were listed separately; and blue-collar and unskilled workers formed a "blue-collar" category. The results are shown in Table 5-5.

The table reveals that while it is true that there is a relationship between one's social status and one's satisfaction with work, most people, even those in professional occupations, do not derive great satisfaction from their work. Less than one-half of the

TABLE 5-5
Involvement in Work

Occupational Category	Low		Medium		High		Total
	%	N	%	N	%	N	N
Professional	12	5	29	12	59	25	42
White Collar	23	15	39	26	38	25	66
Blue Collar	28	9	47	15	25	8	32
Total	20.7	29	37.8	53	41.4	58	140

sample (41.4 percent) claimed to be highly involved in their work and 20.7 percent had low involvement.

In their study of work satisfaction, Bidnick and Lopreato predicted that job alienation would be "directly related to the monotony of the work, and inversely related to the amount of the workers' control over the work process and the products of work" (1972:313). Because they had no data on monotony of work and work control, occupational level was used as a rough measure in the expectation that job satisfaction would vary directly with position in the occupational hierarchy. Table 5–6 shows that their expectation was at least partially correct.

The table shows that professional managerial workers had more job satisfaction than lower white-collar workers, who, in turn, were more satisfied than blue-collar workers. However, there is little difference between the two kinds of clerks; in fact, the difference is in the opposite direction to that expected. In addition, there was no difference in the three grades of manual workers. Nevertheless, Bidnick and Lopreato claim that there is a positive relationship between job satisfaction and occupational level.

The same investigators queried workers about specific job complaints. As expected, the manual workers complained mostly about low wages and poor working conditions (toilsomeness, danger, irregularity, and inconvenience). The nonmanual workers complained of lack of freedom and the incompetence of their

TABLE 5–6
Job Satisfaction in Specific Occupational Categories*

Occupational Category	Job Satisfaction	
	Percent with No Complaints about Job	Total N in Category
Professionals, large proprietors, managers, and functionaries	70	81
Middle clerks	61	138
Small proprietors	55	111
Routine clerks	63	78
Skilled workers	54	261
Semiskilled workers	54	239
Unskilled workers	53	95
Small farmers and sharecroppers	46	232
Farm laborers	45	126
All respondents	54	1361

*From Bidnick, M., and Lopreato, J.: *In* Lopreato, J., and Haxelrigg, L. E., eds., *Class, Conflict, and Mobility*. San Francisco: Chandler, 1972, 314.

superiors. "Beyond these points, the dominating feature . . . is the gradation by skill level of those proportions of persons who reported they 'disliked everything' about their jobs. A person who is a manual worker was at least twice as likely to express this radical kind of disaffection with his job as a person who was a nonmanual worker" (1972:317).

Most studies of worker satisfaction reveal this correlation between occupational level and job contentment. Only one study known to this writer tends to contradict this general finding. Kaplan and Tausky (1972) studied 275 chronically unemployed people—those at the very bottom of the social class hierarchy. The study revealed that even among the hard-core unemployed, commitment to work is as strong as it is for employed white-collar and blue-collar workers. Although the economic function was of primary importance to these persons, there was a definite tendency to value work for its social function—that of conferring respectability on the worker. Finally, there was clear disdain expressed for those who were on welfare and for those who did not wish to work. "The attempts by many of our subjects steadfastly to proclaim their independence and desires to be respected, self-sufficient, and productive members of our society may, in fact, amount to pleas for recognition of their willingness to prove their social worth" (1972:482). This is, of course, not a real contradiction; but the study shows that even the chronically unemployed continue to subscribe to the Protestant Ethic that work is the measure of the human being.

To review our discussion, there seems to be some evidence that the Protestant Ethic is a declining value in the United States, at least in terms of attitudes toward work. Even among those in the highest occupational strata, work is not so intrinsically rewarding as might be expected. Nevertheless, there remains a difference among classes in the ways in which they view their jobs and in how much satisfaction they derive from work.

Associations, Clubs, and Friendship

According to several studies, there are social class distinctions in terms of how men and women interact with other people. For example, every study, in all sections of the country, has shown a clear, direct relationship between social class standing and the number of formal organizations to which a person belongs (Martin, 1952; Scott, 1957; Freeman, Novak, and Reeder, 1957).

Upper-class and middle-class people are joiners, working-class and lower-class people are nonjoiners. Table 5-7 illustrates this fact, as well as the fact that most studies are agreed on this point.

Furthermore, people tend to join those organizations whose membership includes people of their own class (Hollingshead, 1949). However, this finding has been disputed by Cuber and Kenkel. "It was not possible to divide the social-status continuum in such a way that most people would remain within their 'class' for most of their intimate associations" (1954:153). The difference in the two findings may be explained on the basis of time. What was true in 1949 may have been less true in 1954. It is probable that in 1975, memberships in associations would be even more heterogeneous in terms of class than 21 years ago, because more young people from the lower classes are going to college and therefore mixing with each other more.

It has been found that each social class tends to join certain kinds of organizations, and the prestige of the organization reflects the prestige of the members. The Junior League is an example of a national organization of elite young women. Locally, almost every average-size city has its upper-class country club, where members are admitted by invitation only. There are elite athletic clubs, men's clubs, women's "gardening" clubs, and charitable organizations. In addition to this sort of social club, there are upper-class and upper-middle class profession-oriented clubs, chambers of commerce, business and professional associations, service clubs, and college fraternity and sorority alumni clubs.

In contrast to men's clubs, women's clubs are more likely to be local than national, and women are likely to belong to more clubs than their husbands (Hodges, 1964:107). Furthermore, women's clubs are more status conscious than men's. "The quest

TABLE 5-7
Percent Belonging to One or More Formal Associations*

Class Level	Yankee City	Jonesville	National Sample	Peninsula People
Upper	72	100	—	70
Upper-middle	64	100	60	61
Lower-middle	49	55	41	43
Upper-lower	39	50	32	31
Lower-lower	22	30	22	23

*From Hodges, H. M. Jr.: *Social Stratification.* Cambridge, Mass.: Schenkman, 1964, 105.

for social esteem is palpably not the only motive impelling women to join clubs, nor is it necessarily a conscious force. But it appears that it is a compelling one—and, in the instance of upper-middle-class clubs in particular, perhaps even a central compulsion" (Hodges, 1964:108).

Approximately three out of every five people in the upper-middle classes are members of formal associations, compared to two out of every five people in the lower-middle class. However, the upper strata belong to more clubs and to more varied kinds of organization. Lower-middle-class Americans typically belong to fraternal and patriotic clubs, such as the Benevolent and Protective Order of the Elks, the Masons, the Shriners, Optimists, American Legion, Veterans of Foreign Wars, Knights of Columbus, and church clubs.

Members of the working class rarely join these organizations. Genevieve Knupfer gives the following reasons: insufficient income, more strenuous work and therefore less time and energy, fear of intermingling with those above them, and a general nonparticipation in community life (1949:103–114) because the company of well-known kin and neighbors is much more comfortable (Cohen and Hodges, 1963). Dotson found the same nonparticipation in formal associations among working-class families. He contends this does not mean they are social isolates, only that they prefer to spend their leisure time with those they know well rather than with "outsiders" (1961).

For the same reasons that people tend to marry endogamously, they tend to form friendships with those in the same social class. Shared social values and attitudes, even shared language, make friendships more comfortable and social intimacy easier. Warner, in fact, turns this theory around, contending that social classes are the *result* of individuals' tendencies to fraternize with people like themselves, thus forming subgroups (1941).

Whether class causes friendship or friendship causes class is really immaterial. The fact is that the two vary together. One's best friend is likely to be in the same social class, just as one is likely to marry someone from the same social class. Human beings do not interact with everyone; they are selective in their choices of friends. Much, of course, depends on proximity and on special interests and needs, but a great deal depends on social class because an individual is more likely to encounter people at his or her same level in the everyday world and to feel more comfortable with them. Evidence for this comes from observation of children's play groups (Neugarten, 1946; Stendler, 1949) and of teenage groups (Tryon, 1944; Hollingshead, 1949; Havighurst and Taba, 1949; and Gesell et al., 1956).

Kahl and Davis asked their adult respondents to tell them the occupations of their three best friends. They noted that while most adults tend to form cliques with others in the same social stratum, this was most true for those at the highest levels (1955). Table 5–8 shows this relationship, and also shows that as one looks down the social ladder, one can observe that the number of social isolates (those who claimed they had no close friends) increases. Kahl and Davis concluded that "although recreational participation is not completely limited to a given prestige level, in general people associate 'with their own kind.' Furthermore, people at lower levels have less interaction than those at higher levels ... " (Kahl, 1967:138).

There are differences in the ways people on different social levels interact in their friendship groups. In the upper classes and upper-middle classes, interaction with friends occurs spontaneously at least once a week, usually in someone's home. "Drop in if you can around 9 o'clock." Women in these classes often spend their afternoons together, shopping, lunching, or playing cards. Men meet during the day for lunch and in their offices.

Middle-class society is more formal, and meetings are generally by invitation. At parties, behavior is more restrained. There is less drinking and less flirtation than in the higher classes and there is also more competition among the wives to host elaborate suppers and buffets.

Lower-class people are more likely to socialize in same-sex

TABLE 5–8
Percentage Distribution of Status of Best Friends*

Status of Respondent†	Average Status of Three Best Friends						
	N	1	2	3	4	None	Total
1	19	74	16	—	—	10	100
2	34	32	38	15	3	12	100
3	82	10	15	50	12	13	100
4	47	—	9	38	30	23	100
5	17	—	—	35	35	30	100
Total	199						

*Adapted from Kahl, J. A.: *The American Class Structure.* New York: Holt, Rinehart and Winston, 1967: 138.
†Status is in descending order, i.e., 1 is the highest status, 5 is the lowest.

groups and on an informal basis. Women visit in the neighborhood; men meet in taverns. Couples do not often go out together, nor do they invite other couples to their homes (Kahl, 1967:139–141).

It seems clear, then, that people belong to formal organizations and associate informally with those in their own social class. It is also clear that the higher the social class, the greater the amount of interaction, both formal and informal. Such patterning starts in childhood and continues through life. Its principal motivation stems from the individual's attraction to others who share similar values and attitudes, and the fact that intimacy is facilitated with those who are most like ourselves.

Conclusion

In this chapter it has been shown that there are differences between social classes that go beyond the economic factor. Although clearly there is a relationship between differences in life-styles and differences in income and wealth, the factors that probably are most significant in causing the dissimilarities are socialization and association.

It has been noted that social classes have specific ways in which they rear their children, and specific values and attitudes about life that are passed from one generation to the next. This socialization leads to diversified marital relationships, different use of language and communication patterns, and divergent ways of eating and drinking, sex behavior, concepts of leisure-time activities, attitudes to work, and associational behavior.

Evidently there are social entities in the United States which manifest cultural distinctions. Perhaps sociologists cannot observe social classes directly, but they can certainly locate them by noting their cultural patterns.

Bibliography

Baltzell, E. D., *Philadelphia Gentlemen, The Making of a National Upper Class.* Glencoe, Ill.: Free Press, 1958.

Barber, Bernard, *Social Stratification.* New York: Harcourt, Brace, 1957.

Bell, Robert R., *Marriage and Family Interaction.* 3rd ed., Homewood, Ill.: Dorsey Press, 1971.

Bellows, Roger, and Estep, M. F., *Employment Psychology: The Interview.* New York: Holt, Rinehart and Winston, 1954.

Besner, Arthur, "Economic Deprivation and Family Patterns." *In* Irelan, L. M., ed., *Low Income Life Styles*. Washington, D.C.: United States Department of Health, Education, and Welfare, Welfare Administration Publication No. 14, 1966, 15-29.

Bidnick, Marilyn, and Lopreato, Joseph, "Work, Satisfaction, and Alienation." *In* Lopreato, Joseph, and Hazelrigg, Lawrence E., eds., *Class, Conflict, and Mobility*. San Francisco: Chandler, 1972, 303-378.

Bierstedt, Robert, *The Social Order*. 4th ed., New York: McGraw-Hill, 1974.

Billingsley, Andrew, and Billingsley, Amy Tate, "Illegitimacy and Patterns of Negro Family Life." *In* Roberts, Robert W., ed., *The Unwed Mother*. New York: Harper & Row, 1966, 149-151.

Blumberg, Paul, *The Impact of Social Class*. New York: Thomas Y. Crowell, 1972.

Bott, Elizabeth, *Family and Social Network*, 2nd ed., New York: Free Press, 1971.

Brim, O. G., Jr., "Socialization Through the Life Cycle." *In* Brim, O. G., Jr. and Wheeler, S., *Socialization after Childhood*. New York: John Wiley, 1966.

Bronfenbrenner, U., "Socialization and Social Class Through Time and Space." *In* Maccoby, E. E., Newcomb, T. N., and Hartley, E. L., eds., *Readings in Social Psychology*. 2nd ed., New York: Holt, Rinehart and Winston, 1958, 440-425.

Catton, William R., Jr., "Leisure and Social Stratification." *In* Thielbar, Gerald W., and Feldman, Saul D., eds., *Issues in Social Inequality*. Boston: Little, Brown, 1972, 520-538.

Cavan, Ruth S., *The American Family*. 4th ed., New York: Thomas Y. Crowell, 1969.

Clarke, Alfred C., "Leisure and Occupational Prestige." *American Sociological Review* 21:301-307, 1956.

Clawson, Marion, "How Much Leisure, Now and in the Future?" *In* Charlesworth, James C., ed., *Leisure in America: Blessing or Curse?* Philadelphia: American Academy of Political and Social Science, 1964, 1-20.

Cohen, Albert K., and Hodges, Harold M., "Lower Blue-Collar Characteristics." *Social Problems*, 303-334, 1963.

Cooley, Charles Horton, *Social Organization*. New York: Scribner, 1909.

Cuber, John F., and Kenkel, William F., *Social Stratification in the United States*. New York: Appleton-Century-Crofts, 1954.

Dodson, Floyd, "Patterns of Voluntary Association Among Urban Working-Class Families." *American Sociological Review*, 16:687-693, 1961.

Dollard, David, "Drinking Mores of the Social Classes." *Alcohol, Science, and Society*. New Haven, Conn.: *Quarterly Journal of Studies on Alcohol*, 95-101, 1945.

Duberman, Lucile, "Some Thoughts on the Relationship Between the Satisfaction of Central Life Interest in Work and in Leisure and the Possible Social Implications." Unpublished, 1969.

Dubin, Robert, "Industrial Workers' Worlds: A Study of the 'Central Life Interest' of Industrial Workers." *In* Smigel, Erwin O., ed., *Work and Leisure.* New Haven, Conn.: College and University Press, 1963.

Dulles, Foster Rhea, *A History of Recreation: America Learns to Play.* 2nd ed., New York: Appleton-Century-Crofts, 1965.

Dusenbury, D., and Knower, Frank W., "Experimental Studies of the Symbolism of Action and Speech." *Quarterly Journal of Speech, 24:*1938.

Duvall, E. M., "Conceptions of Parenthood." *American Journal of Sociology, 52:*193–203, 1946.

Ellis, Dean S., "The Effects of Limiting the Amount of Exposure Between Interviewers and Interviewees." Unpublished, Communication Research Center, Purdue University, 1964.

——, "Speech and Social Status in America." *Social Forces, 45:*431–437, 1967. Reprinted in Stub, Holger R., ed., *Status Communities in Modern Society.* Hinsdale, Ill.: Dryden Press, 243–251, 1972.

Fadiman, Clifton, "Is There an Upper Class American Language?" *Holiday,* October, 1956.

Frazier, E. Franklin, *The Negro Family in the United States.* Chicago: University of Chicago Press, 1939.

Freeman, Howard E., Novak, Edwin, and Reeder, Leo G., "Correlates of Membership in Voluntary Associations." *American Sociological Review, 22:*1957.

Fullerton, Gail Putney, *Survival in Marriage.* New York: Holt, Rinehart and Winston, 1972.

Gebhard, Ph.H., Pomeroy, W. B., Martin, C. E., and Christenson, C. V., *Pregnancy, Birth and Abortion.* New York: Harper & Brothers and Paul B. Hoeber, 1958.

Gerstl, Joel E., "Leisure, Taste, and Occupational Milieu." *Social Problems, 9:*56–69, 1961.

Gesell, A., Ilg, F. L., and Ames, L. B., *Youth, The Years Between Ten and Sixteen.* New York: Harper & Brothers, 1956.

Gottlieb, David, "The Neighborhood Tavern and the Cocktail Lounge: A Study of Class Differences." *American Journal of Sociology, 62:*1957.

Handel, Gerald, and Rainwater, Lee, "Persistence and Change in Working-Class Life Style." *In* Shostak, Arthur B., and Gomberg, William, eds., *Blue Collar World.* Englewood Cliffs, N.J.: Prentice-Hall, 1964.

Harms, L. S., "Listener Judgments of Status Cues in Speech." *Quarterly Journal of Speech, 47:*164–168, 1961.

Havighurst, Robert J., and Taba, Hilda, *Adolescent Character and Personality.* New York: Wiley, 1949.

Herzog, Elizabeth, "Some Assumptions about the Poor." *Social Science Review, 37:*389–401, 1963.

Hodges, Harold M., Jr., *Social Stratification.* Cambridge, Mass.: Schenkman, 1964.

Hollingshead, August B., *Elmtown's Youth.* New York: Wiley, 1949.

Kahl, Joseph A., *The American Class Structure.* New York: Holt, Rinehart and Winston, 1967.

——, and Davis, James A., "A Comparison of Indices of Socio-Economic Status." *American Sociological Review,* 20:317–325, 1955.

Kaplan, Roy H., and Tausky, Curt, "Work and the Welfare Cadillac: The Functions of and Commitment to Work Among the Hard-Core Unemployed." *Social Problems,* 19:4, 469–483, 1972.

Kerckhoff, Alan C., *Socialization and Social Class.* Englewood Cliffs, N.J.: Prentice-Hall, 1972.

Kinsey, Alfred C., Pemeroy, Wardell B., and Martin, Clyde E., *Sexual Behavior in the Human Male.* Philadelphia: W. B. Saunders, 1948.

Knupfer, Genevieve, "Portrait of the Underdog." *Public Opinion Quarterly,* 11:103–114, 1947.

Kohn, M. L., "Social Class and Parent-Child Relationships: An Interpretation." *American Journal of Sociology,* 68:471–480, 1963.

——, *Class and Conformity.* Homewood, Ill.: Dorsey Press, 1969.

Komarovsky, Mirra, *Blue-Collar Marriage.* New York: Random House, 1962.

Lasswell, Thomas E., *Class and Stratum.* Boston: Houghton Mifflin, 1965.

Lewis, Oscar, *La Vida: A Puerto Rican Family in the Culture of Poverty—San Juan and New York.* New York: Random House, 1965.

Liebow, Elliot, *Tally's Corner.* Boston: Little, Brown, 1967. Reprinted in part in Lejeune, Robert, Ed., *Class and Conflict in American Society.* Chicago: Rand McNally, 1973, 139–144.

Martin, Walter P., "A Consideration of Differences and the Extent and Location of the Female Associational Activities of Rural-Urban Fringe Residents." *American Sociological Review,* 17:687–694, 1952.

McKinley, Donald Gilbert, *Social Class and Family Life.* New York: Free Press, 1964.

Mead, George Herbert, *Mind, Self, and Society.* Chicago: University of Chicago Press, 1924.

Morland, John Kenneth, *Millways of Kent.* Chapel Hill, N.C.: University of North Carolina Press, 1958.

Neugarten, Bernice L., "Social Class and Friendship and School Children." *American Journal of Sociology,* 51:305–313, 1946.

Pear, T. H., *English Social Differences.* London: George Allen & Unwin, 1955.

Perrucci, Robert, "Social Class and Intra-Occupational Mobility: A Study of the Purdue Engineering Graduate from 1911 to 1956." Ph.D. dissertation, Purdue University, 1959.

Putnam, George N., and O'Hern, Edna M., *The Status Significance of an Isolated Urban Dialect.* Washington, D.C.: Catholic University of America Press, 1955.

Rainwater, Lee, Coleman, Richard P., and Handel, Gerald, *Workingman's Wife: Her Personality, World, and Life Style.* New York: Oceana Books, 1959.

——, and Weinstein, Karol Kane, "A Qualitative Exploration of Family Planning and Contraception in the Working Class." *Marriage and Family Living*, 22:238-242, 1960.

Roach, Jack L., "The Crawfords: Life at the Bottom." *In* Roach, Jack L., Gross, Llewellyn, and Gursslin, Orville, eds., *Social Stratification in the United States*. Englewood Cliffs, N.J.: Prentice-Hall, 1969, 213-223.

Scott, John C., Jr., "Membership and Participation in Voluntary Associations." *American Sociological Review*, 22:315-326, 1957.

Schatzman, Leonard, and Strauss, Anselm, "Social Class and Modes of Communication." *American Journal of Sociology*, 60:329-338, 1955.

Shostak, Arthur B., *Blue-Collar Life*. New York: Random House, 1969.

——, "Middle-Aged Working Class Americans at Home: Changing Expectations of Manhood." Paper presented at the Eastern Sociological Society Meeting, Boston, 1972.

Simon, William, and Gagnon, John, "Sex, Marriage, and Social Class." *In* Feldman, Saul D., and Thielbar, Gerald W., eds., *Life Styles: Diversity in American Society*. Boston: Little, Brown, 1972, 86-87.

Statistical Abstracts of the United States 1967. Washington, D.C.: Government Printing Office, 1967.

Stendler, Celia B., "Children of Brasstown." Urbana: *University of Illinois Bulletin, 46:9*, 1949.

Stone, Abraham, "The Kinsey Studies and Marriage Counseling." *In* Himelhoch, Jerome, and Fava, Sylvia Flies, eds., *Sexual Behavior in American Society*. New York: W. W. Norton, 1955.

Strudgill, Peter, *Sociolinquistics*. Baltimore: Penguin, 1974.

Tryon, C. M., "The Adolescent Peer Group." *Forty-Third Yearbook of the National Society for the Study of Education, Part I*, 1944, 217-239.

Vincent, Clark E., *Unmarried Mothers*. Glencoe, Ill.: Free Press, 1961.

Warner, Lloyd W., and Lunt, Paul S., *The Social Life of a Modern Community*. New Haven, Yale University Press, 1941.

Wentworth, Harold, and Flexner, Stuart Berg, *Dictionary of American Slang*. New York: Thomas Y. Crowell, 1960.

White, R. Clyde, "Social Class Differences in the Uses of Leisure." *American Journal of Sociology*, 61:145-150, 1955.

Whyte, William F., "The Wives of Management." *Fortune*, October, 1951, 86-88.

chapter 6

Social Class and Other Institutions:
The Criminal Justice System and Political Life

Throughout this book, it has been emphasized that there are distinct subgroups in American society which can *conveniently* be termed "social classes." The word "conveniently" is used because these subgroups might also be given other names: strata, orders, socioeconomic groups, income groups, occupational groups, and so on. The fact remains that there are discernible social entities, admittedly with blurred boundaries, in American society and in almost all societies in the world. These groups are based primarily on educational, occupational, and income levels, and have different life styles, value different things, have different beliefs, seek different goals, and are treated differently by societal institutions. In this chapter and the next, we will examine the relationship between social class and some other institutions in our society, such as the criminal justice system, the political system, the medical community, and the educational system.

Social Class and the Criminal Justice System[1]

In January 1975, Judge John Sirica pardoned three of the major participants in the most scandalous and dangerous conspiracy ever exposed in the highest echelons of the American government. Three days after this event, Tom Wicker, writing in the *New York Times*, quoted one of the men who was pardoned as saying that his release had renewed his "appreciation and confidence in the essential fairness of America's justice." Wicker wrote.[2]

Mr. Kalmbach's response was worthy of a Kafka story. He got off with six months, mostly in quarters for Government witnesses, and as a result his confidence in the "fairness of American justice" is renewed. *Some people spend more time than that in jail merely awaiting trial on minor larceny charges.* Mr. Kalmbach, who sold an ambassadorship, fancies that his having pleaded guilty to a felony and a misdemeanor, as well as testifying against former colleagues, actually strengthened "the pillars of justice". But first, he and the Watergate gang came as close as anyone has to pulling down those pillars." [Italics added.]

Wicker goes on to describe the generous welcome extended to another of the trio by his neighbors, and comments:

Such generosity is virtually nonexistent, however, when the ordinary convict shuffles out of the prison gate in a state suit with a few grudging state dollars in his pocket and no job, little ability to get one, and no yellow ribbon round the stunted splinter that may pass for a tree in his ghetto neighborhood.

Wicker concludes:

But to the millions of low-income, disadvantaged, unskilled and uneducated Americans, so many of whom have good reason to view the law with fear and distrust, the whole episode is likely to be another demonstration that *there is one kind of justice for*

---

1. Much of this section is based on Clayton A. Hartjen's *Crime and Criminalization*, New York, Praeger, 1974, and on personal conversation with him. The author is deeply indebted to Hartjen for help in the preparation of this section.

2. The following extract's from Wicker's January 10, 1975 column is © 1975 by the New York Times Company. Reprinted by permission.

them, and another for affluent, educated persons with good law-
yers and "standing" in their communities. [Italics added.]

Tom Wicker's column illustrates a generally acknowledged
truth about the criminal justice system in the United States. There
are two distinct kinds of justice: one for the rich, and one for the
poor. Wicker discussed the endpoint—the pardon—but the same
dichotomy occurs through the entire process of crime and punishment.

What are the conditions and factors that compel, motivate, or
lead people into committing illegal acts? How do members of a
society come to be labelled criminals? Why are some so labelled
while others are not, regardless of similar behavior? These are
some of the major issues in the study of criminology. Regarding
the factors involved in the genesis of criminal behavior, it has been
said that:

> Improper socialization, poor peer group relations, poverty, bad
> home environment, psychological or physiological malfunction-
> ing or abnormality, and lack of religious training are just a few of
> the numerous factors that have been said to be the cause of
> crime. Little empirical evidence exists to support any of these
> claims (Hartjen, 1974:40).

Theories of Criminality

The classical school of criminology, which was a by-product of
a judicial reform movement in the eighteenth century, combined
humanism and rationalism to conclude that people are capable of
reasoning, and therefore crime was thought to be the result of a
deliberate decision to break the law. Since people seek pleasure
and avoid pain, the criminal was viewed as breaking the law to obtain pleasure. To stop crime, the pleasure must be replaced by pain
or punishment. Nonsensical as this theory may sound today, it still
underlies the American system of criminal justice. The length of a
prison sentence depends partially on the type of crime. Longer
sentences are required not only to compensate for the pleasure
derived from committing the more outrageous crimes, but also to
provide the public with a sense of revenge.

The theories of the classical criminologists largely are ignored
today, but another explanation for criminal behavior which is still
considered plausible is based on the notion that there are biological differences between people. Some are physiologically "inferior," and the solution to crime is to isolate or sterilize criminals in

order to prevent criminality from passing to the next generation. Cesare Lombroso (1836-1909), a founder of this school of criminology, claimed that criminals are physically identifiable. He proposed that they have distinctive head shapes, long arms, either very large or very small ears, and defective eyes. Lombroso classified three types of criminals: born criminals, insane criminals, and criminaloids. The latter are people who are otherwise normal and sometimes break the law because of loss of self-control (Hartjen, 1974:43). As late as 1939, in line with this theory Ernest Hooton concluded that criminals are "organically inferior," and suggested that the solution to crime would be permanent segregation of lawbreakers. These extreme versions of the biogenic theories of criminality largely have been disproved.

A more modern version of this idea is the theory that some criminals have different chromosomal patterns than noncriminals. The normal female has two X chromosomes; the normal male has one X and one Y chromosome. Some researchers have suggested that a criminal is more likely to have an XYY pattern. Since the "Y" is the masculine chromosome, denoting aggression, biologically the criminal has a more hostile nature. Much attention has been directed to this theory, but in his review of the studies, Richard Fox concludes that research does not support the theory. "The studies done thus far are largely in agreement and demonstrate rather conclusively that males of the XYY type are not predictably agressive. If anything, as a group, they are somewhat less aggressive than comparable individuals with an XY chromosomal pattern" (1971:72-73).

There are also innumerable psychological theories of the etiology of criminal behavior. Some attribute this kind of antisocial behavior to psychosis (Abrahamsen, 1945); while others feel it is caused by neurosis (Glueck and Glueck, 1951). In either case, the criminal is seen as "sick," unable to control his or her impulses and desirous of punishment, whether because of an underdeveloped superego, an inadequate family life, or poor childhood training. The solution lies in "curing" the underlying personality malfunction; the criminal act itself is merely a manifestation of deep psychological disturbance and is therefore unimportant.

Like all psychological and psychoanalytic theories, these theories are difficult to test empirically.

It is undoubtedly true that some lawbreakers do suffer from mental disturbances, as do some nonoffenders. The problem in assessing the validity of psychogenic claims as general explanations of criminality, however, is in determining the extent to which emotional disturbances are causally related to criminal behavior. If, for example, a significantly higher proportion of the criminal population than of the general population suffers from a given mental disorder, it could be argued that this "condition" precipitated the offenders' conduct. However, the studies designed to test psychogenic claims have so far been less than successful (Hartjen, 1974:45–46).

Hartjen explains that in terms of mental illness, there are few differences between incarcerated criminals and the general public. It is possible that both psychological disturbances and criminality are the result of a third factor, and thus are related to each other only indirectly. Second, Hartjen claims that since most psychiatrists see a person after he or she has been accused of committing a crime, the diagnosis of mental disturbance may be predetermined. By definition, the individual cannot be normal or he or she would not have behaved "abnormally" in the first place. Most important for present purposes, Hartjen points out that "there is reason to believe that diagnostic decisions are far from free of cultural or *class* bias. It may very well be that such factors as membership in a certain ethnic or economic group have much to do with determining whether or not legal authorities accuse a person of violating the law" (1974:47. Italics added).

Biogenic and psychogenic theories, then, locate the problem of criminality within the individual. Another explanation is sociogenic; that is, there are factors in the individual's social environment which cause criminal behavior. Again, several theories have been suggested in this area. Sutherland and Cressey identified six social conditions generally assumed to lead to antisocial behavior: (1) other family members are criminal; (2) broken homes; (3) lack of parental interest and control; (4) unhappy, disruptive intact homes; (5) interracial or interreligious marriages; and (6) poverty (1966:217). For some time the second condition, broken homes, was thought to be the most significant factor causing delinquency. However:

> Research has shown that other factors seem to be as closely related to delinquency as is family cohesion. It may be, then, that the broken home is but one of a number of variables that act together to generate illegal conduct. Also, most of the studies relating crime to defective family patterns are biased in that they deal largely or exclusively with lower-class gang delinquents. If

attention were to shift to other forms of delinquent conduct or to other types of delinquents, such as middle-class offenders, the generalization that broken homes are the major cause of delinquency would probably have to be modified (Hartjen, 1974:49).

A major theory explaining criminal behavior was proposed by Edwin Sutherland in 1939 (Sutherland and Cressey, 1966). Rejecting the notion that biology, psychology, or society make a person behave in criminal ways, Sutherland held that criminal behavior is learned during interaction with those who share a criminal value system. One can learn either criminal or noncriminal behavior, depending on *differential association.* Thus, if one lives in a neighborhood in which criminal activities are accepted behavior, one will learn both the motivation and techniques necessary for breaking the law.

Middle-Class versus Lower-Class Delinquency

The theory of differential association inspired many sociologists to explore lower-class juvenile delinquency and to come to the general conclusion that there are factors within the lower-class community which encourage lower-class boys to become more delinquent than middle-class or upper-class boys (Merton, 1957: Cohen, 1955; Miller, 1958; and Cloward and Ohlin, 1961). However, more recently attention has turned to middle-class delinquency, and the findings have revealed discrepancies in the notion that the lower classes have higher rates of juvenile delinquency than the classes above them.

Joseph Scott and Edmund Vaz, for example, remark that:

Most literature on juvenile delinquency describes it as essentially a product of the lower socioeconomic classes. While there has been some speculation over the incidence and quality of middle class delinquency, what evidence exists is largely impressionistic. Nevertheless, the prevailing view is that delinquency among middle-class youth has increased in recent years (1964:115).

Ralph England attempted to formulate a theory to explain middle-class delinquency (1964). England refutes Parsons' explanation that middle-class boys become delinquent because in their efforts to take on a masculine identity, they do not have enough opportunity to interact with their role model fathers, and therefore resort to destructive behavior in an attempt to prove their masculinity (1942). England contends that such a theory is only applicable to urban boys whose fathers work in bureaucratic organizations. It is not applicable to boys who live in small cities or towns and whose fathers are not deeply involved in occupational pursuits. Furthermore, even if a middle-class boy is deprived of a role model, why does he adopt an aggressive stance when a posture of male responsibility is equally available to him?

England postulates that the middle-class teenager, in his desire to be accepted by his peers, rejects the adult values which threaten his peer-group standing and accepts those adult values that he feels will increase his status. Thus, he rejects hard work, thrift, and self-denial in favor of fast driving, drinking, sexual exploitation, income tax cheating, and hedonistic pursuits. England's theory, then "is that some middle class delinquency is the result of an interaction between certain aspects of our general cultural system and an emerging teenage system, producing norms entirely functional to the latter but not to the former" (1964:108).

England's position is similar to that of Scott and Vaz, who contend that teenage behavior is modelled on adult behavior. Middle-class children have access to all the things that they need to be members of the teenage subculture, such as cars, liquor, money, and so on. Just as they acquire *things* from the adults in their class, in the same way they acquire *values*, such as hedonism and competition, which are easily converted into delinquent behavior. "A special set of motives need not be recruited to explain delinquent behavior within the middle class youth culture. At no time does the middle class teenager turn from legitimate to illegitimate means in order to attain his ends. . . . The seeds of middle class delinquency reside in the prominent, culturally esteemed patterns themselves" (1964:128).

Self-Reports versus Official Records

Thus the fact that delinquency is not confined to the lower classes is reasonably well-established. However, it now becomes important to determine whether or not rates of delinquent behavior are higher in the lower classes. Critics of the notion of higher crime rates among the lower classes contend that delinquency is equally prevalent at all social levels and, indeed, might well be higher in the middle and upper classes (Porterfield, 1946; Wallenstein and Wyle, 1947; Nye, Short, and Olson, 1958). Reckless claims that the apparent higher rate in the lower classes results from the fact that agencies of social control are more disposed to classify poor people as delinquents (1950). An important distinction to make in

any analysis of crime is between "official crime" (official delinquency) and "criminal behavior" (delinquent behavior). Official
crime is that behavior which agents of the criminal justice system
deem worthy of their action (arrest and prosecution). Criminal
behavior is that conduct which violates the criminal code, regardless of whether or not it is responded to as such by judicial author-
itites.

Most studies of crime rates use official records of arrests and
convictions to determine the profile of the criminal. They therefore paint a picture of official crime. But several investigators
have come to the conclusion that there is a discrepancy between
these official records and self-reports (officially unrecognized) of
criminal involvement. Eighty-eight percent of the 847 teenagers
interviewed by Williams and Gold admitted to at least one charge-
able offense; yet less than 3 percent had been detected by the
police, and only 22 percent of the respondents had ever had any
contact with police. Williams and Gold note:

Our findings demonstrate that the distinction between delinquent
behavior and official delinquency is indeed useful and necessary:
the distribution of official delinquency among categories of sex,
age, race, and socioeconomic status does not parallel the distribution of delinquent behavior (1972:209–210).

In terms of social class specifically, Williams and Gold found
that, contrary to official records, self-reports revealed that there is
no strong relationship between social class and delinquent behavior. In fact, higher-status boys tended to be more seriously
delinquent than lower-status boys.

It will come as no surprise to students of delinquency that official
measures of delinquency do not accurately reflect delinquent behavior. ... Social status differences characteristically found in
official records of juvenile delinquency contradict the evidence
regarding delinquent behavior reported here. That is, the only
difference in these data identified the *higher* status white boys as
more seriously delinquent than lower status white boys
(1972:226).

Another study by Donald Black (1970) reaches similar conclusions from another perspective: How does deviant behavior come
to be officially recognized? Black studied official reactions to
complaints and concluded, for one thing, that in felony situations
the police gave more attention to complaints made by white-collar
people than to those made by blue-collar people. (This did not

hold true for misdemeanor situations.) Since blue-collar workers are more likely to commit a felony against members of both groups:

> It would follow that the police discriminate against blue-collar citizens who feloniously offend white-collar citizens by being comparatively lenient in the investigation of felonies committed by one blue-collar citizen against another. In this instance, the legal system listens more attentively to the claims of higher status citizens. This pattern is recorded in the crime rate. . . . Thus the life chances of a criminal violator may depend upon who his victim is and how his victim presents his claim to the police (1970:746-747).

Albert Reiss and Albert Rhodes examined the question from a different angle. They found that:

> There is no simple relationship between ascribed social status and delinquency. Both the status structure of the residential community and the extent to which delinquency is a function of a cultural tradition in a residential community affect the delinquency life-chances of a boy at each ascribed social class level (1961:720).

This approach is a more sophisticated application of the differential association theory. In their study of over 9000 white boys, Reiss and Rhodes asked their subjects to report their own delinquent acts in order to determine whether self-reports corresponded to official reports. They came to the following major conclusions: (1) there is more frequent and more serious delinquency in the lower stratum than in the middle stratum; (2) the career-oriented delinquent is found only in the lower stratum; (3) the boys in the lower stratum tended to be conforming non-achievers while the boys in the higher stratum tended to be conforming achievers; (4) peer-oriented delinquency is the most common form at both levels; and (5) the status structure of the area from which the boys come and the rates of delinquency in that area are the most influential factors. More concisely:

> While the life chances of low ascribed status boys becoming delinquent are greater than those of high status ones, a low status boy in a predominantly high status area with a low rate of delinquency has almost no chance of being classified a juvenile court delinquent (1961:729).

John Clark and Eugene Wenninger (1962) offer convincing arguments in two disputed areas: the use of self-reports, and the notion that there are higher rates of delinquency among lower-class youth than among middle-class youth.

Clark and Wenninger reviewed some of the studies of self-reports and official reports and concluded, with Williams and Gold, that the association between delinquency and social class is minimal. What is additionally interesting about the work of these investigators is the attention they give to community size as an important independent variable when trying to relate social class and delinquency. Apparently, the larger the city, the stronger the relationship between class and crime rates. Their study is worth examining in detail. First, they made a comparison between the positions taken by Miller, Cohen, Merton, and Cloward and Ohlin that juvenile delinquency is a lower-class phenomenon, and the work of Nye and Short, and Dentler and Monroe who contended that there is no significant difference between classes in terms of deviance.

Clark and Wenninger found that both these groups of investigators had contributed to the theory of social class as a factor in antisocial behavior; but what they had failed to consider was the size of the community. They found that there was no significant difference in criminal behavior between juveniles in different classes in rural and small urban areas. In large metropolitan areas, however, the pattern of behavior was determined by the predominant class in each area. "This suggests that there are community-wide norms which are related to illegal behavior and to which juveniles adhere regardless of their social-class origins" (1962:833). In short, these researchers contend that social class differences in rates of criminal behavior depend at least in part, on the size of the community itself.

Merton's Typology of Adaptation

Similar factors could, however, affect the members of various social classes differently. Merton's notion of the relationship between cultural goals and legitimate means of attaining them illustrates the point (1938), as shown in Table 6-1. Merton's typology of adaptation indicates that in the United States cultural goals and the means of achieving them are not shared equally by all Americans. If they were, there would be no need for deviance because all people would have equal access to all goals. Instead, people adapt to inequality in different ways. The mode of adaptation refers to role behavior, not to personalty traits. A plus

TABLE 6-1
A Typology of Modes of Individual Adaptation*

Modes of Adaptation	Cultural Goals	Institutionalized Means
Conformity	+	+
Innovation	+	-
Ritualism	-	+
Retreatism	-	-
Rebellion	±	±

*From Merton, Robert K.: *Social Theory and Social Structure*. Glencoe, Ill.: Free Press, 1957:140. Copyright © 1957 by The Free Press, a Corporation.

(+) signifies acceptance, a minus (–) means rejection, and a plus and a minus (±) means rejection of current values and the substitution of new ones.

Merton claims that:

> American culture continues to be characterized by a heavy emphasis on wealth as a basic symbol of success, without a corresponding emphasis upon the legitimate avenues on which to march toward this goal. . . . What, in short, are the consequences for the behavior of people variously situated in a social structure of a culture in which the emphasis on dominant success-goals has become increasingly separated from an equivalent emphasis on institutionalized procedures for seeking these goals? (1957:139).

Conformity is the most common adaptation in a stable society. That is, people have commonly accepted cultural goals and also have access to institutionalized means of attaining them. Examples may be the successful physician or business person. *Innovation* (meaning the reinterpretation and new use of existing culture) is resorted to when the person accepts the goals, but has no institutionalized way of reaching them, largely because he or she is a member of the lower classes and is barred from advancement. "Incentives for success are provided by the established values of the culture and . . . the avenues available for moving toward this goal are largely limited by the class structure to those of deviant behavior" (Merton, 1957:145). Thus, the innovator in this sense is frequently the lower-class criminal.

The *ritualist* is the person who rejects the cultural goals of "success" and "getting ahead," while at the same time rigidly adhering to the rules. Merton feels this is not a truly deviant response because "the adaptation is, in effect, an internal decision and . . . the overt behavior is institutionally permitted" (1955:150). This is the individual who does not "stick his neck out" and who "plays it safe." It is an adaptation illustrated most easily by the timid, lower-middle-class bureaucrat and the industrial worker who carefully conform to the quota they are expected to produce.

Merton claims that *retreatism* is the least common adaptation. Those who adopt this mode are the isolates, the marginal members of society who reject both the goals and the means of acquiring them. Merton includes outcasts, vagrants, tramps, chronic alcoholics, and drug addicts—the dropouts—in this category. "This fourth mode of adaptation, then, is that of the socially disinherited, who if they have none of the rewards held out by society also have few of the frustrations attendant upon continuing to seek these rewards" (1957:155).

Rebellion "leads men outside the environing social structure to envisage and seek to bring into being a new, that is to say, a greatly modified social structure. It [the adaptation] presupposes alienation from reigning goals and standards" (1957:155). Frequently rebels are political activists or renegades, members of a rising rather than a stable class.

Albert Cohen (1955) elaborated on Merton's theory by focusing on the second type of adaptation, innovation. He sought to show how lower-class people, because of their socialization, are blocked from the institutionalized means of achieving accepted goals. Their only escape from status frustration or feelings of status deprivation is to join a delinquent subculture which serves as a substitute means of attaining culturally accepted goals. Lower-class boys break completely with middle-class norms and have no feelings of inhibition as they vent their feelings of frustration and aggression on "respectable" citizens. Cohen, incidentally, has little to say about middle-class juvenile delinquency except to agree with Parsons that it is an attempt to prove masculinity in the absence of a good male role model. Thus, for Cohen, lower-class delinquency derives from status frustration and middle-class delinquency from ego-identification needs. Gursslin and Roach have vigorously attacked Cohen's theory (1969).

Their primary quarrel with Cohen is in his interchangeable use of the terms "lower class" and "working class." They, on the other hand, emphasize the differences between these two strata: basically, the lower class lives at or below the subsistence line, and the working class lives slightly above it. Thus, the two groups have different goals and different access to the means of achieving them. Gursslin and Roach claim that Cohen's assumptions are not valid for the lower class. First, lower-class people have *not* internalized American success goals. Second, lower-class people do *not* perceive the social structure as barring them from opportunity. Third, lower-class people do *not* experience status frustration. Fourth, because lower-class people have weak ego controls, poorly integrated self-systems, limited role skills, and difficulty in shifting perspectives, it is unlikely that they are capable of developing delinquent subcultures. In contrast, working-class individuals do have all these characteristics and abilities. "Adequate grounds are present, therefore, to conclude that Cohen's status-frustration theory is applicable to the working class" (1969:496–497).

Furthermore, Cohen does not believe that his theory applies to middle-class boys. Gursslin and Roach reply that indeed it does, because while opportunities for goal attainment may be available to middle-class boys, not all are capable of taking advantage of them. There are two factors in the middle-class social structure which may create status frustration. First, competition is encouraged in the middle-class, but some children lack the innate ability to rise to the top; and (2) children who are potential failures often are pressured severely by parents. Thus, some middle-class boys fail to achieve and therefore experience status frustration. These researchers suggest that Cohen is correct when he says that working-class children suffer from status frustration; he is incorrect in not recognizing that the same situation exists in the middle class, but does *not* exist in the lower class.

Gursslin and Roach offer an alternative theoretical formulation. Lower-class delinquency is the result of undersocialization; that is, children in the lower class have not internalized the moral values of the society. Thus, lower-class people are more likely than those in other strata to be sociopathic.

> Lower-class adolescents are therefore more likely to commit delinquent acts of a violent nature. . . . Working class delinquency is a result of status frustration. It leads to out-group aggression consisting of rejection of culturally prescribed, essentially middle-class means and goal values. . . . Middle-class delinquency is also the result of status frustration. It leads to in-group aggression involving the rejection of middle-class means but not goal values. This in-group aggression is directed against middle-class parents and the middle-class community in general (1969:498–500).

Class and Adult Criminality

Most of the studies described so far have dealt with juvenile delinquency. Unfortunately, there is a paucity of studies on adult crime as related to social class differences. Edward Green compared two occupational levels for index and nonindex[3] crime arrests (1970). Green reported that the lower occupational groups (semiskilled, unskilled, laborer, and the unemployed) comprise almost one-half of the labor force, but for the sample years 1942, 1950, 1960, and 1965, they were arrested from 7 to 13 times more frequently for nonindex crimes than white-collar workers (professionals, managers, entrepreneurs, clerical and sales workers, and craftsmen). This disparity between the two occupational groups is even greater for index crimes. The lower classes had 40 times as many arrests for such crimes in 1942; 22 in 1950; 12 in 1960; and 26 in 1965.

Green's study confirmed several others that the arrest *rate* for blacks is no higher than the *rate* for whites. While it is true that more blacks in actual numbers, are arrested, this is a function of class, not race. Moreover, the effect of socioeconomic status on arrest rates operates independently of race (1970:490). Green contends that while there is no evidence that the police discriminate against blacks, neither is there evidence that they do not. What is more significant is that the findings in his study clearly show that lower-class people are arrested for criminal acts more frequently than middle-class people, and that the crimes they commit are more serious crimes.

In the state of Florida a judge has the option of withholding adjudication of guilt from defendants who have been put on probation. This is very useful because an accused person can avoid the stigma of "convicted felon" if the judge decides to take advantage of this law. Chiricos, Jackson, and Waldo tried to determine the characteristics of those defendants who were most likely to receive the "adjudication withheld" privilege (1972). They found that defendants who were black, poorly educated, who had a prior record, were older, and were defended by a court-appointed lawyer were those least likely to have adjudication withheld. In other

3. Index crimes are those serious offenses (murder, armed robbery, etc.) compiled annually by the Federal Bureau of Investigation; nonindex crimes are all others.

words, the lower classes were more likely to be labelled "criminal" than the middle or upper classes.

William Chambliss summarized the position of the lower-class person's treatment by the criminal justice system:

> The lower-class person is (1) more likely to be scrutinized and therefore be observed in any violation of the law, (2) more likely to be arrested if discovered under suspicious circumstances, (3) more likely to spend time between arrest and trial in jail, (4) more likely to come to trial, (5) more likely to be found guilty, and (6) if found guilty, more likely to receive harsh punishment than his middle- or upper-class counterpart (1969:86).

In summary, the studies indicate that antisocial behavior at all levels of the social class structure is more or less equal. However, lower-class people more often commit the most flagrant crimes. Partly as a result of the kinds and frequency of the crimes they commit, partly because of economic inability to defend themselves when accused, and also because of the legal bias against the poor and powerless, the illegal behavior of the lower class is more likely than that of other groups to be officially treated as crime.

Crimes among the Respectable—White Collar Crime

What kinds of crimes do middle-class and upper-class people commit? The blue-collar (working) class engages in sensational, alarming crimes: robbery, murder, and rape,—which attract police and public attention and inspire fear. But just *because* Americans are so engrossed in this kind of crime, the fact that the respectable middle classes and upper classes also are acting criminally tends to be obscured. Upper-class and middle-class crimes have been termed "white-collar crimes" (Sutherland, 1949) and may well be more harmful to society than lower-class crime.

Examples of white-collar crime include fraud, graft, embezzlement, false advertising, infringement of patents, price-fixing, bribery, fee-splitting, and so forth. These crimes are less frightening to the public; they also are generally less severely punished, and they are rarely reported in newspapers unless the perpetrator is very well-known or the crime is of great magnitude.

Americans tend not to think of such people as "criminals." But the harm they do to society is incalculable. Consider the pharmaceutical company president who releases a drug before it has been tested properly; or the industrialist who pollutes the air and the water; or the contractor who knowingly uses defective materials in buildings; or the doctor who sends a patient to an inferior specialist in order to obtain a portion of the fee; or consider the public official who uses political power for personal advantage without regard for public welfare. What of the automobile manufacturer who knowingly produces defective cars that endanger thousands of lives—all in the name of profit? Yet this kind of behavior is not labelled antisocial and the people who engage in it are rarely stigmatized by the label "criminal."

Stuart Hill attempted to explain why this kind of illegal behavior goes relatively unpunished in the United States (1971: Chapter 7). There is a comparatively small amount of systematic data and statistics available on white-collar crime, in contrast to the Uniform Crime Reports compiled annually by the Federal Bureau of Investigation which document those acts the public thinks of as criminal and which are known to the police.

In fact, "white-collar crime" is itself not a legal category—much less a homogeneous one—but merely a vague, broad label referring to a variety of disparate offenses committed by businessmen, professional persons, and government officials in the course of their occupations. The patterns these occupational violations take are extremely varied (1971:154).

In spite of the lack of accurate statistics, however, many sociologists and criminologists believe that white-collar crime is very widespread. "And the few social-scientific surveys that have been conducted generally verify these more impressionistic descriptions of pervasive illegal behavior—behavior that results in enormous economic and social harm" (Hill, 1971:155).

The first study of white-collar crime was conducted by Edwin Sutherland (1949) who researched 70 leading American corporations and found that these organizations had committed 779 criminal acts. One corporation had 50 adverse decisions against it; the average for all 70 was 14. Even more interesting was the fact that only 16 percent of these cases were tried in a criminal court; the remainder were handled informally or in civil courts. Sutherland contended that the lack of punishment stemmed from the fact that the offenders had political power or high status, or both, and their offenses did not interest the public. Sutherland apparently could not resist the temptation to make fun of his colleagues who attributed criminal behavior to psychological causes. He noted that "United States Steel did not suffer from any apparent unresolved Oepidus complex, General Motors from any inferiority complex, or the Dupont Company from any desire to return to the womb" (Hill, 1971:156).

Marshall Clinard (1952) studied black market violations of

rationing laws during World War II and found that about 1 in every 15 business corporations had been penalized for serious criminal acts, but the penalties generally had been restricted to modest fines. Furthermore, Clinard found that the actual number of violations was much larger than the official records made it appear; indeed, some of the violations had been serious enough to endanger the war effort. Frank Hartung's study of the wholesale meat market during the same years revealed the same kinds and the same degree of violations, and the same light punishments that is, small fines, suspended sentences, and warning notices (1950).

Consumer fraud has come to the attention of Americans only relatively recently. In one significant investigation, the President's Committee on Consumer Interests documented fraudulent practices in the home maintenance industries. The Commission recorded such dishonest practices as phony sales, misleading financing, worthless guarantees, inferior materials, fake contests, and false advertising. One of the most shoddy aspects of consumer fraud is the victimization of the poor, who are exploited most easily because they are uninformed and lack the education that would help them to avoid being duped or to recover their losses from swindlers.

White-collar crime is prevalent in the professions as well. In medicine, there are numerous reports of fee-splitting (Whitman, 1953), prescribing illegal drugs, unnecessary surgery, Medicare fraud, and false testimony for a fee in accident cases. Yet few doctors are ever arrested, and only very rarely are they tried, convicted, or imprisoned. Lawyers apparently engage in illegal acts in a fashion similar to that of doctors. They have been known to misappropriate funds in receivership, to offer bribes to witnesses, and to chase ambulances for prospective clients. When such practices are discovered, lawyers likewise rarely are criminally prosecuted; they are more likely to be disbarred (Carlin, 1966).

The financial, social, and political costs of these crimes are enormous. Hill estimates an annual amount of between $75 and 100 million in public losses from illegal sales of securities alone; "outstripping by a considerable margin the total theft of the more publicized desperadoes who hold up banks and stores" (1971:167). Others have estimated the financial costs of white-collar crime to be twice as high as the total loss from armed robbery, burglary, automobile theft, and pickpocketing (Hill,

1971:167). The Food and Drug Administration considers that almost $500 million annually is spent for unnecessary, useless, and even harmful medication (Magnuson and Casper, 1968).

In addition to financial costs, white-collar crimes are dangerous to the health and safety of Americans. There is a tendency to fear mugging and street crime, but white-collar crime poses at least as much of a threat of physical and psychological harm. The automotive industry is a good example. An estimated $100 million is spent each year on the repair of defective cars; one-fourth of all new tires cannot meet the manufacturers' own standards. In the mining industry, violations of federal mine safety laws contribute to hundreds of deaths from black lung disease. The examples are endless (Hill, 1971:168–169).

Most white-collar crimes lack the unitary and dramatic predatory nature of rape, robbery, murder, or kidnapping. The serious effects of these occupational violations tend to be spread over an impersonal and anonymous public mass, affecting, sometimes almost imperceptibly, thousands and millions of distant persons. Consequently, it is difficult to document or measure reliably the hazardous effects of various goods and services that result in physical harm through the gradual destruction of human tissues and organs—hazards that are frequently increased by deceptive labeling and advertising which fail to warn the user of the potential dangers to his health or safety (Hill, 1971:169).

White-collar crime also threatens the moral welfare of society. It is hardly necessary to look beyond the Watergate scandal to illustrate this point. Citizens lose their trust and confidence in their government, begin to doubt their leaders' ability to make judgments, and become skeptical of the court system when judges and lawyers are exposed as corrupt. The public display of immorality by citizens who previously have been honored and respected is enormously damaging to the societal morale.

The perpetrator of a blue-collar crime typically is arrested by a policeman, incarcerated for weeks or even months before trial if he or she cannot put up bail, and probably given a long term in prison, especially if he or she has a record of previous offenses. In contrast, middle- or upper-class criminals "are processed through a significantly different kind of legal process, thereby permitting a high degree of immunity from severe punitive sanctions" (Hill, 1971:172). The case of the white-collar criminal is most likely to be heard in a civil court, where the defendant probably is ordered to give up his or her illegal activities, pay a fine, and reimburse those who have been cheated. At worst, he or she may receive a short sentence of a few months, but usually the sentence is suspended. The lower-class person accused, much less convicted, of assault finds it difficult, if not impossible, to get even an unskilled job. On the other hand, the physician, convicted of malpractice may find that his practice increases (Schwartz and Skolnick, 1962).

One may well ask why Americans coddle their white-collar criminals and are so tough with their blue-collar criminals. Two reasons have already been cited: white-collar crime receives far less publicity, and it does not seem as personal as blue-collar crime. Citizens feel remote from it and are less frightened by it. The harm done by white-collar crime is less obvious and, indeed, the victim often is not aware that he or she has been victimized. Furthermore, the effects of white-collar crime are diffused in that they are not immediately or personally experienced. It is "the public" which is cheated or robbed or injured—not you or me. Political slogans of "law and order" apply to street crimes, not corporate crimes. In addition, "underlying the differential and lenient handling of white-collar offenders are a particular set of historical conditions, certain values and ideological beliefs, and the distribution of power and status in American society" (Hill, 1971:181).

Another problem is simply in detecting these crimes. The direct victims are seldom found, for one thing. Second, the crimes are often as much a matter of omission as commission (failure to print warnings on medicine bottles, for example). Third, business crimes may be so intricate that it takes years for teams of experts to unravel the details of the offenses. Fourth, large corporations often engage excellent legal counsel to cope with mediocre lawyers who traditionally staff government agencies. Fifth, who is the culprit? An entire corporation cannot be jailed. The actual crime may be carried out by middle management, but who gave the orders? Magruder and Colson went to prison, but Nixon was given amnesty. The best that can be done is to fine the corporation, but even large fines are trivial amounts of money for multimillion-dollar organizations (Hill, 1971:181–183).

An additional and more elusive problem is the strange reluctance in the United States to punish white-collar crime. Americans have traditionally admired "rugged individualism," "success," unregulated pursuit of profit, and free enterprise. Somehow committing of such crimes is regarded as less reprehensible than being apprehended. The eleventh commandment has always been "Thou shalt not get caught." Thus, "to the degree that such exploitative occupational behavior is normative and intrinsic in much of the American way of life, it would appear that the imposition of criminal sanctions not only will be resisted but also will have minimal 'rehabilitative' impact and limited deterrent efficacy" (Hill, 1971:184).

Finally, the political power and high status of most white-collar criminals are deterrents to punishment. Such perpetrators have the financial, social, and political resources to blunt effective punitive measures against them. George Vold noted cynically, "there is an obvious and basic incongruity involved in the proposition that a community's leaders and more responsible elements are also its criminals" (1958:253).

Summary

Criminality is not an innate characteristic. No one is a "born" criminal and nothing is inherently criminal. Instead, crime is what a society says it is and the criminal is the individual who has been so labelled by the society. The question addressed is: Under what circumstances do some lawbreakers receive the label criminal while others do not? Hill appears to have the answer:

The probability of being labeled as criminal is importantly related to the *location* of various individuals and groups in the structure of the society. One's social and ecological position in the social order—with its related opportunities, deprivations, rewards, life styles, and values—will affect the likelihood of conflict with the legal norms and of possessing the knowledge, resources, and power to avoid the criminalization process (1971:19).

Social Class and Political Life

In Chapter 3 the subjective and the objective aspects of social class were discussed. It will be recalled that the objective aspect refers to the actual inequalities between groups which can be measured, such as income, power, or status. The subjective aspect refers to the perception and meaning of one's location in the social hierarchy. However, the importance of the subjective aspect lies in its effect on behavior. While objective factors no doubt also affect behavior, awareness of one's social class (or class consciousness) will be most influential throughout one's life. Members of different classes are socialized differently and view the world from different perspectives. It can also be expected that members of different social classes will participate in political affairs in different ways and to different degrees, and that they will favor different candidates. Several researchers have found a relationship between social class and political orientation and participation.

Class Consciousness and Political Behavior

Richard Centers postulated that the subjective social standing of individuals conforms to objective criteria, and therefore they will adopt political attitudes which will further the interests of their particular social class. His specific research question was: "Do persons of differing status and role in the economic order (e.g., occupational status) characteristically distinguish themselves from one another by the possession of differing points of view with respect to important political and economic interests?" (1949:55).

The results of his study of over 1000 white males revealed that as one looks down the social ladder, political opinion gradually moves from conservative to radical. Ninety percent of the business executives and managers were either conservative or ultra-conservative, compared with only 20 percent of the semiskilled workers. Centers, then, found a strong relationship between political attitude and occupational status. The highest percentage of conservatives was in the upper strata; the highest percentage of radicals was in the lower strata.

In their study of approximately 1000 people in Elmira, New York, the findings of Bernard Berelson and his associates supported Centers's study. First, they were able to demonstrate that socioeconomic status is related directly to the final vote cast at an election, even if the voter wavers between candidates during the decision-making process. Second, the higher the social stratum the more likely the voter is to be Republican, and the lower the stratum the more likely to be Democratic. Berelson writes:

> Nor is this relationship by any means limited to the so-called objective measures of socioeconomic status. It also appears when socioeconomic status is measured in terms of the respondent's own class identification—his own feeling as to the class in which he belongs. With socioeconomic status controlled, class identification exerts an independent influence upon the vote, especially on the lower socioeconomic status level (1954:56).

Oscar Glantz (1958) came to similar conclusions in his study of businessmen and union workers. Glantz found that 40 percent of the businessmen and 28 percent of the union workers were aware of class membership and that this awareness was related to political solidarity. The class-conscious businessmen voted Republican; the class-conscious unionists voted Democratic. Furthermore, "Class-conscious persons have class-related motives for voting as they did" (1958:371), indicating that they believed the platforms of some candidates would benefit their class. The only point on which Glantz and Berelson are not in agreement is that Berelson found greater class consciousness among the lower classes, while Glantz found the higher strata to be more class conscious. In general, however, the studies agree that most people are aware of their class membership and are likely to vote, in large measure, as a bloc. Furthermore, the higher an individual stands on the social ladder, the more likely it is that he or she will be conservative.

Political Orientation and Social Class

Most researchers agree with Centers's finding that social class is related to political orientation. The upper strata tend to be conservative and to vote Republican; the lower strata tend to be radical and to vote Democratic. Lopreato and Hazelrigg (1972:290) studied 1500 Italian male heads of households and found this division to exist between manual and nonmanual workers, with the lower classes being more leftist than the classes above them. David Knoke and Michael Hout analyzed changes in party affiliation over a 20-year period. They also found that the higher the social class, the greater the likelihood of an individual's being Republican. They noted that socialization is the strongest factor causing an individual to identify with a political party. Sons of blue-collar Democrats became Democrats and sons of white-collar Republicans became Republicans, demonstrating that the parent transmits political preference to the offspring (1974).

Lenski's theory of status inconsistency also has been used to explain why some people vote Democratic (1967). According to this theory, people who are high in one status dimension and low in another experience status inconsistency because they choose to think of themselves in terms of the higher status, while others tend to see them in terms of the lower status. An example is the rich, black man. His notion of himself is that of a rich man; other people are more likely to regard him simply as a black man. The individual response to such a situation is stress, and the reaction to such stress is a tendency to support the political party which favors social change, usually the Democratic party.

David Segal tested Lenski's theory against Lazarsfeld's cross-pressure theory (1948), which states that when people experience pressure from two competing groups, they will select their candidate very close to election day, because conflicting loyalties lead to inertia. Segal found Lenski to be correct, but only when the lower status is visible. However, a person can be cross-pressured because two conflicting statuses are meaningful to him even when there is no external pressure. If this occurs, the voter does not vote until one of the statuses loses political salience. Thus, for Segal, poor people do not vote at all or vote Democratic because their low economic status may conflict with a high religious or ethnic status (1969).

Political Participation and Social Class

People must address their problems on either an individual or a group level. Several sociologists have found that lower-class people opt for the individual solution and thereby avoid joining political organizations. Lee Rainwater (1974) contends that poor people avoid organizational life for several reasons. The organizers often treat the poor as "special" and are patronizing. Also, the poor feel uncomfortable about their clothes and speech, and often the other members tend to manipulate and exploit them. In addition, unlike the organizers who see poverty as a miserable condition, the poor often do not feel a need to be "rescued" and may even view the future with hope. Therefore, lower-class people do not always see the political organization as the best means of solving their problems. What organizers regard as "apathy" can really mean that the poor have too difficult a time simply surviving to pay attention to broader issues.

Most important, according to Rainwater, is lower-class stress on individualism. Poor people believe the best way out of poverty is to dissociate one's self from other poor, rather than joining forces with them. For this reason they may try to move out of the neighborhood, either looking for a better job, better housing, or to avoid bill collectors.

> One can assume, therefore, that except when lower class people feel trapped in their neighborhoods by low income and unem-

ployment or by discrimination they will not be available for
neighborhood organizations. . . . Even when there is this sense of
being trapped, the preferred route of mobility is individual; lower
class people will often have difficulty in seeing a strategy of organized groups as really relevant to their own needs and wishes
(1974:307).

Rainwater contends that lower-class people are not socialized
to be joiners the way middle-class people are. Beginning with
childhood, the middle-class person belongs to the scout troop,
and then goes on to the bridge club, the golf club, and the political
party. Not so in the lower classes. Their parents were not joiners,
and nothing in their adult lives is conducive to a belief that organizations can help them. Rainwater thinks that lower-class people
may be correct in this assessment. "It is possible that if lower-class
people were as skilled and ready for organization as middle-class
people are believed to be, they would still not be able to achieve
their goals by organizational action" (1974:307–308). The literature indicates that lower-class individuals do not believe that
political organizations are responsive to their needs; therefore,
they seldom organize to get their own people into office so that
their voices can be heard in the decision-making process.

Walter Dean Burnham offers an alternative explanation for
the failure of the poor to vote. He notes that fewer eligible voters
exercise this privilege in the United States than in any other Western country. It is a popular assumption that Americans take this
privilege for granted, and that those who do not vote are not especially interested in politics. Burnham suggests "that the lower
turnout in this country may instead be principally a product of an
effort by those in control of governments and legislatures to limit
the number of citizens who vote" (1974:288).

According to Burnham, keeping people away from the polls in
the United States is accomplished by leaving registration up to the
individual, while in other countries the government assumes responsibility for registration. Attempts to register may be met with
barriers of various kinds, especially if the would-be voter is from a
lower class. This can be seen when voter-participation before
1900, when no registration was required, is compared with voter-
participation after the law went into effect. Pre-1900 "the turnout
in a number of states was so high as to make it virtually certain
that lower-class people participated about as fully as did middle-
and upper-class people" (1974:294). Today there are about one-
half as many blue-collar as professional-managerial voters.

Thus Burnham sees voter registration (especially a periodic registration system, which requires a voter to register in person before every election) as a device used to keep undesirable voters, for example, blacks in the South, away from the polls. The costs of voting become too high for the poor, who cannot afford to take time away from work or the expense of transportation to register before an election. Middle-class voters, on the other hand, find these requirements no problem. Burnham claims there is a strong class bias in the American system of voter registration. Even when racial and ethnic factors are considered, "class remains the strongest predictor of turnout and . . . there is a systematic relationship between the two" (1974:295). *It is not lack of class consciousness, apathy, disinterest, lack of faith, nor status inconsistency that keep the poor from voting. It is that those in power create sociological barriers that restrain the poor from exercising the franchise.*

Maurice Pinard found that poor people are never the first to join political movements, although they may eventually become numerically superior and important to the organization. This is not a new finding. Many sociologists, including Karl Marx, have found that extreme poverty is not a sufficient incentive for participation in political organizations. In fact, poverty actually mitigates against participation because it generates apathy and a feeling of hopelessness. The leaders of a radical organization are usually those with rising expectations and hope of improving their life styles. Daniel Bell expressed it this way:

> It is not poverty *per se* that leads people to revolt; poverty most often induces fatalism and despair, and a reliance, embodied in ritual and superstitious practices, on supernatural help. *Social tensions are an expression of unfulfilled expectations* (1962:31).

Pinard suggests four factors that account for the lack of response to political activism among poor people.

1. Poor people are worried people and worry tends to make an individual self-centered. Furthermore, related to worry are hopelessness, fatalism, and despair. The poor do not expect to escape from their situation, and thus collective action has no meaning for them. However, Pinard did find a difference between the working and middle classes in their worry over daily concerns. Still, middle-class people are much more likely to participate in political action. Pinard explains that worry inca-

pacitates the poor, and they do nothing to change situations. On the other hand, worry activates the middle class, causing them to turn to politics for solutions to problems.

2. Lack of sophistication has been suggested as a reason for the disinclination of the poor to try to resolve their difficulties through a political organization. Pinard found an inverse correlation between income level and political savvy, and thus concluded that lack of knowledge is a factor contributing to poor people's lack of political participation.

3. Formal participation in any kind of organization is known to be lower among the poor. Pinard found this to be true among his respondents and agreed it is another factor reducing political activity.

4. Poor people get less exposure to propaganda. They read less, watch less television, and interact less with people outside their immediate world. Pinard found that there was equal exposure to information in his sample, but the lower class was less likely to respond to it than the middle class.

Political Orientation of Downwardly Mobile People

Lipset and Bendix found that when people are moving down the social ladder, they tend to change their political orientation. For example, they become more radical than the members of the middle class which they have left, but less radical than their stable working-class peers (1959:72).

The study of Wilensky and Edwards revealed opposite findings: the skidder continues a middle- or upper-class orientation in hope of reentering the class of origin, or non-acceptance of the fact that he or she has left it, or early socialization proves so strong that the person is able to withstand the class change (1959).

Peter Blau (1956) may have provided some explanations for these opposing views by suggesting that if the skidder maintains contact with the people in the former class, he or she will be unable to "keep up" with them and will continue to feel a failure. If, on the other hand, the individual comes to accept membership in the new class, the pressure to "keep up" will diminish and the failure will be forgotten. The important adjustment is to give up the old, including the political orientation (usually conservative), and accept the new (usually radical).

Lopreato and Chafetz (1970) found that Italians who were downwardly mobile tended to become either more radical or more conservative than the stable working-class members they had joined. These investigators contended that this is because the skidders, formerly members of higher strata, are politically more aware than their fellow class members. They postulate that skidders have a tendency to accept the political stance of the class they enter. However, they cannot completely lose the orientation of their class of origin, and this has the effect of neutralizing the resocialization process. The result is the adoption of a political stance somewhere between the leftist class of destination and the rightist class of origin. This argument comes close to that of Lipset and Bendix.

Political Orientation of Upwardly Mobile People

Most studies show that upward social mobility, especially across the nonmanual-manual line, is accompanied by increased political conservatism. In the United States, the children of manual workers who rise above their fathers give up the family's political orientation and adopt the orientation of the class they have joined (Lipset and Zetterberg, 1959:67; Lipset and Zetterberg, 1964:475; Butler and Stokes, 1969:98; and Lopreato and Hazelrigg, 1972:45). Some researchers have also concluded that when a lower-class person moves up to the middle class in the United States, he or she becomes more conservative than those who are born into that class (Lipset and Zetterberg, 1967:94). In contrast, European upwardly mobile individuals adopt a political position which is between that of the class of origin and that of the class of destination.

As an explanation for his finding Lopreato asserted that upwardly mobile American men are political overconformists. Since occupational success is the highest attainment possible in the United States, he claimed that the achiever feels gratitude toward the social order that made his mobility possible and thus his response is to oversubscribe to middle-class values and become conservative (1967:592).

Hopkins reviewed all the literature on overconformity among upwardly mobile American men, and concluded that the studies compel rejection of this theory. Hopkins particularly cited the work of Maccoby (1954), West (1954), and Thompson (1971) to illustrate his point. Contrary to Lipset and Zetterberg and Lopreato, these three researchers show that upwardly mobile Americans tend to vote the same as those born into the middle class. One study (West) provides data showing that upward-bound people are actually less conservative than the stable middle class. Hopkins concludes:

If anything, therefore, the data support the view that the up-wardly mobile "underconform" to the political norms of the middle class. . . . However, most of the findings yeild no statis-tically significant differences one way or another (1973:147).

Summary

Certain factors stand out clearly in the research that has been done on social class and political life. One, contrary to popular myth, there is a great deal of class consciousness among Ameri-cans, and they tend to vote for the political candidate whom they think will serve their class interests most effectively. Two, the higher up one is in the social hierarchy, the more likely one is to be conservative. Three, status inconsistency is likely to result in support for the Democratic party, which traditionally favors social change. Four, membership in political parties is related to social class; lower-class people do not join organizations, particularly formal ones. The most important reason for this seems to be a lower-class stress on individualism, combined with a belief that political organizations cannot help them. On the other hand, Burnham has demonstrated that those in power make an effort to keep the poor from voting. Probably both factors are operative: the poor do not try to participate and the powerful attempt to discourage their participation. Finally, the literature suggests that when people are mobile in either direction their political orienta-tion changes, but there is no conclusive evidence showing the pre-cise direction of that change. A political stance somewhere be-tween the class of origin and the class of destination is the proba-ble choice of most people because they retain some qualities of the former, while not fully accepting the characteristics of the latter.

Conclusion

All institutions in the United States seem to treat the rich and the poor differentially. In the criminal justice system, beginning with arrest and continuing to release, the poor are given less opportunity to prove their innocence; are more likely to be rep-resented by incompetent or indifferent counsel; and less likely to get short or suspended sentences. Most important, they are more apt than the middle-class person to be presumed guilty. The crimes poor people commit are more dramatic and fear-inspiring than white-collar crimes, although the latter are probably harmful to greater numbers of individuals and to the society in general. Finally, the poor are more likely to be labelled "criminal" and the rich are more likely to escape detection, arrest, conviction, and prison.

The American political system also operates to discourage the participation of the poor in the selection of their representatives. One method described in this chapter shows how the requirement for periodic registration to vote prevents large numbers of the poor from voting. In addition, lower-class values are not conducive to organizational life, so poor people tend to avoid joining political groups. In doing so, they relinquish the right to share in the decision-making process.

In short, the criminal justice system and the political process seem to conspire to prevent lower-class success. This concept will be explored further in Chapter 7, with a look at two more social institutions.

Bibliography

Abrahamsen, David, *Crime and the Human Mind*. New York: Columbia University Press, 1945.

Bell, Daniel, *The End of Ideology*. Revised ed., New York: Collier, 1962.

Berelson, Bernard R., Lazarsfeld, Paul F., and McPhee, William N., *Voting*. Chicago: University of Chicago Press, 1954.

Black, Donald, "Production of Crime Rates." *American Sociological Review*, 35:4, 733-748, 1970.

Blau, Peter M., "Social Mobility and Interpersonal Relations." *American Sociological Review*, 21:290-295, 1956.

Burnham, Walter Dean, "Equality of Voting." *In* Rainwater, Lee, ed., *Social Problems and Public Policy*. Chicago: Aldine, 1974, 288-298.

Butler, D., and Stokes, D., *Political Change in Britain*. London: Macmillan, 1969.

Carlin, Jerome E., *Lawyers' Ethics*. New York: Russell Sage Foundation, 1966.

Centers, Richard, *The Psychology of Social Classes*. Princeton: Princeton University Press, 1949.

Chambliss, William J., *Crime and the Legal Process*. New York: McGraw-Hill, 1969.

Chiricos, Theodore G., Jackson, Phillip D., and Waldo, Gordon P., "Inequality in the Imposition of a Criminal Label." *Social Problems*, *19*:4, 553–572, 1972.

Clark, John P., and Wenninger, Eugene P., "Socioeconomic Class and Area as Correlates of Illegal Behavior Among Juveniles." *American Sociological Review*, *27*:826–834, 1962.

Clinard, Marshall B., *The Black Market: A Study of White Collar Crime.* New York: Rinehart & Co., 1952.

Cloward, Richard A., and Ohlin, Lloyd E., *Delinquency and Opportunity.* New York: Free Press, 1961.

Cohen, Albert K., *Delinquent Boys.* Glencoe, Ill.: Free Press, 1955.

Dentler, Robert A., and Monroe, Lawrence J., "Early Adolescent Theft." *American Sociological Review*, *26*:5, 733–743, 1961.

England, Ralph W., Jr., "A Theory of Middle Class Juvenile Delinquency." *In* Cavan, Ruth S., ed., *Readings in Juvenile Delinquency.* 2nd ed. Philadelphia: Lippincott, 1964, 115–128.

Fox, Richard, "The XYY Offender: A Modern Myth?" *Journal of Criminal Law, Criminology, and Police Science*, *62*:59–73, 1971.

Glantz, Oscar, "Class Consciousness and Political Solidarity." *American Sociological Review*, 23:375–382, 1958; reprinted in Roach, Jack L., Gross, Llewelyn, and Gursslin, Orville, eds., *Social Stratification in the United States.* Englewood Cliffs, N.J.: Prentice-Hall, 1969, 361–372.

Glueck, Sheldon, and Glueck, Eleanor, *Unraveling Juvenile Delinquency.* Cambridge, Mass.: Harvard University Press, 1951.

Green, Edward, "Race, Social Status, and Criminal Arrest." *American Sociological Review*, 35:3, 476–490, 1970.

Gursslin, Orville R., and Roach, Jack L., "Social Class and Delinquency: A Theoretical Restatement." *In* Roach, Jack L., Gross, Llewellyn, and Gursslin, Orville, eds., *Social Stratification in the United States.* Englewood Cliffs, N.J.: Prentice-Hall, 1969, 493–503.

Hartjen, Clayton A., *Crime and Criminalization.* New York: Praeger, 1974.

Hartung, Frank E. "White-Collar Offenses in the Wholesale Meat Industry in Detroit." *American Journal of Sociology*, 56:25–34, 1950.

Hill, Stuart L., *Crime, Power, and Morality.* Scranton, Pa.: Chandler, 1971.

Hooton, Ernest A., *Crime and the Man.* Cambridge, Mass.: Harvard University Press, 1939.

Knoke, David, and Hout, Michael, "Social and Demographic Factors in American Political Party Affiliations 1952–1972." *American Sociological Review*, 39:5, 700–713, 1974.

Lazarsfeld, Paul F., Berelson, Bernard, and Gaudet, Hazel, *The People's Choice.* New York: Columbia University Press, 1948.

Lenski, Gerhard, "Status Inconsistency and the Vote." *American Sociological Review*, 32:298–301, 1967.

Lipset, Seymour Martin and Bendix, Reinhard, *Social Mobility in Industrial Society.* Berkeley: University of California Press, 1959, 11–75.

———, and Zetterberg, H., "A Theory of Social Mobility." *In* Coser, L., and

Rosenberg, B., eds., *Sociological Theory*. New York: Macmillan, 1964, 437–462.

Lopreato, J., "Upward Mobility and Political Orientation." *American Sociological Review*, *32*:586–592, 1967.

——, and Chafetz, Janet Saltzman, "The Political Orientation of Skidders: A Middle-Range Theory." *American Sociological Review*, *35*:3, 440–451, 1970.

——, and Hazelrigg, Lawrence E., *Class, Conflict, and Mobility*. San Francisco: Chandler, 1972.

Maccoby, E., "Youth and Political Change." *Public Opinion Quarterly*, *18*:23–39, 1954.

Magnuson, Warren C., and Casper, Jean, *The Dark Side of the Marketplace*. Englewood Cliffs, N.J.: Prentice-Hall, 1968.

Merton, Robert K., "Social Structure and Anomie." *American Sociological Review*, *3*:672–682, 1938.

——, *Social Theory and Social Structure*. Glencoe, Ill.: Free Press, 1957.

Miller, Walter B., "Lower Class Culture as a Generating Milieu of Gang Delinquency." *Journal of Social Issues*, 14:3, 5–19, 1958.

New York Times, January 10, 1975, p. 37.

Nye, F. Ivan, Short, James F., and Olson, U. J., "Socioeconomic Status and Delinquent Behavior." *In Family Relationships and Delinquent Behavior*. New York: Wiley, 1958, 23–33.

Parsons, Talcott, "Age and Sex in the Social Structure of the United States." *American Sociological Review*, 7:604–616, 1942.

Pinard, Maurice, "Poverty and Political Movements." *Social Problems*, *15*:2, 250–263, 1967.

Porterfield, Austin, *Youth in Trouble*. Fort Worth, Tex.: Leo Potishman Foundation, 1946.

President's Commission on Consumer Interests, "Home Maintenance and Repairs." *Consumer Issues 1966*. Washington, D.C.: United States Government Printing Office, 1966.

Rainwater, Lee, "Lower-Class Life-Styles and Community Action." *In* Rainwater, Lee, ed., *Social Problems and Public Policy*. Chicago: Aldine, 1974, 306–312.

Reckless, Walter, *The Crime Problem*. New York: Appleton-Century-Crofts, 1950.

Reiss, Albert J., Jr., and Rhodes, Albert Lewis, "The Distribution of Juvenile Delinquency in the Social Class Structure." *American Sociological Review*, *26*:5, 720–732, 1961.

Schwartz, Richard D., and Skolnick, Jerome H., "Two Studies of Legal Stigma." *Social Problems*, 10:133–142, 1962.

Scott, Joseph W., and Vaz, Edmund W., "A Perspective on Middle-Class Delinquency." *In* Cavan, Ruth S., ed., *Readings in Juvenile Delinquency*. 3rd ed., Philadelphia: Lippincott, 1975, 103–118.

Segal, David R., "Status Inconsistency, Cross Pressures, and American Political Behavior." *American Sociological Review*, 34:3, 352–359, 1969.

Sutherland, Edwin H., *White Collar Crime*. New York: Dryden Press, 1949.

——, and Cressey, Donald R., *Principles of Criminology*. 7th ed., Philadelphia: J. B. Lippincott, 1966.

Thompson, P. H., "Upward Social Mobility and Political Orientation: A Re-Evaluation of the Evidence." *American Sociological Review*, 36:223–235, 1971.

Vold, George B., *Theoretical Criminology*. New York: Oxford University Press, 1958.

Wallenstein, James S., and Wyle, C. J., "American Law-Abiding Law Breakers." *National Probation*, Mar.–Apr., 107–112, 1947.

West, P. S., "Social Mobility Among College Graduates." *In* Bendix, R., and Lipset, S. M., eds., *Class, Status and Power*. London: Routledge, 1954.

Wilensky, H. L., and Edwards, H., "The Skidder: Ideological Adjustment of the Downward Mobile Worker." *American Sociological Review*, 24:215–231, 1959.

Williams, Jay R., and Gold, Martin, "From Delinquent Behavior to Official Delinquency." *Social Problems*, 20:2, 209–229, 1972.

chapter 7

Social Class and Other Institutions:
The Health and Educational Systems

Social Class and the Health System

When Weber defined class, he used the term "life chances" (see Chapter 2). His frame of reference was economic, but this can be taken to mean life chances in every area of life: the chance to join the "right" clubs and know the "right" people, the chance to live in a good neighborhood, and especially, the chance to get good medical care and to live longer.

Beginning at conception, the upper-class infant has a better chance to be born alive and healthy. The upper-class pregnant woman has the best medical attention, the best foods, and ample time to rest. After birth, the upper-class infant lives in the best possible environment:

sanitary, uncrowded, with good food and good medical attention. During his or her teen-age years, the upper-class young person is less exposed to the risks of street life. Even the time of death is class-related; lower-class people die at a younger age.

Life Expectancy and Social Class

Life expectancy studies which examined records extending over several centuries have revealed that there has always been a direct correlation between social class and life expectancy. Aaron Antonovsky described several such studies showing this relationship (1972). One study he described shows that life expectancy for families in the years between 1823 and 1834 ranged from 28.2 years for families of manufacturers, merchants, and directors, to 17.6 years for families of factory workers, to 9.4 years for families of day laborers, and to 1.9 years for families of spinners, weavers, and locksmiths (1972:470). Antonovsky showed that the life expectancy differences between classes have always existed, but "In recent decades, the class gap has narrowed to what may be the smallest differential in history, but evidence of a linear gradient remains, with a considerable differential, given man's life span" (1972:473).

For example, a study conducted for the year 1839 in a suburb of London showed that the life expectancy for "gentlemen, professional men, and their families" was 45; for "tradesmen and their families" 26; and for "mechanics, servants, laborers and their families" 16 (1972:470).

Antonovsky examined over 30 studies of life expectancy from the nineteenth century up until 1953, and came to "the inescapable conclusion that class influences one's chance of staying alive. Almost without exception, the evidence shows that classes differ on mortality rates" (1972:486–487).

Although the gap in life expectancy between social classes has narrowed since the end of World War II, Table 7–1 shows that differentials continue to exist. The gap is narrower for females, but there is still a considerable difference in the life span between the highest and the lowest classes.

Physical Health and Social Class

Studies of physical health and the use of medical technology have shown that poor people derive less benefit from medical advancements than those in higher social classes. A National Health Center survey conducted in the early 1960s indicated that

TABLE 7-1
Life Expectancy at Birth, by Class, Baltimore 1949-1951*

	Class					
	I (highest)	II	III	IV	V (lowest)	Difference between I and V
White Males	68.5	66.4	65.4	63.9	61.4	7.1
White Females	73.1	72.4	71.2	69.8	68.4	4.7

*From Antonovsky, Aaron, as presented by Mayer, K. B., and Buckley, W.: *Class and Society*. 3rd ed., New York. Random House, 1970.

wealthier people not only live longer, but live healthier lives. The survey revealed that the rates for heart disease, chronic physical illnesses, arthritis, hypertension, rheumatism, and eye and ear diseases were higher among the poor than in any other classes. The same relationship exists for rates of hospitalization, restricted activity, time lost from work, and confinement to bed (1965).

Lee Rainwater has done the outstanding work on the relationship between lower-class characteristics and behavior in terms of health, illness, and the use of medical services. He notes that this group represents about 25 to 30 percent of the American population, and that their problems are manifold. For poor people, life consists of one crisis after another, and therefore no particular crisis is extraordinary. "This means that lower class people . . . will be inclined to slight health difficulties in the interest of attending to more pressing ones, such as seeing that there is food in the house . . ." (1974:180).

Rainwater points out that the world view, the life style, and the belief system of the poor make the meticulous and careful attitude toward health which is held by health professionals and by the middle class seem meaningless. In addition, Rainwater claims, poor people live in "understaffed" households; that is, there is a higher frequency of one-parent families, or even if both parents live in the house, there may be minimal involvement or concern for one another. Attention to personal health is marked by the absence of the practice of preventive medicine; and even if a family member becomes ill, proper attention or care may not be forthcoming.

Poor people are, in one sense, preoccupied with their bodies. This is implicit in their reliance on patent medicines and in their interest in dancing and contact sports. They also tend to confuse

somatic and psychic symptoms and have higher rates of psychosomatic illnesses than among the middle class. On the other hand,
relative to the middle class, they are less likely to be hypochondri-
cal or to seek medical help.

Moreover, because of an inferior environment and lack of opportunity, the poor view their bodies in much the same way they
view the world—as mysterious and potentially threatening and
dangerous. As a result, they do not identify with their own bodies,
nor do they try to improve or cure their bodies. Lower-class individuals have a low self-evaluation and a picture of themselves as
unworthy. Nothing and no one encourages them to value their
own persons. "They do not hold the sacredness of their persons
in the same way that middle-class people do. Their tendency to
think of themselves as of little account is readily generalized to
their bodies" (Rainwater, 1974:182). Just as lower-class people
become resigned to a life that is below standard, so they also
accept a body which does not function normally.

This low opinion of their own bodies extends to their children's physical health. Lower-class parents pay little attention to
minor ailments such as colds, sores, or infection, nor do they
practice preventive medicine or take their children for periodic
checkups. When real illness occurs the doctor's orders are likely to
be ignored.

The low esteem of the world (which extends to one's own
body and the bodies of one's children) combines with a fatalistic
preoccupation with the present to produce a predictable result:
The poor seek medical help only under emergency conditions; all
else is seen as an unavoidable part of life and is accepted. Only
acute, incapacitating illness will compel the poor to seek the help
of a physician.

In the middle class, any symptom that is obvious incapacitates
because it takes away from the kind of more perfect person the
middle class individual likes to think of himself as being. The
lower class person cannot afford the conception of himself, he
attends to physical symptoms, if at all, only when they pose a
crisis in carrying out those functions he considers necessary
(Rainwater, 1974: 184).

Use of Health Facilities and Social Class

Lower-class people have mixed attitudes toward medical doctors. On the one hand, they would like to be cared for by the
omniscient physician because the body is so unpredictable and

unknowable. On the other hand, they fear and are distrustful of physicians because they represent the middle class and symbolize authority, and because clinic medicine is all they can afford.

Their attitude toward medical institutions is somewhat different. The poor are accustomed to the treatment they receive in large hospitals and clinics: long waiting, impersonality, indifference, and disrespect. They may appear docile enough, but the attitudes of hospital personnel are in good part responsible for the lack of motivation among the poor to seek medical assistance (Rainwater, 1974:184).

The lower-class individual encounters additional problems in the bureaucratic hospital clinic. Not understanding the necessary division of labor, he or she wants *a person*, not a group, to administer treatment. Unlike the middle-class individual, the poor person does not have a personal physician to run interference at a hospital. In addition, there is a basic lack of mutual trust and communication between doctor and patient. The middle-class or upper-class doctor often cannot hide contempt for the poor client, and the patient recognizes and resents this attitude; it has been encountered in other situations and will be encountered again. "When lower class people perceive the middle-class professional as blaming, derogating, or hostile toward them, they withdraw quickly into an adaptation of resentful docility, and are then much less available for any real communication or learning" (Rainwater, 1974:186).

Hospitalization may be a dreadful experience for the poor. They often are placed in crowded wards and given a minimum of attention and comfort; relatives often are unable or unwilling to visit them frequently, because transportation is too expensive or perhaps out of sheer indifference. In addition, the poor inpatient is ignorant of what is going to happen to him or her and is understandably frightened. Unable to ask the right questions, the patient is unsure even as to who might have the answers.

Long-trend studies indicate that the relationship between social class and the use of medical services has virtually disappeared (Health Information Services, 1958). For example, in the period between 1928 and 1931, of a sample of 40,000, 5.9 percent of those with incomes below $1200 went into a hospital, compared with 10.6 percent of those with incomes over $10,000. In contrast, in 1953 12 percent of all hospitalized patients were poor, compared to 11 percent of the middle class (Kriesberg,

1972). Thus, within a period of approximately 30 years, the differences in hospital admissions have become miniscule.

One reason why lower strata people now make greater use of medical facilities is the growth of hospital insurance plans. The importance of this can be seen from the fact that in 1953, there was an inverse relationship between hospital admission rates and income among insured individuals. Since it can be assumed that the poor are more sick and sick more often than the middle class, clearly the insurance permitted them to seek treatment (Anderson and Feldman, 1956:59). A second reason is the general rise in real income for all strata, allowing the lower classes more money to spend on medical care. Among other reasons for greater utilization of hospital facilities by the poor are sick leave benefits, increased hospital space, improved public transportation, and greater dependence of doctors on hospital services (Kriesberg, 1972:473–476).

Dental Care and Social Class

Unlike the utilization of hospital facilities, which is apparently losing its class-linked character, there continue to be differences between classes in the use made of dental services. In 1953, when asked if they had seen a dentist within the preceding year, 17 percent of those with incomes under $2,000 replied yes, compared to 56 percent of those with incomes over $7,500. The response to the same question in 1958 was 15 percent of the poor group and 53 percent of the higher income group. Thus, there seems to have been little change (Kriesberg, 1972:476).

Quentin Smith and his associates contend that the differential use of dental services does not stem from differences of income. In their study of a union which provided prepaid dental care, they found that though services were available to all members without charge, the higher strata members were much more likely to take advantage of the opportunity than lower strata members (1959:23–25).

Kriesberg and Treiman used a national survey to examine the relationship between social class and the utilization of dental services (1960 and 1962). They found that when adults had been taken to the dentist as children for preventive treatment, they continued to go later in life and also to take their children for periodic checkups. Interestingly, the parents transmitted a habit to their children, rather than a set of values about preventive dentistry. In addition, dentists who practice preventive dentistry are more likely to have patients from higher strata. The interaction between the dentist and the patient is likely to increase the patient's participation in preventive dentistry. Furthermore, such dentists charge higher fees and have better equipment, so that treatment is actually less painful than it is for the poorer patient.

One other value seems to come into play. Middle-class people are more likely to believe in professional dental care and in keeping their own teeth. Lower-class people probably place less importance on keeping their teeth because they have known many adults who have lost some or all of their teeth. Thus, lower-class people are not motivated esthetically to see a dentist for preventive reasons, nor could they afford such care even if desired.

Mental Health and Social Class

Sociologists also have turned their attention to the social class differences which exist in the diagnosis and treatment of mental diseases. Many studies show that lower-class patients do not use mental health facilities as frequently as middle-class patients; they receive less intensive forms of treatment; and they benefit less from the treatment they get (Riessman, Cohen, and Pearl, 1964). Antonovsky found that slightly more than 9 percent of persons in families with incomes below $2,000 reported mental conditions, compared with 5.4 percent of those with incomes over $7,000 (1972).

Studies show that psychopathology is more common among the poor than among the wealthy. The relationship, however, is not a simple one. For example, while schizophrenia is found more often in the lower classes, this is not true of other types of psychoses (Weinberg, 1967). It is also not clear that social class is related to the occurrence of neuroses (Weinberg, 1967). Nevertheless, even with these exceptions, when all forms of mental illness are combined, most researchers agree that there is a relationship between psychopathology and social class (Srole, 1962). It is generally held that although there is more mental illness among poor people, they are less likely than people in higher strata to seek treatment.

The pioneering work in associating social class with mental health was done by Faris and Dunham in 1939, and Hollingshead and Redlich in 1958. Faris and Dunham studied more than 30,000 people who had been admitted to hosptials for treatment of mental disorders in Chicago over a 12-year period. Their most important conclusion was that the highest rates of psychoses were found among the poorest people in the city; however, only schizophrenia appeared to be class-linked, while manic-depressive psychosis was not. This conclusion has been substantiated by several other investigators (see Kaplan et al., 1956).

Perhaps Faris and Dunham's most significant contribution was that they inspired other investigators to research the topic. Robert Clark, for example, studied the relationship between schizophrenic psychoses and occupational prestige, finding a direct correlation between low occupational prestige and schizophrenic psychoses, and thus corroborating the conclusions of Faris and Dunham (1949).

In their study, Faris and Dunham suggested that social disorder was the cause of the high rates of schizophrenia in slums. This hypothesis has been argued against by later investigators. Some prefer to explain the phenomenon by asserting that psychotics are attracted to lower-class areas, rather than that such areas produce psychoses (Gibbs, 1962). Others claim that social isolation or a low degree of social participation results in higher rates of psychoses among the poor (Jaco, 1954).

Hollingshead and Redlich (1958) studied psychiatric patients in the environs of New Haven, Connecticut. Among their conclusions were: (1) schizophrenia and social class are inversely related; (2) lower-class psychotics do not drift into slum areas; (3) the proportion of manic-depressives is also higher among poor people; (4) people in different classes are treated differently when they become mentally ill. For example, lower-class people are most often treated by residents and interns rather than by psychiatrists. They are more likely to be given shock treatments, frontal lobotomies, and drugs, while middle-class and upper-class people are treated by psychoanalysis and psychotherapy. Myers and Schaffer reported similar findings even before the Hollingshead-Redlich study. They found that high strata individuals were more likely to be accepted for treatment, to be treated by senior personnel, and to be treated over a longer period of time than lower strata people (1954:307).

Hollingshead and Redlich also were attentive to neuroses. Their data led them to assert that the chance of becoming neurotic has a great deal to do with one's social class. They found that neuroses are as prevalent in the middle class as they are in the lower class. Furthermore, types of neuroses are class-linked. Neurotics in the two highest classes (Classes I and II) are dissatisfied with themselves and tend to be depressive. Neurotics in Class III are fearful and antisocial. Those in Class IV feel physically ill. Those in the lowest stratum, Class V, behave badly and display hysterical and psychosomatic reactions (1958:240). Later research has revealed that neuroses are found more frequently in the middle class than in the lower class. It would seem that middle- and upper-class people have more time and inclination to worry about whether or not they were loved by their parents, while lower-class people have more real and pressing problems.

Arnold Green studied middle-class male children and concluded that middle-class parents tend to be ambivalent and anxious, often threatening to withhold love from their children as a form of punishment. This kind of childrearing can generate neurosis (1946). Others have held that because punishment in the middle class is indirect and subtle, as opposed to the direct, physical punishment of the lower class, middle-class children develop feelings of guilt, inferiority, and anxiety. To assuage such feelings, middle-class children repress all feelings and tend to overconform to win approval (Reissman, 1959; Cattrell, 1945).

Summary

In all areas of health, poor people do not share the same life chances as those in the social classes above them. Members of the lower class tend to die younger and to have higher rates of all kinds of illnesses—physical, dental, and mental. Even though they are in a sense preoccupied with their bodies, lower-class people avoid medical and dental care because of mistreatment, lack of consideration, and cost. They seek help only when the situation becomes acute and the illness interferes with other things in their lives. There are good reasons for this behavior: (1) illness is only one of many crises in their lives; (2) they are treated badly in medical facilities and by physicians; (3) they are not accustomed to thinking in terms of prevention or esthetics; and (4) treatment for the poor usually is less successful than it is for the higher classes.

The poor in this country are sick more often and more seriously than any other group. They are more likely to have chronic and acute physical ailments; they are more likely to become psychotic; and they are more likely to have poor teeth. But they do less to improve their health than the middle class, and when they do try to get help, their rate of cure is lower than that of other social classes.

Education and Social Class[1]

Before World War II the role of education in the United States was clearly delineated. High schools were preparatory schools for students who planned to go to college; others went from junior high schools to trade and commercial training schools. Until almost the middle of the twentieth century, 75 percent of all high school graduates went on to further education; today only 33 percent continue on to college. This means that high schools must maintain separate curricula for those who are college-bound and for those who will terminate their education after 12 years. Inherent in this system is the problem caused by those students who change their minds; curricula must be flexible enough so that transfers can be made (Kahl, 1957:280).

College education before World War II served two well-defined functions. The first was to prepare young people, mostly upper-middle-class and upper-class sons, for entrance into graduate and professional schools; the second was to educate students, again mostly sons, in the liberal arts. Today the stated objective is to make college education available to anyone who wishes to take advantage of the opportunity.

Ideologically, then, the availability and purposes of education have changed in the last three decades. Education is venerated because it is considered the best vehicle for upward mobility for the individual, and because Americans believe that knowledge of technology (which they think can only be acquired in school) will solve national problems. Education, then, has become a kind of Holy Grail. In 1957, Joseph Kahl expressed it this way:

The long term trend in the distribution of income is to put more people in the middle, to reduce the numbers at the extremes of rich and poor. The same is true of education. We are approaching a system in which high school is universal, and some college is very common. . . . Our school system creates an atmosphere of equality and an ease of communication that blurs economic disparities. It is probably the most important social factor in creating the American feeling that social-class differences are not important (1957:280-281).

1. The author is grateful to Ralph Larkin for his perceptive criticism of this section.

Since Kahl wrote these optimistic words, events have occurred which may have proved him to be incorrect. The "stated purposes" do not seem to accord with the realities. In this section, the discrepancies between the ideologies Americans hold about education and the realities they practice will be explored. Because of the importance that has been placed on it, American education has been plagued by many disputes and complex issues, most of which deal, at least peripherally, with social class. The two basic questions are as follows:

(1) Does the United States truly offer education for everyone who wishes it or does it still favor children from the higher strata? If the answer to this question is that higher class children are favored, where does the fault lie? Can blame be placed on the child and the kind of family he or she comes from? Or are the schools at fault because they evaluate children in ways which are geared to middle-class abilities and because predominantly middle-class schools have better teachers and facilities? The first question, then, is concerned with whether or not Americans are creating a meritocracy.[2] A second part of this dilemma is whether a meritocracy based on intelligence will replace an aristocracy based on inherited wealth.

(2) Is the stress placed on education by both universities and employers warranted? Do employers demand more education than is really needed for a given position? In other words, is a college degree necessary for *doing* a job or merely for *getting* a job?

"Mass" versus "Class" Education

There are two opposing social principles which are at work in every stratification system. One is a "strain toward aristocracy," which means that parents naturally wish to pass on to their children their wealth, social position, and privileges. The other is a "strain toward equality," which stresses the individual's ability and tries to offer each individual an opportunity to achieve the best position in society.

This is the ancient question of "mass" versus "class" education. Is a college education a right or a privilege? Should young people be allowed to attend college because they can afford it; because they are the brightest; or should everyone be permitted

2. A meritocracy is a society in which a young child is evaluated by the state and is then educated accordingly. The individual's social class position thus is determined by the contribution he or she makes to the welfare of the society (see Michael Young, 1958).

to go? Should all members of society get a mediocre education, or should the elite get a superior education? It is impossible to have it both ways. Since the end of World War II, the United States has claimed that it offers education to everyone.

From the time that this ideology became accepted dogma, it was conceded that not all children were equally prepared for higher education. Headstart programs were begun for very young children and "open enrollment" programs were offered in many colleges and universities, usually with remedial courses available to students who could not demonstrate adequate ability in rudimentary skills.

Innumerable studies have shown that none of these attempts have been successful. Disadvantaged children, on the average, always score lower on all standardized tests, according to every investigator who has ever examined the question. "There are significant differences in intelligence test performance of children and youth from different socio-economic backgrounds, with children from the higher levels always securing the higher intelligence test scores" (Eells, Davis, et al., 1951, 53). Does this mean that lower-class children are duller than middle-class and upper-class children? Some say test scores have nothing to do with intelligence. Poor children score lower because the values and opportunities in their environment are not conducive to learning or even to motivate them to want to learn.

David K. Cohen's discussion of the relationship between schooling, intelligence tests, and income concludes that America is not a meritocracy based on intelligence because I.Q. scores are not the best predictors of success. Instead, Cohen postulates that the relationship between the three variables is quite stable: that is, success depends upon education, opportunity, and intelligence. Poverty and the *appearance of stupidity* are correlated; but intelligence is unrelated to poverty. Cohen remarks that:

Among other factors which lead to a situation in which some people are poor or hold low-status jobs, lower intellectual ability is not a terribly important one. Being stupid is not what is responsible for being poor in America (1974:134).

Time magazine has reported on the relationship of learned values and dropout rates in Detroit, pointing out that by the time children enter kindergarten their subcultural values have already influenced them (1962). Poor children lack the educational privileges of middle-class children. They do not see books and magazines in their homes; they lack opportunities for creative play, as with crayons and drawing paper. Poor parents communicate and interact less with their children than middle-class parents, with the result that the five year old child is less at ease with words, sentences, and abstract ideas. Further, parental financial failure brings a sense of inferiority, stupidity, and rejection and even very young children "get the message" from their parents. They already envision themselves as inadequate or "dumb." A negative attitude toward education is transmitted from generation to generation—an attitude that the child internalizes at a very young age. Thus, the fact that poor children score lower on standardized tests is not proof of biological inferiority. The results instead force us to question what intelligence really is and how it can be measured so that social class will not intrude as an intervening variable.

Intelligence

The average person understands intuitively what is meant by the term intelligence. Generally when one is described as intelligent, it is understood to mean the ability to obtain information, to understand it, and to apply it to diverse situations. Psychologists, on the other hand, have a great deal of difficulty with the concept of intelligence.

Definitions of intelligence can be classified into four major categories: biological, educational, faculty, and empirical (Pinter, 1931). *Biological* definitions are Darwinian inasmuch as they assert that intelligence can be measured on the basis of ability to adapt to the environment. The most intelligent person is the one who adjusts most efficiently and reaches the pinnacle of the social structure. The *educational* definition restricts meaning to the ability of the individual to learn, retain, and utilize data, but does not imply that the individual will necessarily be successful. Those who define intelligence as a *faculty* mean that it is the ability to think abstractly. The *empirical* position states that intelligence is the ability to react favorably to situations. But none of these definitions is wholly satisfactory. Undoubtedly there is a relation between intelligence and heredity; but more and more sociologists and psychologists are giving credence to environmental and emotional factors which may enhance or hold back the basic genetic endowment.

Thus, even though intelligence has never been defined properly, the American educational system continues to measure it.

Although it is not certain what the standardized tests actually measure, the scores are accepted widely and used to sort young people into categories. Invariably, as children are categorized, a meritocracy is created which supposedly is based on intelligence. But in fact the existing class differences are perpetuated because upper strata children persistently score higher. This is not surprising and does not reflect negatively on the children in the lower classes. It simply means that the I.Q. test is a general achievement test that is highly correlated with reading ability, and therefore reflects a pattern common to the upper strata.

For example, Kahl claims that social class standing is the best predictor of success in college. If the father is a professional, his child has a 43 percent chance of graduating from college; if he is a businessman, the chances drop to 19 percent; if he is a salesman or a clerk, the child has a 15 percent chance; and a blue-collar worker's child has only an 8 percent chance of graduating from college (Kahl, 1957:283). Another survey showed that of those students in college in the mid-1960s, only 20 percent came from families with incomes under $3,000 (U.S. Bureau of the Census, 1969).

Sewell and Shah's study of Wisconsin high school seniors shows similar results. These researchers obtained I.Q. test scores and socioeconomic status of students in 1957. Seven years later they contacted the same students to see how many and which ones had gone to college and had graduated. Table 7–2 shows the results of this study and clearly proves that social class is related to college attendance and graduation. For example, the table shows that when intelligence levels were high, 64 percent of the high-strata students graduated from college, compared with 20 percent of the low-strata students. Even when I.Q. scores were low, .3 percent of the lower-class students graduated, while 10.5 percent of the upper-class students did so.

Income

John Porter's discussion of social class and educational opportunity in Canada can be generalized to reflect conditions in the United States because of similarities between the two nations. Of several barriers to equality of educational opportunity in Canada, income is one of the most important. Since private universities in Canada are very expensive, only wealthier families can afford to send their children to such schools. Family size is another determining variable. In a large family only a few of the children, if any

TABLE 7–2
Percentage of 1957 High School Seniors Who Had
Graduated from College by 1964–1965,
by Socioeconomic Status and Intelligence, Males Only*

Socioeconomic Status Levels	Intelligence Levels				
	Low	Lower Middle	Upper Middle	High	Total
Low	.3 (363)	7.9 (267)	10.9 (193)	20.1 (149)	7.5 (972)
Lower Middle	2.3 (300)	7.4 (324)	16.7 (275)	34.4 (253)	14.2 (1152)
Upper Middle	4.4 (273)	9.8 (277)	24.4 (316)	46.7 (289)	21.7 (1155)
High	10.5 (134)	23.3 (232)	38.5 (299)	64.0 (442)	42.1 (1107)
Total	3.2 (1070)	11.5 (1100)	23.9 (1083)	47.2 (1133)	21.8 (4386)

All x^2's for each column and row in this table are significant beyond the .05 level.
Effect parameters: Socioeconomic Status .081   Intelligence: .123

*Adapted from Sewell, W. H. and Shah, V. P. 1967:15.

at all, can be educated; and since poorer people tend to have more children, fewer lower-class children go to college. A third barrier mentioned by Porter is geographic location. Educational facilities vary qualitatively and quantitatively in different provinces, and since going to college far from home entails greater expense than going to college nearer to home, the kind of education available close by becomes significant.

Religion

Religion is yet another factor related to educational inequality. French Catholic children receive less education than English Protestant children. This is partly a function of income level (French Canadians are more likely than English Canadians to be in the lower echelons), and partly a function of family size (French Catholic families are larger than English Protestant families). However, Porter claims that French Catholics do not have as good or as much education as other Canadians because the Church controls the schools in Quebec province (where French Canadians are concentrated), and religious training takes precedence over technical training. Table 7–3 shows the relationship between education and social class in Canada.

TABLE 7-3
Children, Aged 14-24 Years, Living at Home
and Percentage in School*

Class (1 is highest)	Number of Children Living at Home	Percentage of Children in School
Class 1	13,502	71.0
Class 2	173,937	55.2
Class 3	40,130	50.6
Class 4	60,739	45.6
Class 5	573,095	38.9
Class 6	200,517	38.2
Class 7	186,862	34.8

*Adapted from Porter, J., in Curtis, J. E., and Scott, W. G., eds., 1973:127.

For Canada, then, the picture is much the same as in the United States. Level of education is clearly class-linked, with the upper class most likely to attain the highest educational level. Family size and religion are also important determining variables, but they are in turn also related to class. A Protestant is more likely than a Catholic to have a small family, to be wealthy, and to go to a school which stresses the kind of training needed to succeed in an industrialized society.

Higher Education
Kahl notes that most studies show a correlation between I.Q. scores, social class, and going to college. However, he points out that there are many intervening variables which prevent the correlation from being constant. There are a number of reasons why bright youngsters from poor families may not go to college and, conversely, why young people with below average intelligence from wealthy families do go (1957:283-284).

According to Kahl, the father's occupation does not affect the child's school performance in the early grades but by the time fourth grade is reached, a pattern begins to emerge, and by junior high school it is quite definite. This occurs because as a child gets older, behavior is influenced not so much by intelligence, but by the values absorbed from his or her environment. Upper-class children learn that it is necessary at least to get passing grades in school, and even if they are not bright, they understand that if they show interest and are cooperative in school, they will be able to meet their families' and friends' expectations that they go to college. In short, they are socialized to be *students*.

Lower-status children often learn from their parents that college is not for them, and they also see that their friends are not concerned with getting into college. Even the bright lower-class youngster learns early that in his or her environment books and education are not as important as sports, popularity with the opposite sex, and "fun."

The social world of higher-status young people encourages all but the very slowest learner to enjoy school and seek admission to college, while the values of the lower-class world tend to orient even the smartest young people away from college. Obviously, family and peer pressures are as meaningful as intelligence in forming aspirations for a college education.

William Sewell and his associates have been studying the relationship between opportunities for higher education and characteristics not relevant to learning since 1964 (1964, 1965, 1966a, 1966b, 1967, 1968a, 1968b, 1969, 1970, 1971, 1975). Although they used various measures of socioeconomic status (father's and mother's educational levels, parental income, and father's occupation), they consistently found great differences in educational opportunities among various social classes. For example, an upper-class student's chances for education or training beyond high school are 2 1/2 times greater than those of a lower-class student; chances for college are 4 to 1; for graduation, 6 to 1; and 9 to 1 for a postgraduate degree.

> Our findings lead inexorably to the conclusion that in their opportunities for higher education [people] seldom escape the influence of their social origins. The selective influence of socioeconomic background . . . operates independently of academic ability at every stage in the process of educational attainment (1971:796).

Robert Hauser, who has worked with Sewell and who agrees that social class origins are the determining factor in educational opportunities, states: "Success in school is highly contingent on social origins" (1969:609). On the other hand, he finds that "tracking" in high schools is not based on social class. "There is little evidence of discrimination by socioeconomic background in the teaching or marking of students" (1969:611). A more detailed discussion of "tracking" later in this chapter will indicate that Hauser probably is incorrect.

Cultural Deprivation

Most researchers agree, then, that there are correlations between social class and intelligence test scores that are not related to intel-

ligence per se. Rather, the correlation is between cultural deprivation and low I.Q. scores, or between cultural advantage and high
I.Q. scores. This gets the argument back to the four categories into
which intelligence is classified. Cultural deprivation certainly influences, for better or worse, ability to adjust to one's environment,—
to control, exploit and react effectively to it. In short, it is likely
that the consistent correlation researchers find between intelligence and social class is in fact a correlation between test scores
and educational deprivation or advantage. That is, membership in
a social class does not imply that one is more or less able to obtain, retain, and use information. Instead, membership in a social
class has a direct bearing on the amount of personal motivation
and available opportunities to seek education.

It appears that regardless of how much is done to elevate I.Q.
test scores of lower-class children, no matter how much special
attention is given, they continue to do poorly—when compared
with middle-class children—on all measures of intelligence, learning, and achievement because social factors impede all efforts to
help them. The conclusion seems inescapable that while ideologically all American children have equal access to educational opportunities, the system works in such a way that middle-class
children can take advantage of the opportunities while lower-class
children cannot. But social class background cannot be solely
responsible; it is also likely that the educational system operates
in ways that discriminate against the lower-class child. This issue
has been explored by a number of sociologists.

Lauter and Howe describe how, in the 1960's, education
focused its attention on the so-called "disadvantaged student."
The watchword of the times was "equality of educational opportunity," and today all major school systems have special programs
to help poor children "catch up." The philosophy behind such
programs was twofold: There was a desire to help the individual
attain occupational success and an attempt to develop educated
citizens for the benefit of the country as a whole. Lauter and
Howe claim, however, that:

If these are, indeed, the goals of our educational system, it has
severely failed, especially in the urban ghetto. Nearly 81 per cent
of sixth grade Harlem pupils score below grade level in reading
comprehension, 77.5 per cent in word knowledge, 83.3 per cent
in arithmetic (1972:199).

These researchers contend that the failure of the schools results from the incompatibility of the two goals. There are essential jobs in industrialized societies that do not require a good education; therefore, despite the pronouncements of equality of opportunity, schools must see to it that only a limited number actually reach the top. How else can the low level jobs be filled?

Tracking

Schools have means of channelling and directing students, and one way of doing this is called "tracking," defined as classifying pupils in high school according to their talents and abilities. "Tracking" or "ability grouping" was proposed originally to keep children who were bored by study from dropping out of school by individualizing their programs to suit their skills and retain their interest. The idea was that if a student simply did not care about social science, physics, or classical literature, he or she should study what was of interest and of practical value to them, such as automotive repair or hairdressing.

Research has found, however, that this purpose was not achieved. Miriam Goldberg, for example, found that "ability grouping, *per se*, produces no improvement in achievement for any ability level and, as an administrative device, has little merit" (1966:163). Lauter and Howe report that several other studies arrive at the same result: tracking has not succeeded in keeping pupils in school. Indeed, the results have been (1) to perpetuate the cycle of hopelessness, ignorance, and joblessness for the poor; and (2) there has been no increase in the number of talented youngsters. These authors then pose the question: If tracking has proved detrimental, why has it continued for so many years?

They claim that its real purpose is control of manpower. Despite the myth that "any boy can become president," in reality opportunities are strictly limited. The American economy has a greater need for salespersons, production workers, technicians, and white-collar workers than it does for medical doctors, lawyers, college professors, or engineers. Tracking is one way to "ensure that unpopular industries, like the Army, or less prestigious occupations, like sanitation work, are supplied with manpower" (1972:204).

The result of tracking, then, is that the children of the poor end up in tracks which are not college-bound. This is not because they are less intelligent than middle-class children, but because their home life does not prepare them to do well on I.Q. and other standard tests which would place them in more academic tracks. Not only are such children poorly trained for test taking, but the content of such tests does not conform to their experiences as it does to the experiences of middle-class children. In fact, "tracking harms some children, depriving those we call 'deprived,' making them less competent, less about to reach, let alone to use, the instruments of power in U.S. society. In the light of tracking, schools become for such children not the means of democratization and liberation, but of oppression" (1972:206). Lauter and Howe summarize their report:

The track system provides a formal basis for translating these class-based factors into academic criteria for separating students into different groups: those who will drop out; those whose diplomas will not admit them to college; those who will be able to enter only two-year or junior colleges; and the lucky few in the honors classes who will go on to elite institutions and to graduate and professional schools. Thus while tracking may assure the "failure" of lower-class students, as a system it allows the schools to "succeed" in serving middle-class interests by preparing their children to fill the technological and professional needs of corporate society (1972:207).

Subsidies

Hansen and Weisbord (1974) studied the subsidy system in California colleges and universities in which tuition is free. In California, compared with other states, the greatest percentage of high school graduates go to college. The amount of subsidy varies with the type of school attended. For example, in the 1960s, students at the University of California received approximately $5,000; those at a state college got about $3,000; and those at a junior college about $1,000. The hidden agenda is that students from higher social strata are much more likely to go to the University of California and those from lower strata to go to state or junior colleges. Thus, "the selectivity process restricts the availability of large subsidies to all but high income families" (1974:117). The result is that the three educational systems—the universities, the state colleges, and the junior colleges—educate three different classes of students.

According to these authors, California is representative of other states which offer students similar unequal subsidies. On the national level, lower-class students are more likely to drop out of high school than middle-class or upper-class students, and therefore they are cut off from all subsidy. Furthermore, more lower-class students go to those educational institutions at which the subsidy is lowest, and they are less likely to graduate. Once again, the lower classes get a smaller part of the subsidy offerings. Compounding these inequalities are the majority of state tax structures which are mostly regressive, in that poorer families "actually pay a larger fraction of their income in taxes to support higher education than do affluent families" (1974:118), but receive less benefit from it. Hansen and Weisbord conclude:

> The claim that the American system of higher education contributes to equality of educational opportunity is largely fiction. . . . In practice, a perverse redistribution of higher education subsidies from low income to high income families takes place. Those with the most need for higher education are getting the least in terms of public benefits . . . the mythology of equal educational opportunity for all is just that: mythology (1974:116–118).

Achievement

Bradley Schiller's study of success among sons who grew up in welfare families goes far to support those who see the schools as villains in the stratification of educational opportunities. Schiller postulates that socioeconomic attainment is a function of three phenomena: the opportunity structure, which defines the individual's possibilities and the avenues available for attainment; individual personality characteristics, such as intelligence, motivation, skill, and value system; and chance or luck, which may come from the opportunity structure or be inherent in the person.

Comparing a sample of men raised in welfare families with a sample of nonwelfare sons, Schiller concludes that the tremendous achievement differences between the two groups cannot be explained in terms of parental educational levels or occupational status, or a combination of both. "Thus it is concluded that a substantial portion of the AFDC [Aid to Families with Dependent Children] sons' underachievement can only be explained in terms of a relative constriction in opportunities, with the constriction itself based on the economic status of the origin family" (1970:439).

Kenneth Clark documents the discrepancy in achievement between lower-class and middle-class children in terms of the kinds of schools they attend, qualifications of the teachers, facilities available in the schools, and the training pupils receive for taking standard tests. Clark states, "American public schools have become significant instruments in the blocking of economic mobility and in the intensification of class distinctions rather than fulfilling their historic function of facilitating such mobility" (1968:101).

Blau and Duncan assume that father's educational and occupational level leads to the child's educational attainment, which in turn leads to intergenerational mobility. Thus, the influence of class origin on occupational achievement is indirect, mediated through education. This means that if a person does complete a college education, the class of origin has little influence on the class of destination. For Blau and Duncan education is essential because it either mediates or diminishes the effects of class origin on one's final social class standing (1967). In short, the probable answer to the question of whether social class leads to educational opportunity or educational achievement leads to social class standing is that the two variables interact with each other. A high social class facilitates entrance into college, and graduation from college facilitates entrance into a high social class.

Direct and Indirect Discrimination

A slightly different point of view is expressed by Christopher Jencks in his reevaluation of the Coleman Report (1966). The Coleman Report placed the blame for failing to provide adequate education for the disadvantaged child squarely on the school system. Jencks agrees that poor and middle-class children are segregated in schools, but denies that the schools attended by the poor are inferior to those attended by the middle class. He claims that the Coleman Report did not prove that less money is spent per student in lower-class schools, or that the classes are larger, the teachers poorly trained, the physical plants inferior, or that there are fewer textbooks, paper supplies, and other equipment. Jencks reaffirms the position that the observed differences between the achievements and attitudes of children are traceable to the social class from which they come. Lower-class children are socialized to expect to fail. It is this expectation of failure which accounts for their inferior performance, not discrimination by the schools themselves. The schools may not directly discriminate, according to Jencks, but they still fail because they do not compensate the disadvantaged child for an inability to conform to middle-class virtues, such as self-discipline. "It is the school's failure to develop these personal characteristics, not its failure to teach history or physics, or verbal skill, that lies behind the present upheaval in the schools" (1972:225).

The research findings described, except for Jencks, are substantially in agreement that the school system of tracking, the content of the intelligence tests, and sometimes outright discrimination is to blame for the failure of lower-class children to compete successfully with middle-class children in school. This kind of differentiation is harmful in two ways. By acting through the system to ensure that the "right" people get the "right" jobs, the United States is wasting human resources which could benefit the country, and depriving individuals of the opportunity to realize their full potential. The system prevents the poor child from attaining a position which might well have social and economic value to society. Conversely, the rich child often attains a position that he or she is incapable of filling properly.

There are other researchers who assert that the schools do not discriminate against lower-class students, and that the fault lies solely with the child's family and environment.

Social Factors

Adams and Meridam studied almost 1500 white adults in North Carolina in order to discover the social factors that determine college attendance. They found several variables that accounted for whether or not an individual goes to college. For example, in white-collar families the size of the family is not a deterrent until the number of siblings exceeds five. At this point, one's chances for going to college decrease with each additional child. In blue-collar families, an only child has a distinct advantage. Furthermore, male children have a higher probability of going to college than female children, especially in low-status families. However, the study found that father's occupation is the most important variable. "The great disparity in college attendance which is based upon socioeconomic status is apparent in the 76 percent of white-collar offspring in our sample who attended college, as compared with 27 percent of the blue-collar" (1968:233).

Skills, Ability, and Social Class

Barbara Heyns recognizes that most American high schools offer different curricula for college-bound and work-bound students. In her study of 48 urban public high schools, she tried to ascertain whether students were assigned to different ability groups on the basis of social class background or scores on standard tests. Contrary to most studies, Heyns found that "the total effect of socioeconomic status . . . is still less than the unique effects of tested verbal ability" (1974:1440). She acknowledges that upper strata students have some advantage, but "it does not seem sufficiently large to argue that considerable social class discrimination is prevalent in selection mechanisms within schools" (1974:1442).

Heyns, then, argues that "educational stratification largely results from differential performance on achievement tests. . . . The principal determinant of curriculum placement and grades is verbal achievement test scores, not father's occupation, education, or family size" (1974:1449). Heyns appears to ignore the fact that the higher a student's social class level, the greater is the probability that his or her verbal skills will be superior. It has been established quite clearly that middle-class and upper-class children are exposed earlier and more often to the written and spoken word. Furthermore, parents in these classes expect high performance levels from their children, pressure them to produce in school, reward them when they do well, and punish them when they fail. Lower-class parents are much more likely to be indifferent to school performance (see Chapter V). It is not surprising, then, that advantaged children do better on verbal achievement tests. What is surprising is that Heyns makes no attempt to account for these intervening variables.

Summary

An evaluation of the evidence we have presented leads to the conclusion that *although Americans profess a desire to establish equality of educational opportunity, in fact, opportunity frequently has been denied to lower-class children.* Undoubtedly part of the blame must be placed on home environment which is unlikely to motivate the child to seek higher education. But this can hardly be considered "blame" in the sense that poor parents deliberately set out to hurt their children. It is blame in the sense that being poor usually means being ignorant, fatalistic, and unable to do very much to help oneself or one's children.

The lion's share of the responsibility must rest with the school system. It has failed the lower-class child in several ways. It has done little to counteract the negative forces operating in the home environment; it has used tests which are poorly understood by the testers and which clearly discriminate against the disadvantaged child; it has failed to provide the child who must attend secondary school in ghetto neighborhoods with the same level of quality of teacher, physical plant, and supplies that are available to the middle-class child; and it has "tracked" children in such a way that they are labelled for life.

In conclusion, Americans are creating a meritocracy which is ostensibly based on intelligence, but which in actuality is based on wealth, power, and privilege. The "strain toward aristocracy" clearly has won out over the "strain toward equality," despite all protestations to the contrary.

The Value of Education—Credentialism

Education in the United States generally is used as a means to financial stability; and, indeed, for many people this is virtually the only proper use for education (Fountain, 1972). Table 7-4 illustrates this point.

Clearly, for each increment of education, there is a monetary gain. Yet, in a sense, this is an unrealistic evaluation of ability by business employers. While it is true that "many of the attributes that are marketable in the world of work can be learned in school, some are best learned on the job, and some are innate" (Fountain, 1972:175). In effect:

> Education is only one ingredient in financial success. Top executives are rare not so much because of their education but because of unique combinations of education *and* intelligence *and* personality *and* willingness to work 10 hours or more each day (Fountain, 1972:178).

This leads directly to the question of credentialism. Why is it that those with more education are more likely to be hired for a position than those with less? Why is it that level of education is directly related, as Fountain demonstrates, to earned income? Is it really necessary, in most positions, to have attained the "required" level of education? Necessary or not, the United States is a "credential" society. This means that without the essential "passport" (i.e., the B.A., Ph.D., or whatever is demanded), people find access to desirable positions blocked.

TABLE 7-4
Years of Education and Lifetime Income*

Years of School Completed	Income from Age 18 to Death
Elementary:	
Less than 8 years	189,000
8 years	247,000
High School:	
1 to 3 years	284,000
4 years	341,000
College:	
1 to 3 years	394,000
4 years	508,000
5 years and more	587,000

*Adapted from Fountain, Melvin, 1972:174: *In Current Population Reports, Consumer Income,* Series P-60, No. 56, August 14, 1968, Bureau of the Census, p. 9.

Conflict versus Functional Theory

Two theories have been proposed to account for the demand for increased education by employers. The functional theory of education is a specific application of the general theory of stratification (see Chapter 3). It is based on the notion that educational requirements simply reflect the need for technological skills in highly industrialized societies. Conflict theory, on the other hand, contends that these requirements represent the efforts of those in power to monopolize opportunities. Randall Collins (1971), in his consideration of both theories, believes that conflict theory is supported more strongly by the evidence.

Functionalists claim that educational requirements in industrialized society increase because the number of low-skill jobs decrease and the number of high-skill jobs increase. Collins shows that this is only true to any substantial degree during early industrialization. Functionalists also contend that as technology advances greater skills become required in the same jobs; that is, to be a plumber in 1976 requires more knowledge than was necessary in 1926. Collins refutes this, claiming that many people are over-educated for their jobs. Finally, functionalist theory asserts that formal education is the only way to acquire those job skills that are in demand. In contrast, Collins cites evidence to show that better-educated people are frequently less productive in their jobs.

Furthermore, "most skilled manual workers acquire their skills on the job or casually" (1971:1006). The relevance of education to productivity in nonmanual and professional work is difficult to evaluate, because frequently there are legal requirements for each category of job or profession which make a comparative study impossible. However, as many students know, a Ph.D. does not ensure that the holder is a good teacher. In addition, there is scattered evidence that knowledge acquired in classrooms is forgotten rather quickly, and that most students are more concerned with "nonacademic interests or with achieving grades with a minimum of learning" (1971:1007). Summarizing his critique of the functional theory of education, Collins writes:

Economic evidence indicates no clear contribution of education to economic development, beyond the provisions of mass literacy. . . . Education is often irrelevant to on-the-job productivity and is sometimes counter-productive. . . . The quality of schools themselves, and the nature of dominant student cultures suggest that schooling is very inefficient as a means of training for work skills (1971:1007).

In his brilliant defense of the conflict point of view, Collins notes that there is a great deal of evidence showing that the level of skill demanded in most jobs is very flexible. Employers simply do not have clear conceptions of the level of ability a given job requires. Therefore, "it appears that standards of performances reflect the power of the groups involved . . . [and] ascriptive factors continue to be important in occupational success. . . . The social mobility data . . . show that social origins have a direct effect on occupational success, even after the completion of education" (1971:1007–1008).

Collins makes it clear that educational opportunity, like many other things in the United States, is related to power and wealth. Those with power send their children to elite schools; graduates of elite colleges tend to be hired for elite jobs.

Elitism

It has been important not only to possess a college degree in order to succeed in the business world, but also to get a degree from the "right" school (Pierson, 1972). George Pierson acknowledges, however, that this is no longer as true as it once was because the demand for expertise is greater than the elite universities can supply. The result has been that people from less prestigious universities now may be found among the top business executives in America.

In his study of Wall Street lawyers, Erwin O. Smigel reported that in 1957, of all partners in the large law firms, 40 percent had graduated from Harvard, Yale, or Princeton. The 1962 figures reveal the persistence of this pattern, with 41.5 percent of the partners coming from these same elite schools (1969:73). By the late 1960s, however, law firms could no longer maintain these standards. In the revised edition of his book, Smigel writes:

> The law firms still prefer Eastern national schools and Law Review experience. But the realities of the growing competition in the marketplace have forced the firms to change their standards. . . . Law school prestige is . . . of necessity, less important (1969:369).

Education and Productivity

Ivar Berg has vigorously attacked the significance business organizations accord to credentials. Berg notes that in recent years in the United States the employment rate for skilled workers has risen, while rates for unskilled workers have decreased. Efforts to resolve this problem usually focus on educating the unskilled. Berg contends that this solution obscures the real question: "Are academic credentials important for doing the job—or just getting it?" (1974:119). Furthermore, Berg believes that higher education does not mean better job performance. To prove his hypothesis, he collected data from many private companies, the military, public school systems, and federal civil service. Every personnel manager he interviewed asserted that for each increment of education, the worker's attitude improved, trainability increased, adaptation was more rapid, and promotion probability increased. However, these personnel managers had no data to substantiate their assertions, while Berg's data flatly contradicted them.

For example, Berg compared the productivity of 4000 life insurance salesmen and found that the number of policies sold was unrelated to the salesman's educational level. In fact, those with less education and more experience actually were the most productive. In another company Berg examined the performance records of 200 female clerks and found no differences among them which could be attributed to educational background. At a publishing company which hired high school and college educated secretaries, because the employers claimed that college-educated women would be promoted to editorial jobs, Berg found that none of the secretaries went on to join the editorial staff. Instead, particular college graduates from outside the company were selected for such positions. In a New York chemical company, the employers believed that the best technicians were those with the most education. Berg found, to the contrary, that the more highly educated technicians did not perform as well and had higher turnover rates. Among a group of blue-collar workers in Mississippi, the same pattern was observed: the best educated produced less and left the job more quickly. Berg concluded that on every occupational level Americans tend to overestimate the value of education, denying employment opportunities to those with less education and demanding more education than most jobs require.

William Sewell agrees with Berg and criticizes the importance placed on credentials by both colleges and employers. "This criticism is particularly persuasive whenever it can be shown that the educational requirements for entry into an occupation have little bearing on the activities of that occupation" (1971:793). Since the trend of credentialism is likely to accelerate, occupational opportunities will not be equalized until educational opportunities are equal. Opportunities for elite jobs are restricted to those from elite schools. Thus, high educational requirements are set by elite employers who can then limit and control those who will succeed in the occupational hierarchy.

Summary

In summary, it cannot be denied that America is a highly technological society which requires those who have special knowledge and special skills. Unfortunately, the only means readily available to employers for ascertaining job applicants' qualifications is to determine their educational level. Educational systems and industrialization develop together because industrialization is not possible without a system for training technicians, specialists, and others needed to make technology work and expand. Thus, the notion of equality of educational opportunity is closely associated with a nation's economic system. No society with a rigid, inherited occupational system can industrialize; therefore, real equal educational opportunity is beneficial to both individuals and societies.

In America, however, ideology and reality are not the same. Promises of equality are generously expressed but rarely truly attained. Until a way is found to start each child's life with the same advantages, lower-class children will often be denied the chance to go to college, to go to elite colleges especially, and to find their way up the occupational ladder. Up to now, this country has been fortunate in finding enough able people within the upper strata to fill its need for technological and managerial skills. Nevertheless, there has been a vast waste of potential talent—a waste that is costly and wrong.

It has been well-documented, as this review of the literature illustrates, that one's class of origin, one's intellectual capabilities, and one's motivation are, in that order, the determinants of educational attainment which, in turn, influences one's class of destination. While there is no doubt that higher education is of value because it yields personal satisfaction and self-realization, its greatest significance lies in the fact that it is an avenue—perhaps the most direct avenue—for power, privilege, and income. Unfortunately, as Robert Lejuene says, "In industrialized societies formal education has become the most important mechanism for the allocation of persons to positions in the occupational hierarchy" (1972:169). Since the chance to obtain a formal education is greatest for those from wealthy families, we are unquestionably wasting the talents of millions of people who are deprived of higher education because of their social class origins.

Conclusion

The health care system shows the same exclusory pattern we outlined in the previous chapter on the criminal justice and political systems. Not only do lower-class people tend to be less healthy, but also tend to die younger and to receive poorer quality treatment for their ailments. Nothing in the bureaucratic structure of the American health care delivery service encourages the members of the lower strata to try to obtain help when they are ill, or to try to prevent illness from occurring in the first place.

Finally, there is a strong correlation between educational attainment and social class. Those in the higher strata are much more likely than those in the lower strata to be placed in honor tracks in high school, to go to college, to go to elite colleges, to graduate, and to get the more prestigious positions in society which are awarded on the basis of credentialism. This is not because the poor are inherently less intelligent than the rich. It is because poor children are not encouraged by their home environment, their parents, or their peers to seek education. Nor do the school systems do much to help them attain middle-class motivations and aspirations. Indeed, much of educational officialdom is destructive to even the brightest lower-class child.

Most of America's important social institutions seem to conspire, whether overtly or covertly, against lower-class social mobility. While there is opportunity in the United States, it tends to be confined largely to those who can afford to take advantage of it.

Bibliography

Adams, Bert N., and Meridam, Miles T., "Economic, Family Structure, and College Attendance." *American Journal of Sociology,* 74:3, 230–239, 1968.

Anderson, Odin W., and Feldman, Jacob J., *Family Medical Costs and Voluntary Health Insurance: A Nationwide Survey.* New York: McGraw-Hill, 1956.

Antonovsky, Aaron, "Social Class, Life Expectancy and Overall Mortality." *In* Blumberg, Paul, ed., *The Impact of Social Class.* New York: Thomas Y. Crowell, 1972, 467–491.

Berg, Ivar, "The Great Training Robbery." *In* Rainwater, Lee, ed., *Social Problems and Public Policy.* Chicago: Aldine, 1974, 118–124.

Blau, Peter M., and Duncan, Otis Dudley, *The American Occupational Structure.* New York: Wiley, 1967.

Cattell, Raymond B., "The Cultural Functions of Social Stratification: II. Regarding Individual and Group Dynamics." *Journal of Social Psychology, 21:*3–55, 1945.

Clark, Kenneth B., "Alternative Public Schools Systems." *Harvard Educational Review, 38:*Win., 1968.

Clark, Robert, "Psychoses, Income, and Occupational Prestige." *American Journal of Sociology, 44:*433–440, 1949.

Cohen, David K., "Schooling, I.Q., and Income." *In* Rainwater, Lee, ed., *Social Problems and Public Policy.* Chicago: Aldine, 1974, 124–134.

Coleman, James S., et al., *Equality of Educational Opportunity.* Washington, D.C.: United States Government Printing Office, 1966.

Collins, Randall, "Functional and Conflict Theories of Educational Stratification." *American Sociological Review, 36:*6, 1002–1019, 1971.

Eells, Kenneth, Davis, Allison, et al., *Intelligence and Cultural Differences: A Study of Cultural Learning and Problem-Solving.* Chicago: University of Chicago Press, 1951.

Faris, Robert E. L., and Dunham, H. Warren, *Mental Disorders in Urban Areas.* Chicago: University of Chicago Press, 1939.

Fountain, Melvin, "What Is an Education Worth?" *In* Lejeune, Robert, ed., *Class and Conflict in American Society.* Chicago: Rand McNally, 1972, 173–178.

Gibbs, Jack P., "Rates of Mental Hospitalization: A Study of Societal Reaction to Deviant Behavior." *American Sociological Review, 27:*782–792, 1962.

Goldberg, Miriam, *et al., The Effects of Ability Grouping.* New York: Teachers College, 1966.

Green, Arnold W., "The Middle Class Male Child and Neurosis." *American Sociological Review, 11:*31–41, 1946.

Hansen, W. Lee, and Weisbord, Burton A., "Inequalities in Higher Education." *In* Rainwater, Lee, ed., *Social Problems and Public Policy.* Chicago: Aldine, 1974, 116–118.

Hauser, Robert A., "Schools and the Stratification Process." *American Journal of Sociology, 74:*6, 587–611, 1969.

Health Information Service, "The Increased Use of Medical Care." *Programs in Health Services, 7:*Oct. 3–4, 1958.

Heyns, Barbara, "Social Selection and Stratification Within Schools." *American Journal of Sociology, 79:*6, 1434–1451, 1974.

Hollingshead, August B., and Redlich, E. C., *Social Class and Mental Illness.* New York: Wiley, 1958.

Jaco, Gartley E., "The Social Isolation Hypothesis and Schizophrenia." *American Sociological Review*, *19*:567-777, 1954.

Jencks, Christopher, "A Reappraisal of the Most Controversial Educational Document of Our Times." *In* Lejeune, Robert, ed., *Class and Conflict in American Society*. Chicago: Rand McNally, 1972, 217-225.

Kahl, Joseph A., *The American Class Structure*. New York: Holt, Rinehart and Winston, 1957.

Kaplan, Bart, Reed, Robert B., and Richardson, Wyman, "A Comparison of the Incidence of Hospitalized and Non-Hospitalized Cases of Psychoses in Two Communities." *American Sociological Review*, 21:472-479, 1956.

Kriesberg, Louis, "The Relationship Between Socio-Economic Rank and Behavior." *In* Thielbar, Gerald W., and Feldman, Saul D., eds., *Issues in Social Inequality*. Boston: Little, Brown, 1972, 458-482.

——, and Treiman, Beatrice R., "Preventive Utilization of Dentists' Services Among Teenagers." *Journal of the American College of Dentists, 29*:Mar. 28-45, 1962.

——, and Treiman, Beatrice R., "Socio-Economic Status and the Utilization of Dentists' Services." *Journal of the American College of Dentists, 27*:Sept., 147-165, 1960.

Lauter, Paul, and Howe, Florence, "How the School System is Rigged for Failure." *In* Lejeune, Robert, ed., *Class and Conflict in American Society*. Chicago: Rand McNally, 1972, 197-216.

Lejeune, Robert, ed., *Class and Conflict in American Society*. Chicago: Rand McNally, 1972.

Mayer, Kurt, B., and Buckley, Walter, *Class and Society*. 3rd ed., New York: Random House, 1970.

Myers, Jerome, and Schaffer, Leslie, "Social Stratification and Psychiatric Practice: A Study of an Out-Patient Clinic." *American Sociological Review*, *19*:307-310, 1954.

Pierson, George W., "The Educational Backgrounds of American Business Executives." *In* Lejeune, Robert, ed., *Class and Conflict in American Society*. Chicago: Rand McNally, 1972, 179-185.

Pinter, R., *Intelligence Testing*. New York: Henry Holt, 1931.

Porter, John, "Social Class and Educational Opportunity." *In* Curtis, James E., and Scott, William G., eds., *Social Stratification: Canada*. Scarborough, Ontario: Prentice-Hall, 1973, 117-134.

Rainwater, Lee, "The Lower Class: Health, Illness, and Medical Institutions." *In* Rainwater, Lee, ed., *Social Problems and Public Policy*. Chicago: Aldine, 1974, 179-187.

Riessman, Frank, Cohen, Jerome, and Pearl, Arthur, eds., *Mental Health of the Poor: New Treatment Approaches for Low Income People*. New York: Free Press, 1964.

Reissman, Leonard, *Class in American Society*. Glencoe, Ill.: Free Press, 1959.

Schiller, Bradley, "Stratified Opportunities: The Essence of the 'Vicious Circle.'" *American Journal of Sociology*, 76:3, 426–442, 1970.

Sewell, William H., "Community of Residence and College Plans." *American Sociological Review*, 29:24–38, 1964.

——, "Inequality of Opportunity for Higher Education." *American Sociological Review*, 36:5, 793–809, 1971.

——, and Armer, J. Michael, "Neighborhood Context and College Plans." *American Sociological Review*, 31:159–168, 1966a.

——, and Armer, J. Michael, "Response to Turner, Michael, and Boyle." *American Sociological Review*, 31:707–712, 1966b.

——, and Haller, Archibald O., "Educational and Occupational Perspective of Farm and Rural Youth." *In* Burchinal, Lee G., ed., *Rural Youth in Crisis: Facts, Myths, and Social Change.* Washington, D.C.: United States Government Printing Office, 1965, 149–169.

——, Haller, Archibald O., and Ohlendorf, George W., "The Educational and Early Occupational Status Achievement Process: Replication and Revision." *American Sociological Review*, 35:1,014–1,027, 1970.

——, Haller, Archibald O., and Portes, Alejandro, "The Educational and Occupational Process." *American Sociological Review*, 34:82–92, 1969.

——, and Hauser, Robert M., *et al.*, *Education, Occupation, and Earnings.* New York: Academic Press, 1975.

——, and Shah, Vimal P., "Parents' Education and Children's Educational Aspirations and Achievements." *American Sociological Review*, 33:191–209, 1968b.

——, and Shah, Vimal P., "Social Class, Parental Encouragement, and Educational Aspirations." *American Journal of Sociology*, 73:559–572, 1968a.

——, and Shah, Vimal P., "Socioeconomic Status, Intelligence, and the Attainment of Higher Education." *Sociology of Education*, 40:1–23, 1967.

Smigel, Erwin O., *The Wall Street Lawyer.* Revised ed., Bloomington, Ind.: Indiana University Press, 1969.

Smith, Quentin, Pennell, Elliot H., Bothwell, Ruth Dee, and Gailbreath, Mary N., *Dental Care in a Group Purchase Plan, A Survey of Attitudes and Utilization at the St. Louis Labor Health Institute.* Washington, D.C.: United States Department of Health, Education, and Welfare, Public Health Service, Division of Dental Resources, 1959.

Srole, Leo, Langner, Thomas S., Michael, Stanley T., Opler, Marvin K., and Rennie, Thomas A. C., *Mental Health in the Metropolis.* New York: McGraw-Hill, 1962.

Time, March 16, 1962, 63.

U.S. Bureau of the Census, *Current Population Reports.* Series P-20, No. 185, Washington, D.C.: United States Government Printing Office, 1969.

U.S. Bureau of the Census, *Current Population Reports, Consumer Income.*

Series P-60, No. 56, Washington, D.C.: United States Government Printing Office, August 14, 1968.

U.S. National Center for Health Statistics. Series 10, No. 17, Washington, D.C.: United States Government Printing Office, May 1965, Table 17, 28.

Weinberg, S. Kerson, *The Sociology of Mental Disorders.* Chicago: Aldine, 1967.

West, P. S., "Social Mobility Among College Graduates." *In* Bendix, R., and Lipset, S. M., eds., *Class, Status and Power.* London: Routledge, 1954.

Whitman, Howard, "Why Some Doctors Should be in Jail." *Collier's,* Oct. 30, 1953, 23-27.

Young, Michael, *The Rise of the Meritocracy, 1870-2033.* Baltimore: Penguin, 1958.

chapter 8

Caste in the United States:
Racial Groups as Caste Groups

Introduction

Human beings interact not so much in terms of what they actually are but in terms of the conceptions that they form of themselves and of one another (Shibutani and Kwan, 1965, 38).

Up until this point we have been discussing class stratification systems. There are, however, other types of stratification systems, namely, slavery, estate, and caste. No stratification system exists in pure form, and so the following descriptions are presented as ideal types, each of which contains elements of all or some of the others.

Charles Horton Cooley was among the early American sociologists who claimed that the term "caste" was preferable to what we now call "stratum," because continuity and inheritance are basic to class stratification. Cooley argued that differences between classes are perpetuated by heredity, association, culture, and opportunity. Caste features are maintained by life-style differences, a lack of communication between strata, and minimal knowledge about each other (1956:211, 217). In other words, *any* stratification system implies permanence and hereditary inquality, not just "achieved" inequality. Thus, in a sense, even a class system is also a caste system.

Max Weber referred to caste as a closed status group, implying that caste is prestige stratification (1958:39–45). Heller modified the Weberian formulation by stating that prestige in terms of inherited inferiority or superiority and one's position in the hierarchy determines one's economic and power position. What Heller says about a caste system applies in many ways to a class system:

The crucial test of the weight of the status factor in caste stratification is that in those cases of discrepancy between one's economic standing and his status, status decides the caste placement. Furthermore, status in caste stratification . . . is unchangeable. People of low caste who manage to advance economically, nevertheless cannot cross the caste line (1969:57).

Furthermore, every type of stratification system is extremely complex and a precise delineation of the characteristics of each would be difficult, perhaps impossible. Criteria by which various types of stratification systems might be distinguished from one another have been suggested by Heller (1969:52).

1. How *normatively* open or closed is the society? That is, to what degree do the norms permit social mobility or make it impossible or difficult? Slavery and caste systems would be the most closed; estates somewhat more open; and class systems would be the most open of all.
2. How much stress is placed by the society on ascription and how much on achievement? In other words, how much emphasis is put on the unchangeable fact of parentage? Slavery and caste systems stress ascription; estates somewhat less so; and class systems ideally not at all, although it has been shown that in actuality this is not always so.
3. To what degree does institutionalized inequality exist and what types are there? In other words, how equal is access to opportunity? On what basis is inequality permitted—by custom, law, ideology, or any combination of these three? Inequality is most rigidly institutionalized by ideology and customs in caste systems. It is institutionalized by law in slavery and estate sys-

tems. It is presumably not institutionalized at all in class systems, although certainly it is institutionalized to some degree by custom in all systems.

4. What is the most significant factor leading to inequality—power, economics, or status? The economic factor dominates slavery; power and status are most salient in estate systems; all three are meaningful in class systems; and status is clearly the most important factor in a caste system.

Systems of Social Stratification

Slavery

Slavery is a system of stratification which is usually ignored or unrecognized by many sociologists, and yet it still exists in many parts of the world (Sulzberger, 1967). The United Nations Human Rights Commission estimates that there are more than 2 million slaves in parts of South America, Africa and Asia. In this type of stratification system inequality is institutionalized by law and the economic factor is of the greatest significance.

The historian, M. J. Finley, defines slavery as a stratification system in which "a man is in the eyes of the law and of public opinion and with respect to all other parties a possession of another man" (1960:145). *The fact of being owned, rather than the type of work he or she performs, makes a person a slave.* A slave occupies a very low position because he or she is a legal possession, and the slave-owner has complete power over the slave in every sense. Thus, all three factors—economic, power, and prestige—are operable in the slave stratification system.

Finley was writing about slavery among the ancient Greeks and Romans, but several American scholars have demonstrated that slavery in the United State did not differ substantially from slavery in classical times. According to Arnold Sio (1965), for example, the legal status of the slaves and the pervasiveness of the system were no different in the two eras. But the social distinction between slave and free person was much more marked in America than in Greece or Rome (Davis, 1966:30, 47). The important difference between the two systems was that race was the meaningful differentiating factor in the American system of slavery, while heritage and nationality were the differentiating characteristics in the ancient systems.

The tie between race and slavery accounts for all other major differences between American and ancient slavery. First of all, it explains why the American slave, in contrast to the slave of ancient times, was considered *intrinsically* inferior. This supposed innate inferiority was in turn developed into an ideology, a rationalization for the tie between slavery and race. . . . In America it was considered proper and fitting that Negroes be slaves because of their race (Heller, 1969:55).

Estates

Estate stratification systems were common during the medieval period of European history. They evolved out of the nobility, who held a legally endorsed, hereditary, privileged position in the society, and out of the development of a numerically greater group of people who farmed the land and were thus legally enjoined from leaving it because they supplied the food for the privileged minority. Gradually subgroups developed, such as clergy, artisans, and government administrators. All these estates had legal recognition, prescribed rights and obligations, privileges, and hereditary membership. Typically, a medieval society had three major estates: the nobility, the clergy, and the peasantry. All were hereditary, largely endogamous, and sanctioned by law. They were virtually closed strata, with admission by ascriptive means, and some slight allowance for outstanding achievement.

An estate system of stratification was related to land ownership, and consisted of unequal strata with closed membership. With a limited monetary system, land was the basis of power, wealth, and prestige. One's position in the system depended on the amount of land one owned.

Classes

Since much of this book has been devoted to the American class stratification system, it will not be discussed at length here. It is only necessary to describe the ideal type class system.

A class system is . . . a system of inequality, unlike castes or estates, [which] requires no legal or other formally institutionalized support. Since opportunities for social mobility are held out to all members of the society, changes in ascribed status through personal accomplishments frequently occur. The society has no formal restrictions on social relations or on marriage among members of different strata. Thus, social organization along class lines is minimal and class boundaries are blurred. Class consciousness, i.e., awareness of class position and feelings of solidarity among class members, is limited (Roach, Gross, and Gursslin, 1969:75).

The above is an ideal image of a class system as seen in the United States. That it is a distortion of reality is clear from the research conducted by sociologists in recent years. Social mobility is not nearly as widespread as imagined; talent and ability are not the most common means of status advance; social relations between classes are restricted; class lines and class awareness are not blurred; and among the upper and lower classes, especially among the former, there is awareness of solidarity.

Castes[1]

Lopreato and Lewis have provided an ideal type definition of a caste system of stratification:

> A caste system may be viewed as a close approximation to a pure type of social stratification in which class membership is hereditary and the various classes are rigidly segregated by occupational specialization, religious and dietary taboos and by the moral belief that what is, ought to be (1974:412).

India is most often considered to be the best example of an ideal type caste system. There are four major castes or *varnas* in India. The highest is the *Brahmin* caste, whose members traditionally are priests. Just below the *Brahmins* are the *Kshatriyas,* comprising the warrior and administrator caste. The *Vaishiya* is the third-ranking caste, composed of merchants and artisans; and the lowest ranked caste is the *Shudra*, whose members are servants, peasants, or laborers. Below the four castes are the *Harijan*, the untouchables or pariahs, who traditionally sweep the streets, tan animal hides, and clean latrines. In the past, occupations were not merely ways of earning a living, but were sacred obligations. Today, although there are informal pressures on children to follow parental occupations, rigid caste-based occupational specialization is rare.

Each caste is divided into subcastes, called *jatis*, which may contain merely a handful of people or several million. No one knows how many *jatis* there are in India; estimates go as high as 4500. The subcastes are local units, each with a distinctive name, life-style,

1. I am deeply indebted to S. Priyadarsini for her constructive and indispensable assistance with this section.

and vocation. From a prestige point of view, the caste rank is most significant, but because they are regional units, it is the *jatis* that are most salient in the daily life of the Hindu.

Caste systems ensure the most institutionalized inequality because they are maintained by custom, religion, and ritual. Once born into a caste, a person is not permitted to leave it. His children and children's children will always be members of his caste. Furthermore, *jatis* are endogamous, internally homogenous, exclusive, and totally closed—thus maximizing differences between groups. Ritual and custom prevent personal interaction between members of different *jatis*. For example, especially on formal occasions, members of differently ranked *jatis* are not permitted to dine together; nor can a high *jati* member even eat food prepared by a member of a lower *jati*. When such taboos are broken inadvertently, Hindus quite often undergo purification rites to cleanse themselves of the contamination.

In the modern Indian constitution, passed in 1950, laws have been enacted which forbid discrimination on the basis of caste or *jati* membership. In addition, urbanization and industrialization have led to changes in the old patterns of avoidance. When the movement away from the rural areas first began, at the beginning of the twentieth century, Indians could not afford to bring their wives and children to the cities with them, and they were forced to mingle with members of other *jatis*. Later on, after the 1950 constitution had been passed, avoidance patterns had to be ignored because talented people were needed in industry, and those from lower *jatis* could not be excluded on a caste basis alone. However, in the villages and outlying sections of India, the *jati* differentiation and taboos are still rigidly maintained by custom and reinforced by religion.

But the Indian caste system is more complex than this brief description indicates. Although *jati* members are traditionally assigned to certain occupations, the exceptions now are almost as numerous as the rules. Intermarriage is forbidden, but it does occur between members of immediately adjacent *jatis*, particularly among urban Indians. Members of different *jatis* do eat together and socialize with each other, in spite of the fact that intercaste commensality is taboo. In the past wealth and caste varied directly, but today there are almost as many poor and middle-class *Brahmins* as there are rich ones, and there are many wealthy *Shudras* and *Harijans*. Educational levels, however, are still highest for the two upper castes. Thus, nowhere, not even in India, does an ideal caste system exist.

Caste in the United States

The term inequality appears in the title of this book because it is broader and more general than other terms, such as class and stratification, which frequently are used interchangeably. Class differentiation and the stratification of a society along a class continuum are common, perhaps universal. In addition, however, there are other dimensions of inequality. Groups distinguished by age, race, ethnicity and religion, or sex are not classes in the economic sense of the term used earlier in this volume. Instead, they are *caste* groups. This is not because they have the characteristics attributed ot a "true" caste system, but because each has sufficient caste features to justify our reference to them as castes.

Some sociologists will disagree that such social categories should be termed castes. While approving application of the term to ethnic, religious, and racial groups, they strongly resist its use for age and sex groups. It may be that age and sex are *ascribed* statuses and that inequalities can be identified; but, the argument runs, castes represent people of all ages and both sexes, and assignment is based on parentage. These objections are nit-picking. It is more important to identify the "caste-like" features of these categories and to observe their consequences than it is to be concerned with the origin of the inequality.

Certainly if one insists on using commonly accepted definitions of a caste system, it must be admitted that membership in an age or sex group is not the same in every sense as membership in other caste groups. For example, endogamy is not a feature of an age or sex caste; nor, of course, are formal rules of deference enforced. There are no verbalized taboos against eating with members of other age groups or of the opposite sex. Nevertheless, certain features of these groups are very similar to those of caste groups. Occupational mobility is not forbidden, but it is certainly more difficult for females and the elderly than it is for males and the young. Relations of sub- and superordination between members of groups are obvious and well-maintained, if not legal. Individual achievement can go only a short way toward eliminating the ascribed stigma of sex and age. Despite the claim that America and India represent the two extremes of the stratification continuum, there is reason to argue that there are at least four caste-like groupings in the United States: ethnic/religious, racial, age, and sex. Moreover, caste differentiation is as pervasive in this country as class differentiation, and it cuts across class lines in significant ways. For example, it is more desirable to be a white bank president than a black bank president. Furthermore, it is better to be a male bank president than a female one; or a young bank president than an old one; or a Protestant bank president than a Catholic or a Jewish one. It is more advantageous to be a bank president in the eastern part of the United States than in the Midwest. Such caste differences may be found on every class level. Bank president was used as an example, but salesman or janitor would be just as applicable. Just as in India it is preferable to be a *Brahmin* rather than a *Harijan*, regardless of economic class, in the United States it is preferable to be white rather than black, young rather than old, Protestant rather than Catholic or Jewish, male rather than female, and of British rather than of Italian ancestry.

Fig. 8–1 shows how caste membership cuts across class lines, and reveals that one's class status is affected by membership in any of the lower castes.

There are many ways to stratify groups of people, and some ways are more prominent than others in some social systems. But to deny that a caste system coexists with a class system in the United States is to ignore reality. The contrast between India and America may thus be more apparent than real. Ideology may have it that Americans reach certain social statuses because they have demonstrated abilities in open competition with others, and therefore deserve the positions they occupy. But this is not the entire picture. Even when minority caste members do achieve positions of high economic reward, it is still the case that their "caste" characteristics affect their social evaluation by others.

Minority Groups as Caste Groups

In this chapter, then, certain types of minority groups will be discussed. Although not necessarily numerically inferior, a minority group is any group of people which, for various reasons, is in a low-status position, from which they cannot escape, regardless of economic gain. Minority group members are given unequal treatment vis-à-vis the opposing dominant group inasmuch as they are

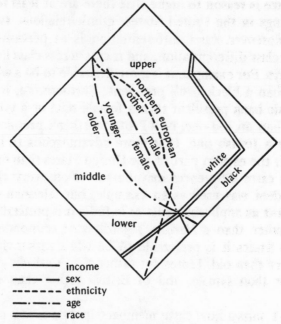

FIGURE 8-1
Class and caste in American society by income, sex, ethnicity, age, and race. Approximate percentages of total population: women, 51%; ethnic group members (self-reported), 35%; over 65, 10%; blacks, 11%. The author is indebted to Clayton A. Jartjen for this figure.

prevented from sharing in the opportunities, resources, and services available in the society. In the United States, minority groups, in many ways, are caste groups, although their positions are institutionalized not by law, but by folkways, mores, and custom.

Many minority groups can best be viewed as caste groups in relation to the extent to which they comply with the traditional criteria of caste. The following features are common to castes:

1. The stratification system is institutionalized either by law, ideology, custom, or any combination of these.
2. Social mobility between castes is either nonexistent or severely limited.
3. Membership is ascribed at birth and unchangeable.
4. Endogamy is the rule, although exogamy occasionally occurs.
5. There is segregation in dwelling areas, places of worship, and occupation.
6. Access to opportunity tends to be restricted.

7. Relationships of sub- and superordination exist between members of different castes.
8. There are rules of avoidance and deference, and sanctions are applied when these rules are violated.
9. Cultural norms differ between castes.
10. Lower-caste members emulate upper-caste members.
11. Members are aware of their membership in their caste.
12. Membership in a given caste affects all other aspects of life.

Several groups in American society resemble ideal caste groups on all or most of these criteria to varying degrees.

Racial Groups as Caste Groups[2]

India versus the United States

A continuing controversy among social scientists is whether or not blacks in the United States constitute a caste. One of the main protagonists in this debate, Oliver Cox, a black sociologist, does not believe that blacks constitute a caste in the United States. He argues that race relations and caste relations are two different phenomena. Castes in India are occupational specialty groups, while in the United States blacks and whites have legal and moral rights to compete for any occupation. In America there is de facto segregation which causes disharmony between the races. In India, on the other hand, caste inequality is considered legally and morally right, and therefore does not disrupt the social system.

The difference between the racial attitudes of whites and the caste attitude, so far as the social ideals of each system are concerned, is that whites *wrongfully* take the position of excluding groups from participating freely in the common culture, while castes *rightfully* exclude outsiders from participating in their dharma [obligatory duty] (1974: 429).

Cox writes that the black seeks to be accepted by and integrated into the white sector of American society.

The ideal of Negroes is that they should not be identified; they evidently want to be workers, ministers, doctors, or teachers, without the distinction of being *Negro* workers, *Negro* ministers, and so on. In short, they want to be known unqualifiably as American citizens, which desire, in our capitalist society, means assimilation and amalgamation (1974:429).

2. Much of the information in this section is from Alphonso Pinkney, *Black Americans.*

Cox further claims that in caste systems occupations are legally monopolized, and thus there is no need for any one caste to exploit another. In American social organization, the economic system is such that exploitation of the lower-class black by the upper-class white is not only possible, but probable. Unlike castes, races are not identified with occupations and open competition is destructive and unfair to the black.

Racial rivalry divides a society vertically, while a caste creates stratification by status hierarchy. Both systems prevent social mobility, but the caste system prevents occupational mobility, while the racial system prevents mobility across the color line.

Cox has made two major points: First, inequality exists in both societies but it is illegal in the United States and legal in India; Second, castes do not exploit each other economically, while whites have exploited blacks in America.

The problem with this argument is that it does not accurately reflect the Indian system. For one thing, the Indian constitution legally prohibits discrimination against low-caste members and *Harijans*, just as the American constitution legally prohibits discrimination against blacks. Thus, *both* societies are illegally excluding a number of groups from "participating freely in the common culture." Furthermore, while no group in either country is actually barred from any particular occupation, blacks and *Pariahs* often have the lowest paying and least prestigious jobs within any occupation. While neither is *legally* assigned to sweep the factory floor, that is what the lower-caste member in India and the United States is more likely than the upper-caste member to be doing. Blacks and *Harijans* have the unenviable distinction of commonly being relegated to the lowest occupational groups or the lowest prestige positions within occupations, and of being exploited economically and discriminated against in both societies.

A difference Cox does not take account of is "color." India, for all practical purposes, does not have a "color problem." A *Brahmin* is not easily physically distinguishable from a *Shudra* for example. In the United States, with rare exceptions, blacks and whites are readily identifiable by skin color and sometimes by other features as well. Race relations, then, are concerned with physical differences; caste relations are not. Crossing the color line is an issue only in the United States, not in India. The effect of discrimination by color or caste on occupation (class) is the

TABLE 8-1
Employed Workers by Occupation and Race,
United States, 1972*

Occupation	Black	White
Total number employed, in thousands	8628	73,074
White-collar workers	29.8%	50.0%
Professional and technical	9.5	14.6
Manager and administrator	3.7	10.6
Sales workers	2.2	7.1
Clerical workers	14.4	17.8
Blue-collar workers	39.9	34.4
Craftsmen	8.7	13.8
Operatives	5.5	3.7
Transportation workers	15.8	12.3
Nonfarm laborers	9.9	4.6
Service workers	27.2	11.8
Private household	6.8	1.2
Other	20.5	10.5

*Adapted from U.S. Bureau of the Census, *The Social and Economic Status of the Black Population in the United States,* 1972:49.

same, however. Mobility across occupational lines, income distribution, and unemployment are all functions of caste in India and color in the United States. Both groups vary directly on these three criteria, as indicated in Table 8-1.

Occupational Status, Income, and Educational Level of Black Americans

The table clearly reveals that whites are concentrated in the white-collar categories; there is an almost equal distribution in the blue-collar categories, although there is a higher percentage of blacks; and blacks are overrepresented in service occupations. Blacks, in short, comprise the bulk of the manual worker-service worker castes in the United States.

Even though there has been a degree of occupational upgrading among blacks over the past decade (for example, in 1960, 16.1 percent of blacks were in white-collar jobs, 27.9 percent in 1970, and, as the table shows, 29.8 percent in 1972), blacks are still predominant in the low-skill, low-paid jobs, and relatively absent in the high-skill, well-paid jobs. Furthermore, "even when blacks are employed as professionals in private industry their chances for advancement are minimal" (Pinkney, 1975:83).

Table 8-2 shows how employment discrimination against blacks, evidenced by their presence in the lowest paid jobs, is re-

TABLE 8-2
Median Family Income in the United States,
Nonwhite and White, 1965-1972*

Year	Nonwhite	White	Ratio, Nonwhite to White
1965	3994	7251	.55
1966	4674	7792	.60
1967	5094	8234	.62
1968	5590	8937	.63
1969	6191	9794	.63
1970	5516	10236	.64
1971	6214	10672	.63
1972	7106	11549	.62

*Adapted from U.S. Bureau of the Census, *The Social and Economic Status of the Black Population in the United States*, 1972:17.

flected in their incomes. Moreover, the differential between black and white incomes appears to be generally consistent. It has been slightly above 60 percent of the median white income since 1966. Interestingly, the gap was narrower before the *Brown* v. *the Board of Education* decision of the Supreme Court in 1954, which was considered a first step in eradicating discrimination against blacks.

Table 8-3 indicates that in addition to being in the poorest paid jobs and earning the lowest wages, blacks are also more likely to be unemployed than whites; indeed, twice as likely in almost any given year. Furthermore, once unemployed, blacks are more likely to remain out of work for longer periods of time. Although the differential in unemployment rates is often explained as a

TABLE 8-3
Nonwhite and White Unemployment Rates,
United States, 1965-1972*

Year	Nonwhite	White	Ratio of Nonwhite to White
1965	8.1	4.1	2.0
1966	7.3	3.3	2.2
1967	7.4	3.4	2.2
1968	6.7	3.2	2.1
1969	6.4	3.1	2.1
1970	8.2	4.5	1.8
1971	9.9	5.4	1.8
1972	10.0	5.0	2.0

*Adapted from U.S. Bureau of the Census, *The Social and Economic Status of the Black Population in the United States*, 1972:38.

TABLE 8-4
Number of Years of School Completed for Black and White Populations,
25 Years of Age and Over, United States, 1970*

Race	-5 Years	8 Years	12 Years	13-15 Years	16+ Years	Median School Years Completed
Total all races:	5.3	13.4	34.0	10.2	11.0	12.2
Blacks	15.1	4.2	23.4	5.9	4.5	9.9
Whites	4.2	13.6	35.2	10.7	11.6	12.2

*Adapted from U.S. Bureau of the Census, *The Social and Economic Status of the Black Population in the United States,* 1972:112.

function of the low position of blacks in any given industry, Pink-ney claims that the more valid explanation is simply discrimination on the basis of color (1975:87).

Since much of one's occupational status and income result from one's level of education, it is necessary to take a step backward to see how blacks and whites compare on this dimension.

Table 8-4 shows a gap of more than two years between blacks and whites in the median number of years of education completed. Less than one-fourth of all blacks completed high school compared with over one-third of all whites. The gap is even wider at the college level, where two and one-half times more whites than blacks completed college.

In addition, there is clear evidence that the schools attended primarily by blacks are inferior at every level to those in which whites are numerically dominant. For example, in 1966, 43 percent of black children in elementary schools in the Northeast, compared with 18 percent of white children, were housed in buildings that were over 40 years old. Furthermore, 44 percent of all black college students attend predominantly black colleges, most of which are located in the South and are not accredited. Faculty members in such schools are less likely to hold advanced degrees, they are paid lower salaries, and the student-faculty ratio is higher than in other colleges (Pinkney, 1975:75-81). Given this initial handicap in educational opportunity, it is not surprising that blacks are in the lowest occupational brackets. Thus, to return to Cox's argument, although there may be a majority of black people who would choose to cross the color line if offered the chance, this is not the key issue. They probably prefer to cross the *economic* line but few of them do, and it is in this sense that Cox's argument is fruitless. Economically speaking, then, blacks represent a caste in this country.

Cox also does not fully understand the caste and racial implications of intermarriage either in India or the United States. He acknowledges that in India intermarriage occurs between *jati* members, usually with the male being in the higher *jati*. Hypergamy (the woman marrying up) also occurs between races, but more commonly interracial marriage in the United States is hypogamous (the higher-caste white woman marrying the lower-caste black man). Cox believes, however, that caste identity is not lost when Hindus intermarry, while interracial marriage eventually blurs racial identity. Once again, we are obliged to take issue with Cox. Caste identity is definitely lost after intermarriage, because in India the wife and children take the man's caste. Racial identity, on the other hand, is rarely lost. Indeed, one researcher calculated that, provided all Americans cooperated, complete amalgamation of the two races in the United States would take 13 generations or 351 years, at which point black-white physical distinctiveness would disappear (Heer, 1965:7–9). Cox actually has the situations reversed. Caste membership is lost while racial membership is not lost when exogamy occurs.

One other point in this area is stressed by Cox in his claim that:

> Endogamy is of different significance in caste and race relations. The caste is socially and contentedly locked within its immediate marital circle; the race, on the other hand, is opportunistic and will intermarry or refuse to do so as its interest or cultural strategy demands (1974:429).

Data on intermarriage clearly show this is not the case. As of 1970, interracial marriage represented only .7 percent of the 2,277,000 marriages that occurred in America (*New York Times*, 1973:4). If blacks were marrying whites "opportunistically," one would expect a much higher rate of interracial marriage. Clearly endogamy is an almost totally accepted rule for both Hindus in India and blacks and whites in America.

The trap of accepting the ideal for the real is a common failing among sociologists, as in Cox's misunderstanding of the Indian caste system. Another example is the claim by Johnson that a caste system is stable and social change is not socially possible. Since no member of the society expects or wants change, no energy is required to maintain the system. Unlike race relations in the United States, then, people in India simply accept the way things are (Johnson, 1941). Simpson and Yinger also fall into the trap of accepting the ideal for the real. They contend that race relations are not caste relations because there is no religious justification for a rigid stratification system. In fact, many racists invoke biblical injunctions to justify their bigotry.

Gerald Berreman provides the best arguments against those who claim that blacks and whites in the United States are not in a caste relationship. He states that when these researchers depict Indians of low castes as content to be degraded, disadvantaged, and exploited, they misunderstand the caste system (1974:431). Americans who reject the notion that the racial system in the United States is a caste system believe that caste is passively accepted and endorsed by all Indians on a religious and philosophical basis while black-white relations are characterized by "dissent, resentment, guilt, and conflict." However, these Americans have an idealized image of India. From his study in Sirkanda, a hill village in northern Uttar Pradesh, Berreman cites evidence that low-caste Indians are not content. Low-caste members expressed specific complaints about lack of prestige, poverty, and the fact that high-caste men have access to low-caste women, while low-caste men dare not attempt relations with high-caste women. His subjects did not voice these discontents in the presence of higher-caste people, but they made it clear to the investigator that they were well aware of exploitation on many levels and that it was deeply resented.

Berreman notes that although the Indian caste system contains several unique features that are not found in caste systems on other parts of the world, such as Arabia, Polynesia, Africa, Guatemala, and Japan (Chapple and Coon, 1942; Nadel, 1954; Tumin, 1952; Donoghue, 1957), there is no reason why the term caste cannot be defined more broadly. Thus, a caste system is "a hierarchy of endogamous divisions in which membership is hereditary and permanent" (1974:432).

Berreman also delineates specific points of similarity between caste relations in India and race relations in America. In both systems there are rigid rules of avoidance, and certain kinds of contact (i.e., eating, dancing, touching, especially sexual relations and marriage) are believed to be contaminating. Enforced deference and punishment for lack of deference is present. Color may be the differentiating characteristic in the United States, but complex religious customs and rules have a similar effect in India. These, however, are merely "cultural details." In both systems, the higher caste rationalizes its superiority philosophically, religiously, psychologically, and genetically. Furthermore, caste membership and racial membership are predetermined by birth and are ascribed and unalterable.

> The essential similarity lies in the fact that the function of the rules in both cases is to maintain the caste system with institutionalized inequality as its fundamental feature. . . . From the point of view of the social psychology of intergroup relations, this is probably the most important common and distinct feature of caste systems (1974:433).

Blacks in the United States, then, constitute a class because they are economically deprived and politically castrated. They also constitute a caste because, while there are blacks in all classes, the reactions of whites are more often based on racial characteristics than on economic status. Thus, in speaking of blacks, caste is a more salient classification than class.

In Pinkney's review of the history of black people in the United States, beginning with the arrival of the first slaves in 1619 in Jamestown and ending with the Supreme Court decision to end racial segregation in public schools in 1954, he concludes that "a caste system developed which continues to relegate the former slaves and their descendants to a subordinate position in society" (1975:35–36).

Demographic Characteristics of Black Americans
One fundamental difference between the two major races is their respective population statistics. In 1970 blacks represented the largest visible minority group in this country, approximately 90 percent of the nonwhite population. The population of blacks has steadily increased from the time of the first census in 1790, until in 1970 there are over 23 million (or 11 percent of the total population) blacks in America (Pinkney, 1975:39–40).

The black fertility rate is higher than the white fertility rate. In 1970 the rate for every 1000 white women was 15.5, compared to 25.2 for every 1000 black women (U.S. Bureau of the Census, 1973). Fertility rates are always functions of other social factors. Blacks and whites in the same social class have the same birth rates; but since most blacks have resided in the rural South and have been in low-status occupations, the black rate has been higher. However, migration to urban areas or mobility to higher socioeconomic status results in a decline in black birth rates. It might be expected, then, that as more and more blacks leave the rural South (in 1970, 80 percent of all blacks resided in urban centers, compared to 73 percent of all whites), the black birth rate will decline. However, the economic gap between the races is getting wider, and this could mean the fertility differential will be unlikely to narrow (Pinkney, 1975:42).

The gap in death rates for blacks and whites has narrowed considerably since the beginning of the twentieth century. In 1900 the rate per 1000 blacks was 25 percent compared with 17 percent per 1000 whites. In 1970, the black rate was 9.5 percent, the white rate, 9.4 percent (U.S. Bureau of the Census, 1972:57). However, more blacks than whites die of diseases which modern medicine has controlled. For example, three times as many blacks as whites die of tuberculosis, syphilis, diabetes, gastritis, kidney infections, measles, influenza, and pneumonia. Blacks are four times as likely to die of hypertension, cardiovascular diseases, and cancer. They are eight times more likely to be murdered. Black women are six times more likely than white women to die in childbirth. For every 100,000 blacks in the population, 34.5 of the infants die of birth injuries, compared to 19.2 of white infants. Similar rates hold for infant mortality and life expectancy. For every 1000 live births, the black rate is 31.4 and the white rate is 17.4. In 1970 black males could expect to live 64.6 years, while white males could expect to live 71.7 years (Pinkney, 1975:42–43).

Another demographic characteristic of the black population is that it contains more young people and fewer old people than whites. In 1970, 42.1 percent of all blacks were under 18 years of age, compared with 33.2 percent of the whites. Black people over 65 represented 6.9 percent of all blacks, while white people over 65 represented 10.3 percent of all whites. The problem is that when added together, about 50 percent of the black population is either too old or too young to work. While it is also true that 43.5 percent of all whites must be supported by the rest of the white population, the problem is more serious for blacks because of their lower incomes (U.S. Bureau of the Census, 1972:32).

By way of a summary comparison, "the similarities between blacks in the United States and people in developing nations, on demographic characteristics, are striking" (Pinkney, 1975:52). Both have high birth and death rates; life expectancy is lower for them than for the dominant group; too many people are either too young or too old for the working portion of the population to maintain them on their low incomes; they die from controllable diseases more often than the dominant group; and they are migrating rapidly into urban areas where they are shunted into the most neglected sections of the cities.

Family Life of Black Americans
The demographic features of black and white families also differ considerably. It is a popular myth that most black families are fatherless, but Table 8–5 shows that although there are more black fatherless families than white, almost two-thirds of all black families contain two parents.

Black families are, on the average, larger than white families. In 1971 the white family consisted of 3.5 people, and the black family contained 4.2 people (U.S. Bureau of the Census, 1972:39). This is partly because black women have more children, but also because extended kin and unrelated people are sometimes family members. In some black households two complete families may live together. In 1970, for instance, 6 percent of all black families were subfamilies, compared with 2 percent of all white families (Hill, 1972:42). In spite of the larger size of the black family and in spite of the fact that more black than white wives work (55 percent compared to 44 percent), the average family income is lower for blacks. In 1972 the median black income was $6864, which is 59 percent of the median white income of $11,549. Furthermore, more white than black families own their own homes; 42 percent of blacks and 65.8 percent of whites in 1970 (Pinkney, 1975:101).

These demographic factors, combined with the history of black slavery, discrimination, segregation, and poverty, have contributed to the notion of the "disorganized black family." The evidence indicates that middle-class black and middle-class white family life are almost identical. Unfortunately, most blacks are in the lower classes, and since lower-class life tends to be more disorganized than middle-class life, it is class position, and not race, which make it *appear* that black families are less stable than white families.

The Moynihan Report (1965) which attributed the apparent deterioration of black society to the disorganization of the black

TABLE 8–5
Composition of American Families, By Race, 1973*

Race	Husband and Wife Present	Wife Only	Husband Only	Total
Black	61.4	34.6	4.0	5,265,000
White	87.8	9.6	2.5	48,477,000

Adapted from Pinkney, A.: *Black Americans.* 2nd ed., Englewood Cliffs, N.J.: Prentice Hall, 1975:100.

family, contributed heavily to the image of black inferiority. Moynihan charged that one-quarter of all urban black marriages were dissolved; nearly one-quarter of all black babies were illegitimate; one-quarter of all black families were female-headed; and that in recent years there had been a remarkable increase in the number of black families on the welfare rolls. Many people criticized this Report, but the most serious criticism was that it contained an implicit assumption that blacks were to blame for their condition. When Moynihan's charges are examined carefully, they turn out to be distorted. Actually, the stability of the black family is remarkable.

It is true that the divorce rate for blacks is higher than it is for whites. In 1970, for example, among white men the ratio was 33 divorced per 1000 married; among black men it was 60 divorced per 1000 married (U.S. Department of Commerce, 1971:2–3). However, within particular social classes—lower, middle, upper— no difference in divorce or desertion rates exists between races (Kephart, 1955:462). The higher the class, the lower the divorce rate, and because less than one-third of all blacks are in white-collar occupations (see Table 8–1), it follows that there are more black than white divorces. Furthermore, the black husband will sometimes "leave" his family when he cannot support them in order to make them eligible for welfare assistance. Thus, some marriages are recorded as dissolved when, in fact, they are intact (Lincoln, 1966:60).

Another reason why black families are more likely to be female-headed is that, since the days of slavery, blacks have been forced to find alternative arrangements to the traditional nuclear family pattern. Occupational discrimination against black men makes it difficult for them to support their families and therefore they may desert, or occasionally relatives may move into the house.

According to Pinkney, the 1967 Bureau of the Census report, which estimated white illegitimate births at 9 percent of all live births and 65 percent of all black live births is erroneous (1975:104). Pinkney claims that the discrepancy lies in the fact that white mothers of illegitimate children get preferential treatment from hospitals and medical personnel. Furthermore, whites are more likely than blacks to terminate premarital pregnancies by abortion. Before abortions were legalized, it was estimated that 90 percent of the two million abortions per year were performed on white women. Blacks are less likely to regard illegitimacy as stigmatizing and more likely to keep their babies at home; whites more often put illegitimate children up for adoption (Ladner, 1971:220–225).

Moynihan's charge that more blacks than whites are on the welfare rolls should be examined with care. Ninety percent of the black children on welfare had no father living in the home, compared with 73 percent of the white children on welfare. To state this in another way, when the father is present in the black family, the family is less likely to be on welfare than in a similar situation in the white family (Hill, 1972:49). When possible, then, the black father is more apt than the white father to support his children.

No doubt the black family finds the going difficult in white America. However, it "has demonstrated an amazing degree of resilience, adapting to the social and economic forces emanating from the larger society. . . . Its members must not be blamed for the problems imposed by the larger society" (Pinkney, 1975:107).

As the above statistics show, many of the stereotypes and prejudices about the black family are unfounded. Contrary to popular myth, in the majority of black families, the husband and wife are both present and share power equally. Although one-third of all families are female-headed, they are the poorest blacks and to be a poor black implies a lower class standing that that of the poor white. Among middle-class blacks, however, the family pattern is quite similar to that of middle-class whites. Thus, the difference in pattern results from economic differences, which in turn, result from caste differences.

Finally, the black family has several unique features which give it unusual strength. Blacks have strong kinship bonds, are work-oriented, family roles are flexible, and they have strong religious and achievement orientations (Hill, 1972:4). Certainly the black family has more than its share of problems, but in the face of these it has survived, adapted, and remained reasonably stable.

Political Life of Black Americans

Blacks in the United States have failed to participate significantly in political life either in the electoral process or as public office holders. One reason is that blacks, particularly in the South, were systematically and legally kept from the polls by the imposition of such hurdles as periodic voter registration, literacy tests, the requirement of property ownership, and so on. In spite of several civil rights acts dating from 1866, black Americans were largely disenfranchised. The Voting Rights Act of 1965 finally served to remove most of the obstacles on the road to the voting booth.

By means of this legislation and the growing cohesiveness of black people and increased organizational solidarity of black communities, black Americans are becoming aware that there is strength in unity and that relief from many of their problems—in housing, education, and employment—may be obtained by voting for those candidates who will attend to their interests.

This new political activism, however, must not be overrated. Even in Atlanta, where there is a large, well-organized, black middle class which participates in the political life of the city, blacks are still relatively powerless in the decision-making process despite the fact that the city has a black mayor. In other cities, where there are fewer affluent blacks and less cohesion, there is even less effective political action. One reason for this is that, even when blacks are numerically strong in a geographic area, most of the black population falls into the lower classes and lower-class people participate less than middle-class people in all organizational life (see Chapter 5). In addition, economic and personal problems are frequently so overwhelming that there is little time or inclination to take part in political activities. Further, the political leadership in most cities is controlled by white middle-class individuals, who do not encourage blacks, particularly poor blacks, to enter political life, since their interests are clearly not compatible. Even when the leadership is black, the same discouragement of the poor occurs. Since most blacks are poor, they are effectively excluded as a group from political participation.

Black participation in the electoral process, then, is gradually increasing, although the pace is slow. In the election of 1970, for example, in the South 58 percent of eligible blacks registered and 37 percent voted, compared to 70 percent registered whites, with 46 percent voting (U.S. Bureau of the Census, 1971:117).

The same trend can be seen in public officeholding. Since the

Civil War, with the exception of the years 1901 to 1931, blacks have always held some seats in either the House of Representatives or the Senate. In 1973–1974 there were 17 blacks in Congress, 16 representatives (4 of whom were women) and 1 senator. Blacks currently hold positions at state, municipal, and county government levels. There are several black judges on the U.S. Court of Appeals, U.S. District Courts, and the U.S. Supreme Court. There are black ambassadors, and blacks in the foreign service. There were 38 black mayors in 1973. Nevertheless, blacks are underrepresented in public life. While they constitute almost 12 percent of the total population, they hold less than 1 percent of the total number of elective and appointed positions at all levels (Pinkney, 1975:118).

However, the total picture is more encouraging. Black people are becoming a force in American political life. They are voting in increasing numbers; they are getting elected and appointed to more political positions and to positions with more power. Nevertheless, many of the problems of blacks will not be resolved politically. Legislation is one thing; mores and prejudice are another. It will require more than law to change the attitude of the dominant white majority and to bring the black minority caste into full citizenship.

Religion among Black Americans

During the antebellum period in the South, slave owners generally did not encourage religious participation by slaves, and the slaves themselves showed little inclination to adopt Christianity. However, Methodists and Baptists enthusiastically received prospective converts because these denominations held a special appeal for the uneducated, emotional slave, and their religious tenets did not threaten the owners because they focused on the hereafter rather than the present (Frazier, 1964:8). From this time until the 1960s, religion has played an important role in the black community. It has provided an outlet for many frustrations and the churches have served as centers for social life, especially in the South. The black minister was usually the leader of the people politically as well as spiritually, acting as a mediator between the white community and the black congregation. This was not always in the best interests of the blacks. "The preacher's . . . function became to transmit the whites' wishes to the Negroes and to beg the whites for favors for his people. . . . To this degree the Negro

Church perpetuated the tradition of slavery" (Myrdal, 1944:861). In the South, then, black religion was actually a boon to the white establishment to the extent that it defused black desire to change life on earth.

Northern black churches and ministers tended to be more independent of whites. Their ministers were more sophisticated and less easily subjected to intimidation, and therefore they rarely regarded the dominant whites with fear or awe. However, this did not imply that they were leaders who sought change. By the 1920s, when blacks began to move North in large numbers, the black churches failed to respond to their needs because they had patterned themselves after white churches. "Storefront" churches and sects proliferated in response to the need of the relocated blacks for "that old-time religion" which established black churches could not provide. It was not until the great civil rights movement in the 1960s that the black church regained leadership among lower-class blacks.

The Census Bureau does not collect data on religious affiliation and therefore black church membership can only be estimated. Apparently about 44 percent of all blacks belong to 30 denominations, but of those, approximately 87 percent are either Methodists or Baptists. The remainder are Roman Catholics (about 700,000), Seventh-Day Adventists (about 168,000), Black Muslims (about 250,000), or members of small cults sometimes numbering only a few hundred. In general, it can be said that the higher the social class, the more likely the blacks are to be members of an established, sometimes integrated church. The lower the social class, the more likely they are to belong to fundamentalist sects which still stress emotionalism, separatism, and life after death. These groups are found most often in the South, where their churches are small, dilapidated buildings and the congregations are led by ministers who often have only grade school educations.

Since there is little doubt that the church and religion are significant in the lives of many blacks, especially lower-class people, it is important to assess the help organized black churches have given to the black struggle for equality in the United States. Gary Marx's study showed that there is an inverse relationship between religosity and civil rights militancy (1969:94–105). That is, strongly religious blacks are less likely than others to be actively involved in the civil rights movement. In addition, people who belong to black churches are less militant than those who belong to integrated churches. Perhaps this may reflect the fact that blacks who join integrated churches are usually more militant and aggressive about integration in the first place. Marx also found that members of small sects were the least militant of all. Marx concludes that before religion can become a radicalizing agent for blacks, it must relinquish its power over the people or change its ideology from a belief in the power of God and life after death to a belief in the power of people and the importance of life before death.

In spite of these findings, however, the notion of black nationalism has been instrumental in helping black ministers develop pride and a sense of power among their congregants. While most black churches do keep themselves apart from the movement, there is a small but important minority of black ministers "without which the movement might never have achieved the success it has" (Pinkney, 1975:130).

Crime and Black Americans

The portrayal of blacks as a caste group in the United States can be seen most clearly when one compares their relationship to the criminal justice system with that of whites.

It is well known that crime reports are inaccurate because states and municipalities have differing methods for compiling records (see Chapter 6). Nevertheless, studies have shown that blacks are more likely than whites to be arrested, indicted, and convicted, and that they are less likely to receive short sentences, to be pardoned, to be parolled, or to get suspended sentences (Cressy, 1966).

Pinkney asserts that "policemen, like citizens in general, operate with a set of assumptions about black people which predispose them to differential treatment" (1975:133). Blacks are arrested "on suspicion" more often than whites, and police are more likely to use force to obtain a confession from them. Judges and juries also are likely to impose harsher punishments on blacks. For example, between 1930 and 1963, of 3833 offenders who were executed in the United States, 54 percent were black (*Negro Handbook*, 1966:111). Furthermore, in every category of crime the rate of arrest is higher for blacks than whites. Although they comprise only 12 percent of the population, 27.5 percent of all persons arrested are black. Even the average sentence is longer for blacks than for whites—45.4 months to 34.8 months, respectively. Blacks serve, on the average, 22.9 months in prison, compared with 17.7 months for whites (Federal Bureau of Prisons, 1973:38).

Such statistics do not indicate that blacks *commit* more crimes than whites, nor do they indicate that blacks *deserve* sterner treatment. They do show that because of their inferior social position, blacks probably experience greater frustration in any encounter with police officials. Gunnar Myrdal contends that because blacks are a caste group they are unable to identify with the larger society and its laws and therefore do not feel the laws apply to them. Furthermore, Myrdal claims that the legal system itself is "rigged" against the black person (1944:975–976). In addition, blacks commit the kinds of crimes that make headlines, just as white lower-class people do. Blacks and poor whites are not in a position to commit "white-collar crimes," which go largely unnoticed, unreported, and unpunished (see Chapter 6).

A look at juvenile delinquency reveals similar statistics. In 1973, 23 percent of all arrests of people under 18 years of age were black (Federal Bureau of Investigation, 1973:132). Once again, this does *not* indicate that young blacks are more inclined toward criminal conduct than young whites, but rather that police use different criteria in making assessments of criminals, e.g., clothing, demeanor, race, attitudes, and so on. In one study the investigator found that of all black youthful offenders, 76 percent were referred to juvenile court by the police, compared with 63 percent of the white youth. The difference was not explainable in terms of behavior or attitude (Ferdinand and Luchterhand, 1970).

Apparently, since the police were white, they tended to be less familiar with the black youngster and used more superficial evidence (such as the juveniles' style of dress) to decide their fates. Because they were more familiar with white juveniles, they employed more refined criteria to decide their fates (Hartjen, 1974:89).

It seems that the same act is called a "crime" when committed by blacks, but is considered a light offense or a "prank" when committed by whites. "What would pass for youthful cavorting among certain categories . . . is sometimes interpreted as blatant delinquency in others" (Hartjen, 1974:170). Thus, blacks are more likely to be arrested. They are also more likely to be convicted because they cannot afford to pay fines or hire private law-

yers. Once in prison they are usually assigned to the most menial
tasks and are less likely to be pardoned or parolled, in part because
they lack political power (Pinkney, 1975:134).

Edward Green's study of the black-white arrest rate differential succinctly summarizes the situation. He found that the higher
official crime rate for blacks resulted from the fact that blacks
predominate in the lower classes. Indeed, socioeconomic status
has an effect on crime rates independent of race. Most important:

> The findings lend no credence to the explanation of the Negro-
> white crime rate differential in terms of some distinctive aspect of
> Negro culture or in terms of racial conflict, whether viewed as the
> Negro's reaction to the frustrations resulting from racial discrimi-
> nation or the expression of racial bias by the police (Green,
> 1970:490).

Conclusion

In summary: Black Americans can readily be considered a
lower-caste group in the United States. They are assigned to a
racial group at birth and escape from that group is rare and difficult, largely because of their high visibility. Blacks are very much
aware of their low status, which affects every aspect of their lives.
Access to avenues of social mobility, such as education, is limited.
Even when a black person reaches a high social class, the caste status
remains more salient to the individual and to the society. Relations
with the dominant white group are restricted in terms of dwelling
areas, church membership, occupation, and personal interaction,
especially between members of the opposite sex. These rules of
segregation, although not legalized, are firmly entrenched in American society by custom and mores. Black Americans are not and
never have been an integral part of white American society. Some
progress has been made, but it is slow, with the result that decades
may pass before blacks lose their caste-like status.

Bibliography

Berreman, Gerald D., "Caste in India and the United States." In Lopreato,
    Joseph, and Lewis, Lionel S., eds., Social Stratification. New York:
    Harper & Row, 1974, 431–437.
Chapple, E. D., and Coon, C. S., Principles of Anthropology. New York:
    Henry Holt, 1942.
Cooley, Charles Horton, Social Organization. Glencoe, Ill.: Free Press, 1956.

Cox, Oliver C., "Race and Caste: A Distinction." *In* Lopreato, Joseph and Lewis, Lionel S., eds., *Social Stratification.* New York: Harper & Row, 1974, 422, 430.

Cressey, Donald, "Crime." *In* Merton, Robert K. and Nisbet, Robert A., eds., *Contemporary Social Problems.* New York: Harcourt, Brace, 1966.

Davis, David Brian, *The Problem of Slavery in Western Culture.* Ithaca: Cornell University Press, 1966.

Donoghue, J. D., "An Eta Community in Japan: The Social Persistence of Outcaste Groups." *American Anthropologist,* 59:1,000–1,017, 1957.

Federal Bureau of Investigation, *Crime in the United States, 1972: Uniform Crime Reports.* Washington, D.C.: United States Government Printing Office, 1973.

Federal Bureau of Prisons, *Statistical Report, Fiscal Years 1971 and 1972.* Washington, D.C.: Bureau of Prisons, 1973.

Ferdinand, Theodore N., and Luchterhand, Elmer G., "Inner-City Youth, the Police, the Juvenile Court, and Justice." *Social Problems,* 17:510–527, 1970.

Finley, M. L., *Slavery in Classical Antiquity.* Cambridge, Eng.: W. Heffer & Sons, 1960.

Frazier, E. Franklin, *The Negro Church in America.* New York: Schocken, 1964.

Green, Edward, "Race, Social Status, and Criminal Arrest." *American Sociological Review,* 35:3, 476–490, 1970.

Hartjen, Clayton A., *Crime and Criminalization.* New York: Praeger, 1974.

Heer, David, "Negro-White Marriage in the United States." *New Society,* 6:1965.

Heller, Celia S., ed., *Structured Social Inequality.* New York: Macmillan, 1969.

Hill, Robert B., *The Strengths of Black Families.* New York: Emerson Hall, 1972.

Johnson, C. S., *Growing Up in the Black Belt.* Washington, D.C.: American Council on Education, 1941.

Kephart, William M., "Occupational Levels and Marital Disruption." *American Sociological Review,* 456–465, 1955.

Ladner, Joyce, *Tomorrow's Tomorrow: The Black Woman.* New York: Doubleday, 1971.

Lincoln, C. Eric, "The Absent Father Haunts the Negro Family." *New York Times Magazine.* November 28, 1966.

Lopreato, Joseph, and Lewis, Lionel S., eds., *Social Stratification.* New York: Harper & Row, 1974.

Marx, Gary, *Protest and Prejudice.* New York: Harper & Row, 1969.

Moynihan, Daniel P., *The Negro Family: The Case for National Action.* Washington, D.C.: Office of Policy Planning and Research, Department of Labor, 1965.

Myrdal, Gunnar, *An American Dilemma.* New York: Harper & Brothers, 1944.

Nadel, S. F., "Caste and Government in Primitive Society." *Journal of the Anthropological Society of Bombay*, New Series, 8:Sept., 9-22, 1954.

Negro Handbook. Chicago: Johnson Publishing Company, 1966.

New York Times. February 18, 1974, Section E, 4.

Pinkney, Alphonso, *Black Americans.* 2nd ed., Englewood Cliffs, N.J.: Prentice-Hall, 1975.

Roach, Jack L., Gross, Llewellyn, and Gursslin, Orville R., eds., *Social Stratification in the United States.* Englewood Cliffs, N.J.: Prentice-Hall, 1969.

Simpson, G. E., and Yinger, J. M., *Racial and Cultural Minorities.* New York: Harper & Brothers, 1953.

Sio, Arnold A., "Interpretation of Slavery: The Slave Status in the Americas." *Comparative Studies in Society and History*, 7:3, 289-308, 1965.

Sulzberger, C. L., "Foreign Affairs: Slaves and Science." *New York Times*, March 1, 1967, 42. (This article notes that a report by the United States Human Rights Commission estimates that there are more than two million slaves in Asia, Africa, and South America.)

Tumin, M. M., *Caste in a Peasant Society.* Princeton, N.J.: Princeton University Press, 1952.

United States Bureau of the Census, "Birth Expectations and Fertility: June, 1972." *Current Population Reports*, Series P-20, No. 248. Washington, D.C.: United States Government Printing Office, 1973.

——, "Marital Status and Family Status: March 1970." *Current Population Reports*, Series P-20, No. 212. Washington, D.C.: United States Government Printing Office, 1971.

——, *The Social and Economic Status of the Black Population in the United States.* Washington, D.C.: United States Government Printing Office, 1971.

——, *The Social and Economic Status of the Black Population of the United States.* Washington, D.C.: United States Government Printing Office, 1975.

——, *Statistical Abstract of the United States 1972.* Washington, D.C.: United States Government Printing Office, 1972.

Weber, Max, *The Religion of India.* Glencoe, Ill.: Free Press, 1956.

chapter 9

Caste in the United States:
Caste Groups Based on Ethnicity, Religion, Age, and Sex

Ethnic Groups

Just as membership in a racial group is basic to one's self-identification, so ethnic and religious memberships are at the core of an individual's self-concept. Americans, even those whose families may have been in this country many generations, tend to think of themselves and to be thought of by others as having ethnic labels which precede that of "American." Thus, there are Irish-Americans, German-Americans, Italian-Americans, Jewish-Americans, and so on. An ethnic group, then, can be defined as consisting "of people who conceive of themselves as being alike by virtue of common ancestry, real or fictitious, and are so regarded by others" (Shibutani and Kwan, 1965:572). In addition, community organization leads to the placement of individuals into a hierarchial order, "not in terms of their personal aptitudes but in terms of their supposed ancestry" (Shibutani and Kwan, 1965:572).

Shibutani and Kwan use the term, "ethnic group" from the German word *Volk*, meaning "a people," to refer to individuals of the same national origins, race, or religion. The term will be used here only to refer to a religious group or a group of people with a common national origin, since racial groups were discussed in the previous chapter, and there are important differences between the two kinds of stratification.

Criteria of Ethnic Stratification

Donald Noel has proposed a theory of the origin of ethnic stratification (1968), claiming that three elements must be present in a social system before ethnic groups become stratified: ethnocentrism, competition, and differential power. All three conditions must exist before super-subordination patterns emerge. Continuous contact between two or more distinct ethnic groups will not ensure inequality. Such groups may live together and interact, even develop stable relations, without stratification. If even one of the three elements is absent or weak, stratification according to ethnic membership will not occur.

The concept of ethnocentrism was introduced by William Graham Sumner, who defined it as a "view of things in which one's own group is the center of everything, and all others are scaled and rated to it" (1940:13). This means that the in-group perceives its own values and behaviors as morally superior and more "natural" than those of all other groups. The result, of course, is that other groups are considered inferior to the in-group. According to Noel, the outsiders are viewed as fair game. No allegiance is owed to them, and exploitation in economic relations is commonly practiced. Frequently members of different ethnic groups engage in sexual congress, but endogamy prevails; indeed, endogamy helps to ensure ethnocentrism.

As noted, ethnocentrism alone does not guarantee ethnic stratification. Groups may coexist harmoniously, with mutual respect and acknowledgement that each has superior qualities in different areas. However, when there is competition for scarce goods, the danger of stratification increases. This can be avoided only if both groups view each other as noncompetitive, if the competition is minimal, or if it centers on relatively unimportant objects.

Even when ethnocentrism and competition are both present, groups must have differential power before stratification appears (see Chapter 3). One group must be in a position to impose its will upon other groups. If there is equal power, despite ethnocentrism and competition, the relations between the groups will be conflictual, symbiotic, or pluralistic. But once dominance is established, the superior group will use its power to restrict the lower groups and to short-circuit their efforts to compete. Noel summarized his theory as follows:

When distinct ethnic groups are brought into sustained contact (via migration, the emergence and expansion of the state, or internal differentiation of a previously homogeneous group), ethnic stratification will invariably follow if—and only if—the groups are characterized by a significant degree of ethnocentrism, competition, *and* differential power. Without ethnocentrism the groups would quickly merge and competition would not be structured along ethnic lines. Without competition there would be no motivation or rationale for instituting stratification along ethnic lines. Without differential power it would simply be impossible for one group to achieve dominance and impose subordination to its will and ideals upon the other(s) (1968:163).

In some ways ethnic stratification resembles racial stratification, with the outstanding feature of both systems being that distinctions are made among people. The lower strata are usually kept separate from the higher strata in as many ways as possible. Those in lower strata groups are permitted to marry, worship, work, play, live in decent housing, and educate their children.

However, these things must be done within the confines of the ghetto—whether geographic or fictive.

People become upset only when there is a violation of their sense of propriety; the discomforts and protests arise when someone is seen doing something he has no *right* to do. Objections arise when something happens to violate one's conception of the manner in which social relations are supposed to be ordered (Shibutani and Kwan, 1965:28).

In another way, however, ethnic stratification is markedly different from racial stratification. Among ethnic groups there is a decided tendency for assimilation to occur. Although there are those who advocate cultural pluralism in the belief that variety enriches society, and there are those who advocate ethnic segregation because they believe there are "natural" differences among groups, the fact is that integration invariably occurs as the result of contact between members of ethnic groups.

> In virtually all instances of inter-ethnic contact, no matter how great the initial difference between the groups, people sooner or later become integrated into a single unit and convinced of their descent from a common ancestor (Shibutani and Kwan, 1965:571).

The reasons for this breakdown of consciousness of kind and ethnocentrism are: (1) proximity, which leads to shared interests, values, goals, and so on; (2) a common language develops (foreigners learn to speak English) and communication lines open and become effective; and (3) intermarriage occurs between many members of different ethnic groups. Thus, according to Shibutani and Kwan, social distance grows narrower after a time, permitting people to see and accept their similarities.

There are some sociologists, and the present author is in agreement with them, who argue that segregation of ethnic groups remains high and integration is actually minimal. Nathan Kantrowitz (1969) studied ethnic neighborhoods in New York City and concluded that ethnic segregation there continues into the second generation. Admittedly, his evidence is weak, although it supports data from Chicago and other major cities. Kantrowitz finds that residential segregation of European groups nearly equals that of racial groups. Indeed, in order to achieve ethnic integration, Kantrowitz estimates that over 50 percent of the population which is of southern European origin would need to be redistributed among areas inhabited by those of northern European origin.

According to a 1969 United States Census Bureau survey, 75 million Americans defined themselves as members of one of seven major ethnic groups. These are individuals who differ from the white, Anglo-Saxon Protestant (WASP) in their language, religion, and/or culture. Distribution is shown in Table 9–1.

Americans classify each other in terms of economic position and ethnic affiliation, so that one's social status in the United States depends upon one's standing in the class structure and in the ethnic stratification structure. In many ways, although hardly to the extent that it holds true for blacks, ethnic identification is unalterable. And in those areas in which ethnic identification is salient, such identity restricts one's social advancement.

TABLE 9-1
Population by Ethnic Origin*

Group	Millions
German	20.0
English	19.1
Irish	13.3
Spanish	9.2
Italian	7.2
Polish	4.0
Russian (mostly Jews)	2.2

*From U.S. Bureau of the Census: *Current Population Reports.* Series P-20, No. 221, "Characteristics of the Population by Ethnic Origins," Washington, D.C.: U.S. Government Printing Office, November, 1969.

It is reasonable to refer to ethnic or religious groups as stratified castes because they are believed, by themselves and by others, to be natural divisions of people. Such beliefs are both subjective and objective (see Chapter III), but with qualifications.

The beliefs are subjective in that they are accepted with the certitude that characterizes religious convictions, but one cannot place oneself into any ethnic group. They are subjective also because usually there is a sense of "we-ness" in an ethnic group: consciousness of kind, a sense of cohesion, and sometimes an awareness of belonging which permits concerted political behavior in the group's behalf.

Ethnic groups are subjective also in the sense that emotional ties between members are generated and sustained by their shared heritage and experiences. Social distance is small, permitting members to empathize with and relate to each other's sorrows, fears, and triumphs. There is a feeling of safety in each other's company, a sense of belonging which allows members to lower their defenses and permits relaxation. There is also a conviction that "others" are different, and therefore members of the ethnic group have little or no sense of obligation to "them," only to "us."

Perhaps most important, people within an ethnic group regard it as a reference group. (A reference group is a social category used by individuals to help define their personal values, goals, attitudes, and behavior.) Thus, when people feel themselves to be part of an ethnic group, they will conform to group mores, norms, and culture in order to win acceptance as a bona fide member.

Ethnic groups are objective because they are groups believed by most people to have very specific differentiating characteristics. Americans think of Jews, for example, as being "good with money." Germans are thought of as "thrifty," Italians as "criminal," and Japanese as "sly." There are descriptive characteristics for every ethnic label. Furthermore, ethnic groups are objective because they exist independently, they are social facts sui generis— apart, above, and beyond the control of any individual. They are a matter of consensus and a part of the external world to which all people must adjust.

Variations in Ethnic Stratification Systems

Shibutani and Kwan have discussed the variations in ethnic stratification systems (1965:48–54). Although all systems have some common features, i.e., the basis for division is assumed ancestry and the groups are hierarchal, there are many dimensions along which the systems vary. One dimension of variation is in complexity and magnitude, and this depends on the size of the total population. If many ethnic groups are represented, the system will be more complex and the distinctions will appear more obvious. If only two or three groups coexist, the system probably will be simple and the distinctions either will be blurred more quickly or maintained more rigidly.

A second dimension of variation is the extent of the actual differences between the groups. For example, one can distinguish readily between a Japanese-American and a German-American. One can distinguish less readily between an English-American and a Welsh-American. Shibutani and Kwan claim that assimilation into the larger society occurs most quickly when differences are minimal, because visibility cannot be maintained. Therefore, "whenever underprivileged people attempt to improve their lot, the extent to which they succeed often depends upon the degree to which they no longer stand out" (1965:50).

The third way in which ethnic stratification systems differ is in the degree of solidarity within each group. Broadly speaking, the smaller a group is numerically, the greater the consciousness of kind, even despite geographic distances. The importance of group solidarity lies in the fact that without it there can be no concerted political effort and therefore no way for the group to elevate itself in the hierarchy.

The fourth dimension of difference is the degree of social mobility which is permitted by the larger society. According to Shibutani and Kwan, mobility in ethnic stratification is more difficult to achieve than mobility in class stratification, because financial success cannot erase the physical characteristics of ancestry (1965:51).

All ethnic stratification systems are based on a belief by members in biological or psychological differences or both, between the different groups. However, a fifth way in which these systems are distinct is in the extent to which such differences are stressed. Some groups firmly believe that they are inherently superior to others; in other systems such beliefs are only vague; and in some others they are nonexistent or considered ridiculous.

Shibutani and Kwan consider the sixth dimension the most important: To what extent are the ethnic stratification systems institutionalized? If they are well-entrenched systems, the beliefs are unquestioned and the relative positions of each group are taken for granted and morally justified. In societies in which consensus is weak, people ignore the rules and question the ideology. Because consensus among most ethnic groups in the United States is strong, it is justifiable to refer to ethnic stratification as a caste stratification system.

Religious Stratification

Religious stratification will be considered first as a special form of ethnic stratification. Many historians have contended that early Christianity was responsible for anti-Semitism because it created the image of the Jew as the "Christ killer." Some sociological studies have shown that in modern times there is a relationship between Christian religiosity and anti-Semitism. Those with no religious affiliation are least anti-Semitic while Catholics and members of major Protestant churches are most anti-Semitic (Sanford, 1950).

Jews as a Caste Group

Glock and Stark forcefully point out that there are certain Christian theological beliefs which are direct causes of modern anti-Semitism (1966). Christians, they argue, believe that ancient Jews were to blame for the death of Christ, and this belief is generalized and extended to the modern Jew. To test their hypothesis, Glock and Stark questioned almost 3000 white members of Christian churches in California. Briefly, they were able to show that belief in religious dogma is positively associated with anti-

Semitism; that *religious* hostility is directly related to *secular* hostility; and that religious bigotry is associated with a tendency to engage in anti-Semitic behavior. A replication of the California study on a national scale yielded similar results. These authors concluded:

> Conservatively, these findings would suggest that at least one-fourth of America's anti-Semites have a religious basis for their prejudice. . . . Far from being trivial, religious outlooks and religious images of the modern Jew seem to lie at the root of the anti-Semitism of millions of American adults (1966:205).

Many investigators have challenged the Glock and Stark findings, principally on the basis of methodology. Indeed, the criticism became so sharp that it led Stark to comment that if the findings had been reversed, little attention would have been paid to the methods (1970:151). One of the critics is Russell Middleton, who, in a similar study, questioned a national sample of nearly 2000 Christians (1973). Middleton's findings flatly contradicted those of Glock and Stark in that he found no correlation between religious orthodoxy and secular anti-Semitism.

Nevertheless, whether anti-Semitism is based on theological beliefs and dogma or on secular jealousies and irrationality, Christians consider Jews in the United States as part of an ethnic minority that is "different," and often treated them as an inferior group, regardless of class standing.

Religion and Occupational Level

The significant question is whether anti-Semitism has restricted the opportunities of Jews to participate in the common culture. When socioeconomic status differences among religious groups are examined, for example, almost all research indicates that Jews generally occupy the highest levels, followed by Protestants and then by Catholics. However, Sidney Goldstein modified these findings somewhat by controlling for place of residence (urban or rural), education, and occupation, and discovered that when these variables are taken into consideration, the differences between the three religious groups narrow considerably. "The conclusion seems warranted that both education and occupation play a much more crucial role than does religion itself in influencing the income levels of members of the three religious groups" (1969:612). In another study which broke down the "Protestant" classification into denominations, the same findings obtained. "For only three groups (Congregationalists, Episcopalians, and Jews) does the effect of membership in a religious group produce an adjusted annual family income which departs more than $500 from the grand mean" (Gockel, 1969:647). It would appear then that religion does not constitute an important differentiating factor in income levels in the United States. Despite the fact that Jews may be singled out for some forms of discrimination, they clearly are not barred from the educational and occupational opportunity structures in this country which closely affects income.

A study of the relation between religion and occupational achievement among Catholics and Protestants revealed that Protestants are more likely than Catholics to be in high-status nonmanual occupations and more likely to be upwardly mobile, even when father's occupation is the same (Jackson, Fox, and Crockett, 1970). The differences are attributed to religious factors because several possible intervening variables (ethnicity, region of birth, age, generation, and size of community) were controlled for. This conclusion can be interpreted in any of three ways. One, although the observed differences in occupational achievement are religious in origin, they are too small to be theoretically significant. Two, even if the differences are religious in origin and theoretically important, they are related to religious values and not to economical values (such as Catholics having larger families so that fewer Catholic children can be educated; or prejudice against Catholics among those who control access to high-status occupations; or the fact that many upwardly mobile Catholics convert to Protestantism). Three, the differences are religious in origin, theoretically significant, and the result of economically relevant religious values. The investigators opt for the third interpretation, but they acknowledge that more research is needed before a definitive relationship between religion (at least Protestantism and Catholicism) and occupational achievement can be established.

Ethnicity, Education, and Income

One determinant of occupational achievement is educational attainment. Therefore it is important to know if ethnic groups vary in their levels of educational achievement and if they differ from whites of native parentage in this respect. Table 9-2 shows these comparisons and indicates that, with the exception of Jews from Russia, Poland, and Austria, more native Americans of native

TABLE 9-2
Educational Attainment of Native-Born Persons of
Selected Background, 25–34 Years of Age:
New York City, 1960 (Males Only)*

Origin	Number	Median Years of School Completed	Completed High School (%)	Completed College (%)
Native white of native parentage	149096	12.6	66.9	24.4
USSR (Jews)	29291	14.2	85.3	37.8
Poland (Jews)	17637	13.3	80.8	33.8
Austria (Jews)	8893	13.1	79.9	32.2
U.K.	7162	12.7	70.5	22.2
Germany	5903	12.6	72.5	19.8
Ireland	14653	12.6	69.2	18.1
Italy	59422	12.0	49.6	8.5
Puerto Rican	4951	11.2	40.0	4.5

*Adapted from Rosenwaike, I.: 1973:73.

parentage are likely to finish college than any ethnic group. Thus ethnic background plays an important role in determining one's standing in the social structure. Given the fact that the educational levels of ethnic groups will influence generations to follow, differences in social class will continue to be associated with ethnicity in the future (Rosenwaike, 1973:76).

When we look at the income levels of the various religious groups, we can detect a similar pattern (Table 9-3). Jews have the highest incomes, followed by Protestants in the most prestigious denominations and Protestants in the less prestigious denominations; Catholics have the lowest incomes.

Ethnic Upward Mobility

Shibutani and Kwan noted that ethnic upward mobility is more difficult to achieve than class mobility because physical characteristics are difficult, if not impossible, to erase. Norbert Wiley (1967) has elaborated on this notion. He claims that ethnic mobility is complicated because of discrimination, but more importantly, because of the characteristics within the ethnic structure itself. For one thing, most ethnic groups are not only stratified in relation to the larger society, but also they are stratified internally. For example, among Jews, the Spanish Jew ranks highest, the German Jew second, and the Jew from eastern European countries ranks lowest. Therefore, there are inter- and intragroup opportunities which sometimes may limit the upwardly

TABLE 9-3
Family Income by Religion*

Religious Group	Number	Family Income
Jewish	242	9839
Episcopalian	199	9173
Congregationalist	127	9067
Presbyterian	435	8013
Methodist	1031	7185
Catholic	1936	7132

*Adapted from Matras, J.: 1975: 125.

mobile individual. In addition, complications arise if the entire ethnic group is upwardly bound. The individual then must decide whether to move with or against the group, and this makes him or her more vulnerable to the "mobility trap," defined as "an opportunity for mobility which offers a great deal less than it seems to, and, once pursued, permits release only at the cost of some downward mobility" (Wiley, 1967:148).

The most common metaphor used to describe a stratification system is that of the "social ladder," which conjures up an image of continuously rising levels with no steps missing. It implies that the ladder *can* be climbed, that the distances between steps are equal, and that the means of arriving at the next highest rung are all the same. Other images which have opposite implications of physical restraint also are used in talking about stratification systems, e.g., "beating one's head against a stone wall," "running down a blind alley," or "being on a treadmill." These phrases illustrate another kind of stratification system, one in which the strata are not continuous and climbing upward is forever unlikely, a pessimistic picture which hints that mobility is almost impossible.

Wiley's "mobility trap" is a compromise between these two extremes. Instead of a ladder, he visualizes the opportunity structure as a tree, and the movement is tree climbing, which can be done either via the trunk (the major mobility route) or out on the limbs (dead ends). "The limbs are its distinctive part. The limbs are like strata, leading gently upward but primarily outward and away from all chances of serious ascent" (1967:148–149). The trap is the limb, and Wiley identifies four types of traps.

The first is the "age-grade trap," in which young people accept standards and goals which are out on limbs, moving away from the trunk, which represents the established prestige standards of the older age groups. A second is the "overspecialization trap," in which people with highly specialized jobs find themselves "out on a limb" because they can go only to dead-end limits that lead away from the trunk. A third is the "localite trap," in which people move upward on a local limb and cannot return, once they get out too far, to the national trunk where the real mobility occurs. The fourth type, which is of interest here, is the "minority group trap," and within it Wiley includes not only ethnic groups, but racial groups, religious groups, females, and political radicals. People in such traps can advance only on the limb controlled by their own "ghetto." Excellent examples are the black student who is encouraged to major in "black studies"; the Jewish student in "Hebrew studies"; and the female student in "women's studies." Bachelor's degrees in such areas offer extremely limited opportunities in the occupational structure, and the student on such a limb soon discovers there is no return to the main tree trunk without real downward mobility, e.g., repeating a few years of college with a new and more realistic major. Wiley argues that the ethnic mobility trap is very comfortable because it keeps the mobile ethnic safe within his or her own group. However, real opportunity is lost:

> It is the in-group career that is the classic ethnic trap, for while it is attractive and emotionally rewarding, it usually has a low ceiling, and there is no easy way out into the world at large (Wiley, 1967:151).

It is difficult to speak of ethnic and religious groups in terms of categories used earlier for racial groups such as political participation, religious life, family life, and treatment by the criminal justice system, because there is so much variation among different ethnic and religious groups. We can say, in general, that the groups which enjoy the most prestige and wealth are those which most closely resemble the white Anglo-Saxon Protestant, with the exception of Jews who rank highest in occupational status, educational level, and income level but who have limited access to such things as membership in elite associations, community participation, and political power.

Conclusion

If we return to the list of caste features outlined on pages 236–237, we can now decide if we are justified in referring to ethnic and religious groups as caste groups. Membership in such groups is ascribed at birth and usually unchangeable, although names, facial features, accents, mannerisms, and styles of life can be consciously altered. Ethnic groups do tend to live in segregated areas, to worship in different places, and to some extent they engage in different occupations. They experience some restriction on social mobility and access to opportunity, although this is partly self-imposed because of the group's values. Clearly there are differences in cultural norms among groups; there are rules of avoidance and relationships of super- and subordination. Members of ethnic groups certainly are aware of their membership; the second generation tends to emulate the dominant group; and belonging to an ethnic or religious group affects most other aspects of social life, especially personal relations, which are mostly endogamous, such as marriage.

From this analysis it seems apparent that it is logical to consider ethnic and religious groups in this country as castes, although not to the same degree that races can be so considered.

Age Groups

It is perhaps more difficult to see the aged in American society as a lower caste group. In many respects, however, old people are relatively isolated and deprived. They are more likely to die unnecessarily (from malnutrition, for example); their income levels are lower than the national average, very frequently below the poverty line; they are excluded from the labor force on the grounds of age alone rather than incompetence, which is against the law; and they participate less in the social and political life of society.

Furthermore, the elderly are unable to help themselves. One reason is that people over 65 comprise only 10 percent of the population in this country, and therefore they have little political clout. In addition, they are often chronically ill and financially underprivileged, making them dependent on relatives or public organizations for survival. Finally, they are often socially isolated and therefore do not interact very much with others.

In modern America the old have a low status. They have no place in a society which stresses youth, beauty, skills, talent, work, and ambition. As a result, they are often excluded from positions which could provide rewards and satisfactions. The elderly in our society are thus an out-caste group.

Defining Old Age

Defining "old age" is a difficult problem, especially in an industrial society in which assignment to an age grade is often arbitrary. One can be considered "old" based on chronology alone, but even then there are variations, depending on who is doing the assigning. For example, 62 is the earliest date for retirement under the Social Security Act; yet widows are eligible for Social Security at age 60. The federal civil service permits its employees to retire after 30 years, regardless of chronological age. The Department of Labor has programs for "older workers," beginning at age 55. The Department of Housing and Urban Development accepts people at age 62 for "elderly housing" projects.

Another way of defining "old age" is the ability to function well physically. At 40, an athlete's career is usually over while at the same age a business person may be just beginning to reach the top of a career.

Robert Atchley claims that aging cannot be clearly defined because it varies with individuals and because it is gradual. Some people are old at 50; some are young at 70. No one wakes up "old" one morning. Atchley identifies three stages of advanced adulthood: middle age, later maturity, and old age (1972:6).

Middle age, usually during the forties and fifties, is the time when people first begin to realize they are growing older. They recognize they have less energy and they are less likely to seek physical satisfactions, replacing them with more sedentary ones. Middle-aged people are likely to begin to notice that their vision and hearing are less acute, and perhaps that chronic illnesses are beginning. Menopause in both men and women can lead to irritability, frustration, and oversensitivity. This is also the time of life when people come to grips with the fact that they will die some day. Death is no longer thought of as something that happens only to other people.

Later maturity, the years of the sixties and seventies, is a period characterized by a gradual increase in the processes which occur during middle age. In addition, there is a decreasing interest in the future, decreasing physical activity, and increasing chronic illness. This is the time when people retire and experience a concomitant reduction in income. Their social world narrows, partly as a result of retirement, partly because children move away, and partly because friends and relatives die. This shrinking of their world can be further increased for women if they are widowed, which is true for most women over 65.

In spite of these signs of increasing senectitude, later maturity has its pleasant aspects. Most people in this age group are in reasonably good health; they are active; and they have freedom from responsibility. The greatest problem is financial.

Old age, over 80 years, is a time of life characterized by disability and invalidism. All one's faculties are greatly diminished. The past becomes more important than the present or the future. Activity decreases, and loneliness and poverty generally increase. In the following discussion of older people as a caste group, we will use 65 as the cut-off age, since it generally is accepted as the onset of old age.

The proportion of older people has increased enormously during the twentieth century. In 1900 people over 65 represented 4 percent of the population; by 1950, the number had doubled to 8.1 percent; by 1970, it was up to 9.6 percent; and it is predicted that by 2000 people over 65 will represent 11.1 percent of the population (U.S. Bureau of the Census, 1971). This means that there were 3 million old people in this country in 1900, and over 20 million in 1970.

Age and Income

Aging is, of course, a biological process. However, social factors greatly increase the hardships of old age. The most important of these is income. Fifty-four percent of older families have incomes that are less than one-half of what they were when the couple was between the ages of 45 and 55. In fact, two-thirds of all retired Americans live below the poverty line, which is approximately $3000 for married couples and $2000 for single people.

In 1969 the median income for those over 65 was $4803, which is less than one-half the median income ($10,085) for younger families. About 10 percent of the older group live on incomes over $5000, and 65 percent have incomes under $2500 (Stark, 1975:393).

Social Security provides the majority or all of the income for most elderly people, but it is far from adequate. This system specifies that in order to qualify for a retirement pension a person must have been in the labor force for 10 years and must be at least 62 years old. In 1967 Social Security, as the major source of income, paid a median annual income of $2187 to married couples, $1368 to single men, and $1044 to single women. The Supplementary Security Income, which replaced Aid for the Aged in 1974, guarantees every elderly American $130 monthly regardless of years worked. Like Social Security, this is barely a subsistence level of income. Since neither Social Security nor Supplementary Security Income provide adequate levels of income, and since most elderly people have no other source of income, the United States has not provided sufficiently for its older citizens.

About one-sixth of the older population is still in the labor market, and these people do not collect Social Security or Supplementary Security Income. Clearly, their financial status is better. The average income for working older people is $6470, nearly double the income of those on Social Security. Other sources of income are interest and dividends on savings and investments. But although two-thirds of the people in this age grade report they have such income, the median amount is under $200 annually. About 12 percent receive monies from private pensions, but again this is not an important source of income because private pensions are relatively new and most older people have not contributed to them long enough to make much difference. Furthermore, private pensions are loaded with restrictions: small business people rarely are covered by them; and companies can go out of business, resulting in a smaller return for those fully paid into the pension plan and a total loss of money for those who have partially paid. Also the funds from a pension plan in Company A cannot be transferred when the worker moves to Company B. Generally this means that if a person changes jobs, enough money cannot be accumulated to be meaningful. Schultz quotes a Labor Department official on the private pension plan:

> In all too many cases the pension promise shrinks to this: If you remain in good health and stay with the same company until you are sixty-five years old, and if the company is still in business, and if your department has not been abolished, and if you haven't been laid off for too long a period, and if there is enough money in the fund, and if that money has been prudently managed, you will get a pension (1970:39).

Older citizens also are discriminated against in the employment structure. Once unemployed, they remain out of work longer than younger people, even when their skills are comparable, and despite laws which forbid discrimination on the basis of age. Most discrimination is based on notions that the older worker is more likely to become ill or that his or her skills are obsolete. However, a study by the Department of Labor revealed that there is less absenteeism among older workers than younger; that older people have lower turnover rates; and that their productivity is equal to that of younger people in both blue- and white-collar jobs (1970). Table 9-4 shows the percentage of older males in the labor force in 1960 and in 1970. The table is based on a report to the president from the Department of Labor, which revealed that participation in the labor market for elderly workers continues to drop. The report (1971) predicted that by 1985, only 21 percent of men over 65 will be employed.

Briefly, then, the overall economic picture for aged people is gloomy. Social Security payments and Supplementary Security Income are much too low. Private pension plans are not secure. Old people cannot and do not want to depend on relatives. Assets such as home ownership, although of value, are rarely large enough to help significantly. Most gerontologists are far from optimistic about the future. For example, Atchley writes that "the prospects for the future are not encouraging. The incomes of older people have increased over time, but *relative* to the general rise in income throughout the country, they have remained at a standstill" (1972:147).

Age and Health

Health is a central concern in everyone's life, but it takes on additional meaning for older people. One's state of health has great influence on one's social participation in all aspects of life, i.e., the family, work, recreation, and the community. It is therefore necessary to look at the health of older people as well as their finances in order to determine if they can be regarded as a caste group in this country.

Illnesses can be divided into acute and chronic. Acute illnesses are temporary and generally curable, and include minor ailments such as a cold and major ailments such as appendicitis. Chronic illnesses are either long-term or permanent, such as heart disease,

TABLE 9-4
Labor Force Participation by Older Americans by Age:
1960 and 1970*

Age	Percent in Labor Force	
	1960	1970
Total age 65 and over	32.2	26.8
65–69	45.8	40.7
70 and over	23.5	16.9

*Adapted from Manpower Report of the President, 1971:291.

arthritis, diabetes, or paralysis. Young people are more susceptible
to acute conditions, older people to chronic conditions. This
means that as a group, young people are more likely to recover
from their illnesses, while old people are more likely to have to
live with disability and restrictions for the rest of their lives. Table
9–5 shows the distribution of chronic ailments by age.

Not only are the elderly more likely to be chronically ill than
younger people, but they also take longer to recover from acute
illnesses because their recuperative powers are weakened (Confrey
and Caldstein, 1960:173). Furthermore, there is more mental illness among the aged, a condition more likely to be chronic than
acute. Riley and Foner found that psychosis occurred in 3.5 cases
of 1000 people between 15 and 34 years of age, compared to 40.0
cases per 1000 people 65 years of age and older (1968:370).

The problems of economic need and poor health are related.
As people age they develop more illnesses which are more serious,
require more care, and take longer to cure if they are not chronic.

TABLE 9-5
Percent Distribution of Persons, by Chronic Condition,
United States: July 1963–June 1965*

Age	No Chronic Condition	One or More Chronic Conditions Which Limit Major Activity	One or More Chronic Conditions Which Do Not Limit Major Activity	Total Disability
All ages	54.2	6.6	37.0	2.2
Under 45	64.8	2.5	32.3	0.4
45–64	34.2	11.6	51.4	2.8
65–74	19.6	25.3	45.4	9.7
75 and over	12.6	29.9	33.8	23.7

*Adapted from Atchley, R. C., 1972:116.

At the same time they have less money to spend on medical care, nutrition, and medicines. Cooper and McGee found that the average annual medical bill for an elderly person was $791 in 1970—six times higher than for a young person and three times higher than for a middle-aged person. They also found that while various kinds of insurance paid for most medical services, a person under 65 paid $100 personally, compared to $226 paid by someone over 65.

Medicare was designed to help older people finance their illnesses and almost everyone over 65 is eligible. However, Medicare is useful for short-term health care rather than for chronic, debilitating illness to which the old are more prone. In addition, Medicare does not cover preventive medicine, dental care, eye care, hearing aids, or prescription drugs.

Even if Medicare payments were adequate, most old people would still not receive the care they require to treat their illnesses because they do not have sufficient funds to buy proper food and medicine, they cannot use public transportation with ease, and they rarely own or drive cars.

Rehabilitation is a neglected aspect of all health programs for the aged. Facilities to house old people are more than inadequate; conditions in such homes often do not meet the health and safety requirements of the law or minimal Medicare standards, and many cheat their elderly residents out of their lifetime savings without providing good care, privacy, dignity, comfort, sympathy, or even kindness. "The sad reality is that people in the county [and nursing] homes are out of sight and therefore out of the mind of the public" (Stark, 1975:410).

In conclusion, like income security, health care for older Americans is glaringly indadequate.

Retirement

Retirement is a relatively new phenomenon. It is found in industrialized societies, and results from the productive power such societies generate. There is a higher proportion of older people in such populations because of the advances of medical technology, and room must be made for younger people to enter the job market. Thus in most industries employees are required to retire at a given age, usually between 60 and 70, most frequently at 65. Streib and Schneider conducted an extensive study of almost 2000 males and females employed in a variety of occupations. White, urban, high-status, and high-income people are over-represented in their sample. Since most older retired people are poor, the findings of the study cannot be considered representative of the retired population. The subjects were contacted twice: one year prior to retirement, and again after retirement.

Typically, retirement age for both men and women is either 65 or 70. People with higher-status occupations, more education, and higher incomes are likely to continue to work longer than those in lower strata. The percentage of people who retire voluntarily is almost the same as the percentage who are forced to retire.

These investigators were able to dispel several myths about retirement among the more affluent segment of the elderly. First, they found only a moderate self-reported decline in health, but this is not the result of retirement, since the same decline was reported by people who did not retire. Second, retirement did not bring about an identification of the retiree with old age. In fact, one-third of the subjects at age 70 reported that they considered themselves "middle-aged," whether retired or not. Although there was actually a 50 percent drop in income after retirement, two-thirds of the respondents felt thay had "enough" income to supply their needs. Only one-quarter of the subjects reported that they felt "useless," although retirees reported this feeling more frequently than those who continued to work. One surprising finding was that contrary to popular belief, retired women felt more useless than retired men. Although the researchers found a general overall dissatisfaction with life among older people, this was not necessarily the result of retirement, since the feeling was expressed by both retired and nonretired people. Streib and Schneider summarized their findings:

> The cessation of the work role results in a sharp reduction in income, but there is no significant increase in "worry" about money in the impact year of retirement. There is no sharp decline in health, feelings of usefulness, or satisfaction in life after retirement. Neither do respondents suddenly think of themselves as "old" when they stop working (1971:163).

Age and Social Integration

Irving Rosow studied the social integration of elderly people (1967). He found that older middle-class people had more friends than older working-class people because they were less likely to be dependent on their immediate neighborhood for friendships. Furthermore, older middle-class people were more willing to make new friends and thus were able to enlarge their social environment. However, regardless of social class position, older people sought out friendships with their age cohorts only, and not with younger men and women, although family contact remains important.

Older people are segregated from the general society for social reasons. The loss of an older person's major role is accompanied by role ambiguity, which means that elderly people have no structured roles, no clear expectations, and therefore almost no ambition to seek new roles. Further, Americans tend to devalue the old and to treat them in stereotyped, negative ways. Finally, old people, like other minority groups, unfortunately frequently accept the diminished view of themselves and their peers and behave accordingly—like second-class people. They are marginal members of society, who are ignored, rejected, and discriminated against by younger people. Rosow writes:

Thus, there are endemic forces in modern life which seem to alienate old people as a sheer function of their aging. Although their beliefs do not significantly change in the later years, older people's social integration is steadily weakened on . . . two crucial dimensions: the loss of their social roles and group memberships. These are almost irrevocably undermined so that the basis of their social participation is eroded. Consequently, the net effect of modern trends is alienating (1967:10).

Rosow concludes then, that to the extent that old people can maintain the patterns of middle age, they remain integrated in the society. When old age brings change—in health, work, and income—the result is isolation and anomie.

Conclusion

To review the findings of our discussion, to be old in this country is to be stigmatized. The widely held stereotype of the aged frequently is based on false notions of capability and adequacy. But this stereotype has a powerful impact on the lives of the elderly in that it influences their self-images and their self-expectations. It also relegates them to a societal position that is considered of little importance or use. Thus, the old people in the United States occupy a low caste position.

Membership in an old age category is ascribed and unchangeable. Often the elderly live segregated lives, if not physically then certainly emotionally. They are discriminated against in the labor force, and young people tend to avoid them. Old people are well aware of these prejudices, and they affect all aspects of their lives.

Sex Groups as Caste Groups[1]

Before beginning this discussion, two terms require definition. A *sex status* is a biologically ascribed position in society, which is acquired at birth and which is unalterable for almost everyone. A *gender role* is the sociologically achieved behavior attached to the sex status. Thus, one is born into a sex status—male or female. During socialization one acquires the characteristics which accompany the status—masculine or feminine. Sex is ascribed; gender is achieved.

Socialization is usually so successful that members of a society come to see certain behaviors as "naturally" masculine or feminine. Males "naturally" are athletic, good at mathematics, brave, strong, able to control their emotions, etc. Females "naturally" are passive, nurturing, emotional, weak, dependent, etc. These characteristic differences between the sexes come to be taken for granted; indeed, they come to seem almost sacred and immutable (see chapter 5).

Sexual Stratification

Stratification theorists have been particularly derelict in their attention to sexual stratification. Joan Huber (1973) has constructed a typology of male sociologists' reactions to accusations that sexism exists. One reaction is *simple denial*; a number of sociologists have maintained that the only reason there are so few women in universities is that such women are not available. If qualified women could be found, they would be hired. A second reaction is *simple paranoia*. The male believes that inferior women are getting jobs instead of superior males, who probably have families to support. Still another reaction, *classical liberalism*, is expressed by the male sociologist who swears he has never had any objection to his wife's working and he is convinced all men feel the same way. Of course he would prefer that his wife's job be less

1. Much of the information in this section is discussed in depth in Lucile Duberman, *Gender and Sex in Society.*

prestigious than his own. The *laissez-faire individualist* claims that childrearing is the responsibility of the family, not of the society, and that day care centers are evil substitutes for parents. Of course, fathers should supply the money and mothers should supply the personal, 24-hour-a-day attention. The *jokster* sociologist takes the feminist movement light-heartedly, and kids the "little ladies" in their efforts. The *pseudo-radical* is seriously concerned with re-organizing all of society, provided it does not interfere with his own domestic arrangements. Finally, the *kindly humanitarian* genuinely is sorry for women, but sees no alternative to their situ-ation. Societies would die out if women did not stay home and care for their families.

Since sociology itself is dominated by males, sexual stratifica-tion has almost been ignored. In recent years a few female sociolo-gists have come to recognize that men and women in American society are stratified into caste groups (Hacker, 1951; Andreas, 1971; Acker, 1973; and Chafetz, 1974). Each sex has ascribed characteristics and "proper" statuses and roles in society. Al-though both are boxed into positions that may be uncomfortable, clearly women are the members of the lower caste.

Joan Acker specifically addressed the problem of why sexual stratification has been ignored. One reason is the assumptions that are held about women in stratification literature.

(1) The family is the unit in the stratification system.
(2) The social position of the family is determined by the sta-tus of the head of the household.
(3) Females live in families; therefore, their status is deter-mined by that of the males to whom they are attached.
(4) The female's status is equal to that of her man, at least in terms of her position in the class structure, because the family is a unit of equivalent evaluation.
(5) Women determine their own social status only when they are not attached to men.
(6) Women are unequal to men in many ways, are differen-tially evaluated on the basis of sex, but this is irrelevant to the structure of stratification systems (1973:937).

The first assumption—that the family is the unit of study in stratification—underlies all the other assumptions, and taken to-gether they state very clearly that the female position in the class system depends on the male to whom she is attached. Acker then proceeds to show how invalid and illogical these assumptions are.

The choice of the family as a representative stratification group is falsely based on the notion that everyone lives in families. This is clearly not true. According to Abbott Ferriss, there is a definite upward trend in the percentage of people who live alone or with nonkin. In 1948, slightly less than 10 percent of all households were "primary individual households," compared to almost 18 percent in 1968 (1970:32). Thus the first assumption ignores 18 percent of the population.

Furthermore, by using the male's status as the criterion by which to stratify the family, the sociologist is implying that women have no educational levels, income levels, or occupations in their own right—no personal status resources. This is clearly untrue. If sociologists can rank men on these continua, they can also rank women on them, provided that the occupation "housewife" is ranked among occupations.

Acker concludes that sociologists can no longer claim that females are not relevant subjects of study in stratification analyses, and therefore it is time to reconsider sex and class together. She suggests that first and most important, the unit of study must be the individual, not the family. Second, it must be acknowledged that "females can be viewed as constituting caste-like groupings within social classes" (1973:941). Third, once females are viewed separately from males, the occupation "housewife" must be ranked among other occupations. Such changes in the assumptions about women in stratification studies could broaden our concept of society and new patterns of mobility might emerge:

> As the traditional nuclear family becomes less and less the dominant form in our country, the contribution which sex makes to the class and caste structure and to the social status of the individual will become more visible. In addition, as women become more powerful through greater participation in the labor force and through political organization as women, their position in the total social structure will become a more legitimate problem for the sociologist (1973:944),

Sexual Stereotyping

Stereotyping is a way all human beings have of categorizing other human beings. It is a set of generalizations that one group of people holds about another group. Stereotyping is essential in society because it enables members to identify each other rapidly, and to produce behavior that is considered proper for one's role and status. For example, a student seeing a person approaching down a school corridor makes a rapid, almost unconscious decision about that individual's status. The decision triggers the kind of greeting the student considers appropriate for the approaching person. Such lumping together of people, then, is partially justified because people who share certain characteristics very often share others. It is also justified because it helps the individual to classify the myriad of stimuli with which human beings are bombarded every day. If we could not label people in a general way rather rapidly, we probably could not cope with the hundreds of interactions we encounter daily.

On the other hand, stereotyping is harmful because it de-individualizes people. Most often a stereotype held by a person or a group has emotional overtones, is highly resistant to change, is reinforced by the members of one's own reference group, and is not susceptible to modification even when confronted with contradictory empirical evidence. It is usually negative, exaggerated, and oversimplified. Americans stereotype people along many dimensions, but no stereotypes are as powerful as those applied to males and females.

Chafetz compiled a list of traits showing the characteristics most Americans attribute to males and females, which is reproduced in Table 9-6.

Phyllis Chesler asked 46 male psychotherapists and 33 female psychotherapists to describe a mentally healthy adult female. Both sexes agreed she was "submissive, emotional, easily influenced, sensitive to being hurt, excited, conceited about appearance, dependent, not very adventurous, less competitive, unaggressive, and unobjective" (1971:97).

Myron Brenton defines the commonly accepted male stereotypical characteristics as: aggressiveness, sadism, violence, stoicism, emotion repression, protectiveness toward women, concern about making money, courage, bravery, athletic and mechanical ability (1966, Chapter 2). Kagan and Moss (1962) defined masculinity as sexually active, independent, courageous, competitive, athletic, and dominant.

Other researchers have focused on the core elements of the female role. In one study, for example, it was shown that three statuses are stressed for women, namely, wife, mother, and sex object.

TABLE 9–6
Sex Role Stereotype Traits*

Characteristics	Masculine Traits	Feminine Traits
Physical	Virile, athletic, strong, sloppy, worry less about appearance and aging, brave	Weak, helpless, dainty, non-athletic, worry about appearance and aging, sensual, graceful
Functional	Breadwinner, provider	Domestic, maternal, church-going
Sexual	Sexually aggressive, experienced, single status acceptable, male "caught" by female	Virginal, inexperienced, double standard, must be married, female "catches" spouse, sexually passive, uninterested, responsible for birth control, seductive, flirtations
Emotional	unemotional, stoic, doesn't cry	Emotional, sentimental, romantic, can cry, expressive, compassionate, nervous, insecure, fearful
Intellectual	Logical, intellectual, rational, objective, scientific, practical, mechanical, public awareness, contributor to society, dogmatic	Scatterbrained, frivolous, shallow, inconsistent, intuitive, impractical, perceptive, sensitive, "arty," idealistic, humanistic
Interpersonal	Leader, dominating, disciplinarian, independent, free, individualistic, demanding	Petty, flirty, coy, gossipy, catty, sneaky, fickle, dependent, over-protected, responsive, status conscious, competitive, refined, adept at social graces, follower, subservient, submissive
Other Personal	Aggressive, success-oriented, ambitious, proud, egotistical, confident, moral, trustworthy, decisive, competitive, uninhibited, adventurous	Self-conscious, easily intimidated, modest, shy, sweet, patient, vain, affectionate, gentle, tender, soft, not aggressive, quiet, passive, tardy, innocent, noncompetitive

*Reproduced by permission of the publisher, F. E. Peacock Publishers, Inc., Itasca, Ill., from Janet Saltzman Chafetz, *Masculine/Feminine or Human? An Overview of the Sociology of Sex Roles,* pp. 35–36. Copyright 1974.

(1) A concentration on marriage, home, and children as the primary focus of feminine concern.

(2) A reliance on a male provider for sustenance and status. This important component of the wife role is symbolized by the woman taking her husband's name and sharing her husband's income.

(3) An expectation that women will emphasize nurturance and life-preserving activities, both literally as in the creation of life and symbolically, in taking care of, healing, and ministering to the helpless, the unfortunate, the ill. Preeminent qualities of character stressed for women include sympathy, care, love, and compassion, seemingly best realized in the roles of mother, teacher, and nurse.

(4) An injunction that women live through and for others rather than for the self. Ideally, a woman is enjoined to lead a vicarious existence—feeling pride or dismay about her husband's achievements and failures or about her children's competitive standing.

(5) A stress on beauty, personal adornment, and eroticism, which, though a general feature of the female role, is most marked for the glamour girl.

(6) A ban on the expression of direct assertion, aggression, and power strivings except in areas clearly marked woman's domain—as in the defense of hearth and home. There is a similar ban on women taking the direct (but not the indirect) sexual initiative (Keller, 1974:417).

In contrast, Warren Farrell gives the "Ten Commandments of Masculinity:"

(1) Thou shalt not cry or expose other feelings of emotion, fear, weakness, sympathy, empathy or involvement before thy neighbor.

(2) Thou shall not be vulnerable, but honor and respect the "logical," "practical," or "intellectual"—as thou defines them.

(3) Thou shalt not listen, except to find fault.

(4) Thou shalt condescend to women in the smallest and biggest of ways.

(5) Thou shalt control thy wife's body, and all its relations, occasionally permitting it on top.

(6) Thou shalt have no other egos before thee.

(7) Thou shalt have no other breadwinners before thee.

(8) Thou shalt not be responsible for housework—before anybody.

(9) Thou shalt honor and obey the straight and narrow pathway to success: job specialization.

(10) Thou shalt have an answer to all problems at all times (1974:32).

Thus there are definite characteristics and attributes that men and women, carry around with them. They are given to children as "received" doctrine at birth, and reinforced all through life by peers, books, the mass media, songs, and advertising. Everywhere one looks one encounters the rules that bind people into sex stereotypes, from which it is almost impossible to escape without stigma and pain.

Even before they enter nursery school young children learn what is "normal" or right for boys and what is "normal" or right for girls. Andreas reported that one study of nursery schools showed that clear distinctions were made between the sexes by nursery school teachers. Each sex was given access to different kinds of toys and activities. Boys played with trucks, girls with dolls. Boys were permitted to be more active, dirty, and noisy. Children were segregated by sex, and one way teachers were observed to punish boys was to make them sit in the girls' section. Conversely, it was considered a privilege for a girl to be allowed to sit in the boys' section! (1971:28–29).

Studies of preschool age books reveal the extent to which traditional masculine-feminine stereotyping is reinforced. Table 9–7 shows how male and female people are depicted in a representative sample of story books for children.

Chafetz further shows that schoolteachers believe that many of the traits associated with sex are biologically determined, as is indicated in Table 9–8.

To summarize: Both men and women in the United States are stereotyped and forced to enact gender roles which are related to their sex status. Gender roles are considered synonymous with sex status. The fact, is, however, that to be born male does not ensure masculinity. To be born with male genitalia does not guarantee

TABLE 9–7
Set Stereotypes as Reflected in 27 Preschool Children's Books

Characteristic	Number of Books in Which Female Characters Exhibit Characteristics	Number of Books in Which Male Characters Exhibit Characteristics
Functional role		
Provider	1†	17
Domestic	18	3
Unclassifiable	8	7
Play activity		
Physically active	3	14
Physically passive	10	3
Unclassifiable	14	10
Personality		
Dominant	3	11
Passive	13	3
Unclassifiable	11	13
Intellectual		
Realistic, logical, objective	2	10
Idealistic, illogical, subjective	15	8
Unclassifiable	10	9

*Reproduced by permission of the publisher, F. E. Peacock Publishers, Inc., Itasca, Ill., from Janet Saltzman Chafetz, *Masculine/Feminine or Human? An Overview of the Sociology of Sex Roles*, p. 84. Copyright 1974.

†Schoolteacher.

TABLE 9-8
Characteristics Assigned Males and Females by Grade Schoolteachers*

Characteristic	Biologically Innate to:		No Difference %	Cultural Trait of:		Total N
	Males %	Females %		Males %	Females %	
Aggressive	40	6	26	26	1	147
Practical, objective	15	15	34	20	15	116
Compassionate, sentimental	3	39	26	1	30	148
Idealistic	3	19	48	5	25	151
Verbal ability	8	11	54	16	11	149
Follower	4	18	31	1	45	144
Moral, trustworthy	3	13	67	5	13	150
Intuitive	3	41	33	2	21	150
Abstract reasoning ability	16	10	47	20	6	152

*Reproduced by permission of the publisher, F. E. Peacock Publishers, Inc., Itasca, Ill., from Janet Saltzman Chafetz, *Masculine/Feminine or Human? An Overview of the Sociology of Sex Roles*, p. 89. Copyright 1974.

aggressiveness, bravery, or athletic ability. Males learn how to act as if they were aggressive, brave, or athletic in order to prove they are "masculine." Likewise, to be born female does not ensure femininity. Having ovaries and a vagina cannot make a woman feel that doing housework is wonderful. But most women will act as if having a well-waxed kitchen floor were the end-all and the be-all of life. Masculinity and femininity are learned behaviors within a societal context. Few escape the constant reinforcement of these behaviors by society, just as few escape any caste categorization. However, although both sexes lead circumscribed lives because of these labels, women are in the lower caste.

Women are considered inferior by both sexes in all aspects of life except those pertaining to the home and children. However, since these are in themselves inferior status areas, to excell at them is still to be in an inferior position. In addition, women set lower goals for themselves than men do; they are less frustrated than men when their goals are not realized; and they avoid situations which demand risk-taking, aggression, and nonconformity. Finally, women see themselves as subordinate to the dominant sex. They allow themselves to be dependent on men for economic support and status placement. They display deferential behavior toward men: they ask the questions and men supply the answers. They have limited access to certain opportunity structures in society. There are many ways to illustrate that women are the lower sex caste, but it can best be demonstrated by examining their positions vis-à-vis men in the home and in the occupational structure.

Randall Collins uses a Freudian and a Weberian perspective to construct a conflict theory of sexual stratification (1971). After demonstrating that women are concentrated in the lower echelons of the occupational ladder and on the bottom rungs of each occupation, Collins shows that this is a manifestation of women's subordinate place in the general society.

> The principle of this system is that women take orders from men but do not give orders to them; hence only men can give orders to other men, and women can give orders only to other women. . . . Women's subordinate position at work may be viewed as a continuation of their subordinate position in the home. . . . The female role in the home continues to center around that of domestic servant. The married woman has primary responsibility for cooking, dishwashing, laundering, housecleaning, and child care—occupational roles that are classified as low prestige service positions (1971:5-6).

Women in the Home

Traditionally husbands are the breadwinners in the family and wives are the homemakers, mothers, and sex partners. Homemaking, however, is a very peculiar occupation. It is a job which takes 7 days a week and 24 hours a day. It is nonpaying and it is almost impossible to be fired or to quit, short of death or divorce. Thirty million women today are classified as full-time housewives. Housework is considered a low prestige occupation because it is open to anyone; no special training or qualifications are needed; there are no standards of performance; no financial rewards are offered; and no promotion is possible.

In addition, to be a housewife is to be dependent upon one's male partner. One kind of dependency is *social.* Adult women, especially those with small children, do not interact very much with other adults during the day, and are dependent upon their husbands for sociability in the evening. The housewife is also *economically* dependent, and the amount of money she gets for her personal needs depends solely on the generosity of her husband. Last, a housewife is dependent upon her husband for *social status*, since she has no independent social identity. These dependencies go a long way toward perpetuating the myth that the male is the most important person in the family.

Mothering is also part of the wife status, and since technology has freed women from many household tasks and from bearing more children than they want to, mothering one or two children has become a central concern in the lives of most married women. Biologically a woman is a mother when she gives birth to a child, but then she must learn the social role of mother that is attached to the status. Mothers spend incredible amounts of time reading, discussing, listening to, and understanding the vast quantities of literature which tell them how to be better mothers.

Most young women are socialized from childhood to want to be mothers, and 83 percent of all American women attain this goal (Lopata, 1971:190). However, according to Lopata, few realize the long-term consequences of having children. Most daydream about a little angel lying in a cradle, and are not prepared to cope with the demands made by a child upon their time, energy, health, attention, social life, and sexual life.

The role of wife, which includes homemaker, sexual partner, and mother, is clearly subordinate to that of husband, who is expected to go out into the world and succeed. The male is not expected by society to perform any of the menial tasks involved in running a home and taking care of children. According to Collins, this subordination of women in the home continues into the occupational sector of society.

Women at Work

Although the majority of married American women are primarily housewives, there has been a radical change in the proportion of working wives in the labor force over the past 30 years. In 1940, 15 percent of all married women worked, compared to 43 percent in 1970. Only 26 percent of all women with children in school worked in 1940, compared to 52 percent in 1970. Only 11 percent of mothers of preschool age children worked in 1940; in 1970, 32 percent were employed full time (Nye and Berardo, 1973:271).

Occupations are, of course, stratified, but they are also sex-linked. Men occupy the more "important" positions, women the helping positions. Doctoring is superior to nursing; pilots have more prestige than stewardesses. Some occupations are almost completely male, such as the ministry or accounting; some are almost completely female, such as nursing or elementary school teaching. Women who enter traditionally "male" occupations are

TABLE 9-9
Millions of Year-Round Full-Time Civilian Workers*

Occupation	Male	Female
Professional and technical:†		
Self-employed	.5	.1
Salaried	5.0	2.3
Managers, officials, proprietors		
(nonfarm)	6.1	.9
Sales workers	2.0	1.7
Craftsmen, foremen	7.7	.4
Clerical	2.7	5.8
Operatives	7.2	2.3
Service (except household)	2.1	2.0
Laborers	1.8	.2
Farmers and farm managers	1.5	.2
Farm laborers	.5	.1
Private household workers	.05	.3

*From Ferriss, A., *Indicators of Trends in the Status of American Women* p. 143. New York, Russell Sage Foundation, © 1971.

†Although classified as professional, most women in this category are semiprofessionals, like nurses or teachers; they are not in medicine, law, or university teaching.

considered to have moved upward; men who enter traditionally "female" occupations are considered to have moved downward. Table 9-9 shows how males and females are differentially employed.

Income traditionally is associated with educational level, occupation, length of experience, age, and race. But it is also very much associated with sex. This is difficult to prove because women more frequently than men work intermittently or part time, but pure discrimination accounts for differentials of between 10 and 20 percent in the earnings of men and women (Stein, 1973:16). Table 9-10 shows the consistent differences between the salaries of men and women within each occupational group. Note especially the last column, which shows the ratio of the female's median income to the male's. For example, in 1968 the total median income for women was $4457, which is 58 percent of the median earnings for men that year.

Professional Woman

In the economic world women experience sex-labelling and unequal income distribution regardless of their social class posi-

TABLE 9-10
Number and Median Earnings of Year-Round Full-Time
Civilian Workers, by Occupation and Sex, and
Female/Male Ratio of Earnings, 1968*

Occupation	Median Earnings		Female/Male Ratio (× 100) of Earnings
	Male	Female	
Total	$7664	$4457	58
Professional and Technical:			
Self-employed	17358	–	–
Salaried	10243	6634	65
Managers, officials, proprietors (nonfarm)	9794	5101	52
Sales workers	8292	3388	41
Craftsmen, foremen	7958	4315	54
Operatives	6773	3956	59
Clerical	7324	4778	65
Service (not household)	5898	3159	53
Laborers	5606	3490	62
Farmers, farm managers	3353	–	–
Farm laborers	3870	–	–
Private household workers	–	1464	–

*From Ferriss, A., *Indicators of Trends in the Status of American Women* p. 142. New York, Russell Sage Foundation,© 1971.

tion, and this can be demonstrated best by looking at professional women, partly because there has been more research among professional groups than among white-collar and blue-collar groups. Table 9-11 shows the percentages of women in certain selected professions. It should be clear that although women currently are represented in all professions, they are grossly underrepresented in all of the professions, except the "female" professions (the last three listed).

The table shows that except for minor gains in the fields of medicine and biology, in 1960 there actually were fewer women in the professions than there were in 1950. Athena Theodore contends that women do not enter the higher professions because their socialization discourages such ambition. For males the primary status is occupational; for females it is domestic. Thus even bright, well-educated women willingly give up careers for husband, home, and children (1971: Chapter 1).

Matina Horner (1970) studied "success-avoidance" tendencies in college women, and showed that when ambitious young women are faced with a choice between pursuing their ambitions and maintaining their feminine image, they will choose to behave in ways that reflect their internalized gender role images.

These occupational (class) differences between males and females are, we suggest, a function of the relative caste positions of

TABLE 9-11
Women in Selected Professional Occupations
(Percentage of all Workers)*

Occupation	1930	1940	1950	1960
Lawyers	2.1	2.4	3.5	3.5
College presidents, professors, instructors	32.0	27.0	23.0	19.0
Clergy	4.3	2.2	8.5	5.8
Doctors	4.0	4.6	6.1	6.8
Engineers	—	0.3	1.2	0.8
Dentists	1.8	1.5	2.7	2.1
Scientists	—	—	11.4	9.9
Biologists	—	—	27.0	28.0
Chemists	—	—	10.0	8.6
Mathematicians	—	—	38.0	26.4
Physicists	—	—	6.5	4.2
Nurses	98.0	98.0	98.0	97.0
Social workers	68.0	67.0	66.0	57.0
Librarians	91.0	89.0	89.0	85.0

*Adapted from U.S. Bureau of the Census, Census of Population, 1960. Vol. 1, Table 202, 1960:528-533.

each sex. An analysis of the status of women within three major professional groups is especially revealing in this regard.

Women as University Professors

A study of women sociologists disclosed that of the 8095 graduate students in 1968-1969, 33 percent were women; of 5882 students in 1971-1972, 36 percent were women. The study also revealed that women students were getting more than their share of assistantship money (37.5 percent), which indicates that some reverse discrimination was operative and attempts were being made to encourage and recruit women into sociology (Hughes, 1973). A less flattering but perhaps more realistic way to evaluate the higher proportion of women assistants is to say that male professors prefer women assistants because women perform better in the subordinate role and are more willing than men students to take orders and attend to detail. One could say women in academia make better assistants because they are socialized to accept the "helping" role.

Once out of school, however, the women sociologists do not fare as well. Although they represented 36 percent of the graduate student body in 1972, they represented only 12 percent of the faculty, and they were clustered in the lower ranks. Table 9-12 shows this clearly.

Furthermore, as evidenced in Table 9-13, even at the same rank female sociologists earn less money than their male colleagues.

Ann Davis contends that women are discriminated against in universities because they threaten their male counterparts, not because they are inferior according to objective standards.

TABLE 9-12
Faculty Members, all Graduate Sociology Departments,
1970, 1971, 1972, by Sex and Rank*

Rank	1970		1971		1972	
	Total Faculty	Women (%)	Total Faculty	Women (%)	Total Faculty	Women (%)
Full professor	900	4	1079	4	1035	5
Associate professor	672	10	744	11	686	12
Assistant professor	996	13	1163	12	1115	16
Lecturer	76	12	114	21	106	30
Instructor	212	16	106	29	84	29
Total	2946	9	3249	10	3026	12

*From Hughes, H. M., ed., *The Status of Women in Sociology*. Washington, D.C.: The American Sociological Association, 1973:11.

TABLE 9-13
Salary Differentials Between Male and Female Sociologists
on Four Levels, 1967-1968, by Sex*

Academic Rank	Salary Differential
Professor	$1100
Associate professor	600
Assistant professor	400
Instructor	400
All sociologists	1700

*Adapted from Hughes, H. M., ed., *The Status of Women in Sociology*. Washington, D.C.: The American Sociological Association, 1973:15.

> We continue to be faced with the fact that good intellectual abil-
> ity among women is being wasted as a social and national re-
> source and that lack of clarity about the female role may be
> productive of personal unhappiness (1969:99).

Women as Medical Doctors

Although Table 9-11 indicates that there has been very little increase in the number of women medical doctors over a 30-year
period, there is evidence that the proportion of women admitted
to medical schools is increasing. In 1968, 9.7 percent of all medical students admitted were women. However, other studies have
shown that the woman physician is accepted neither by her colleagues nor by her patients (Williams, 1964).

In their study of the role conflicts of women doctors, Kosa
and Coker (1965) found that sex and professional roles restrict
each other. In order to cope with the conflict, women in medicine
choose specialities that are most compatible with the feminine
image, such as public health. By selecting such a medical speciality
the female physician can schedule convenient hours that are compatible with her family role and avoid the possibility of competing
with male doctors, because she has a salaried position.

Kosa replicated the study in 1971 and found that several
changes had taken place. The black civil rights movement, the
women's liberation movement, and the gay liberation movement
all had been instrumental in changing the status of women in
medicine. It had become easier to get into medical school; there
were more salaried positions available; there was more public and
colleague acceptance; and women were entering some of the
"male" specialties. Kosa concluded that there had been some
progress, but not nearly enough to free the woman doctor from
the shackles of femininity.

Women as Lawyers

In 1960, only 3.5 of all lawyers were female; but by 1973 the percentage had risen to 16.0 (*New York Law Journal*, 1974:1, and 4). This is still a low percentage and much of the blame can be laid at the door of outright discrimination against women. James White examined income differentials among male and female lawyers and consistently found that women earned less than men in the legal profession. His exhaustive study ruled out a number of other alternatives as accountable for the differences: there were no more part-time female workers than male; the women were as experienced as the men; and both males and females were equally high in class rank, in law review participation, attended equally prestigious schools, and were employed by the same kinds of law firms. His conclusion was inevitable: women lawyers are discriminated against by law firms for no other reason than sex (1967).

Of the three professions discussed, the law seems most promising for women in the future. A survey by the American Bar Association revealed a sharp rise in the number of female law students: 16,760 out of 106,102 in 1973, an increase of 38 percent over 1972 (*New York Law Journal*, 1974).

Conclusion

To summarize: Women, especially professional women, are discriminated against at work. Within the professions they are found disproportionately in sex-segregated specialites; they are underpaid in relation to their male counterparts; and they are promoted far less frequently. The expectations and norms surrounding women workers are essentially different from those that apply to men, creating conflicts, ambiguity, limited careers, and personal unhappiness.

Women, then, like blacks, ethnic group members, and elderly people, constitute caste-like groups within the United States. The notion of women as inferior is institutionalized by custom and by ideology. Membership in a sex status is ascribed at birth and remains unchangeable. Female social mobility rates are lower than male social mobility rates because access to opportunities is restricted. Males and females both observe commonly accepted rules of avoidance and deference, and the relationships between them, both personal and business, are those of subordination of females and superordination of males. Women are acutely aware of their second-class status and it is significant in all areas of their lives.

Conclusion

It has been shown in this chapter that the United States is far from an open class society. It has, indeed, many features that closely resemble the Hindu caste system. Certain groups, especially blacks, ethnics, old people, and women, are discriminated against continually and systematically deprived of their rights within the common culture.

In a heterogeneous society there are three ways to deal with minority groups. A *pluralistic* method suggests that all the diverse subgroups should coexist on an equal basis because each group's culture enriches the whole society. An *assimilationist* model encourages minority group members to enter the mainstream of society—to become one of "us." A *hybrid* model seeks to reconstruct all of society, redefining roles and statuses in such a way that labels are no longer meaningful.

Some of these ways of treating minority groups work better for some kinds of groups than for others. A pluralistic model would work best for ethnic and religious groups because it would allow this country to retain its remarkably varied and distinctive groups, which can so greatly enhance the whole culture. Assimilation seems the best solution for the black caste, although none of the models is easily workable for the blacks. Prejudice against this caste is so strong that there is little hope of full acceptance in the near future. The hybrid model would serve women by removing the labels which stigmatize them and prevent their entrance into "male" domains. It would also help men to throw off their restrictive labels and allow them to show their humanness and their involvement with things other than money and success.

Bibliography

Acker, Joan, "Women and Social Stratification: A Case of Intellectual Sexism." *American Journal of Sociology*, 78:4, 936–945, 1973.

Andreas, Carol, *Sex and Caste in America*. Englewood Cliffs, N.J.: Prentice-Hall, 1971.

Atchley, Robert C., *The Social Forces in Later Life*. Belmont, Calif.: Wadsworth, 1972.

Brenton, Myron, *The American Male*. Greenwich, Conn.: Fawcett, 1966.

Chafetz, Janet Saltzman, *Masculine/Femine or Human?* Itasca, Ill.: Peacock, 1974.

Chesler, Phyllis, "Stimulus/Response: Men Drive Women Crazy." *Psychology Today*, 5:1971.

Collins, Randall, "A Conflict Theory of Sexual Stratification." *Social Problems*, 19:1, 3-21, 1971.

Confrey, Eugene A., and Caldstein, Marcus S., "The Health Status of Aging People." *In* Tibbitts, Clark, ed., *Handbook of Social Gerontology*. Chicago: University of Chicago Press, 1960.

Cooper, Barbara, and McGee, Mary, "Medical Care Outlay for Three Age Groups." *Social Security Bulletin*, 34:May, 1971.

Davis, Ann, "Women as a Minority Group in Higher Academics." *American Sociologist*, 4:2, 95-99, 1969.

Duberman, Lucile, *Gender and Sex in Society*. New York: Praeger, 1975.

Farrell, Warren, *The Liberated Man*. New York: Random House, 1974.

Ferriss, Abbott L., *Indicators of Change in the American Family*. New York: Russell Sage Foundation, 1970.

———, *Indicators of Trends in the Status of American Women*. New York: Russell Sage Foundation, 1971.

Glock, Charles Y., and Stark, Rodney, *Christian Belief and Anti-Semitism*. New York: Harper & Row, 1966.

Gockel, Galen L., "Income and Religious Affiliation: A Regression Analysis." *American Journal of Sociology*, 74:6, 632-647, 1969.

Goldstein, Sidney, "Socioeconomic Differentials Among Religious Groups in the United States." *American Journal of Sociology*, 74:6, 612-631, 1969.

Greeley, Andrew M., "Political Participation Among Ethnic Groups in the United States: A Preliminary Reconnaissance." *American Journal of Sociology*, 80:1, 170-204, 1974.

Hacker, Helen M., "Women as a Minority Group." *Social Forces*, 30:60-69, 1951.

Horner, Matina, "The Motive to Avoid Success and Changing Aspirations of College Women." *Women on Campus: 1970, A Symposium*. Ann Arbor, Mich.:

Huber, Joan, "Editor's Introduction." "Changing Women in a Changing Society." *American Journal of Sociology*, 78:4, 763-766, 1973.

Hughes, Helen McGill, ed., *The Status of Women in Sociology*. Washington, D.C.: The American Sociological Association, 1973.

Jackson, Elton F., Fox, William S., and Crockett, Harry J., Jr., "Religion and Occupational Achievement." *American Sociological Review*, 35:1, 48-63, 1970.

Kagan, Jerome, and Moss, Howard, *Birth to Maturity: A Study of Psychological Development*. New York: John Wiley, 1962.

Kantrowitz, Nathan, "Ethnic and Racial Segregation in the New York Metropolis, 1960." *American Journal of Sociology*, 74:6, 685-695, 1969.

Keller, Suzanne, "The Female Role: Constants and Change." *In* Franks,

Violet, and Burtle, Vasanti, eds., *Women in Therapy.* New York: Brunner/Mazel, 1974, 411–434.

Kosa, John, "Women and Medicine in a Changing World." In Theordore, Athena, ed., *The Professional Woman.* Cambridge, Mass.: Schenkman, 1971, 709–719.

——, and Coker, Robert E., Jr., "The Female Physician in Public Health: Conflict and Reconciliation of the Sex and Professional Roles." *Sociology and Social Research, 49*:3, 294–305, 1965.

Lopata, Helene A., *Occupation: Housewife.* New York: Oxford University Press, 1971.

Matras, Judah, *Social Inequality, Stratification, and Mobility.* Englewood Cliffs, N.J.: Prentice-Hall, 1975.

Middleton, Russell, "Do Christian Beliefs Cause Anti-Semitism?" *American Sociological Review, 38*:1, 33–52, 1973.

New York Law Journal. January 15, 1974, 1 and 4.

Noel, Donald L., "A Theory of the Origin of Ethnic Stratification." *Social Problems, 16*:2, 157–172, 1968.

Nye, F. Ivan, and Berardo, Felix M., *The Family: Its Structure and Interaction.* New York: Macmillan, 1973.

Riley, Matilda, and Foner, Ann, *Aging and Society. Vol. 1,* New York: Russell Sage, 1968.

Rosenwaike, Ira, "Interethnic Comparisons of Educational Attainment: An Analysis Based on Census Data for New York City." *American Journal of Sociology, 79*:1, 68–77, 1973.

Rosow, Irving, *Social Integration of the Aged.* New York: Free Press, 1967.

Sanford, R. Navitt, "Ethnocentrism in Relation to Some Religious Attitudes and Practices." *In* Adorno, T. W., et al. eds., *The Authoritarian Personality.* New York: Harper & Brothers, 1950, 208–221.

Schultz, James H., "Pension Aspects of the Economics of Aging: Present and Future Roles of Private Pensions." *Report to the Special Committee on Aging,* U.S. Senate, January 1970.

Shibutani, Tamotsu, and Kwan, Kian M., *Ethnic Stratification.* New York: Macmillan, 1965.

Stark, Rodney, "Rokeach, Religion, and Reviewers: Keeping an Open Mind." *Review of Religious Research, 11*:Win., 151–154, 1970.

——, *Social Problems.* New York: Random House, 1975.

Stein, Herbert, *New York Times,* July 11, 1973, 16.

Streib, Gordon F., and Schneider, Clement J. *Retirement in American Society.* Ithaca, N.Y.: Cornell University Press, 1971.

Sumner, William Graham, *Folkways.* Boston: Ginn, 1940.

Theodore, Athena, ed., *The Professional Woman.* Cambridge, Mass.: Schenkman, 1971.

United States Bureau of the Census, "Characteristics of the Population by

Ethnic Origins." *Current Population Reports*, Series P-25, No. 221, Washington, D.C.: United States Government Printing Office, November 1969.
——, "Projections of the Population of the United States by Age and Sex, 1970 to 2020." *Current Population Reports*, Series P-25, No. 470, Washington, D.C.: United States Government Printing Office, 1971.
United States Department of Labor, *The Law Against Age Discrimination in Employment*. Washington, D.C.: United States Government Printing Office, 1970.
——, *Manpower Report of the President*. Washington, D.C.: United States Government Printing Office, 1971.
White, James J., "Women in the Law." *Michigan Law Review*, 65:6, 1967.
Wiley, Norbert F., "The Ethnic Mobility Trap and Stratification Theory." *Social Problems*, 15:2, 147–159, 1967.
Williams, Josephine J., "Patients and Prejudice: Lay Attitudes Toward Women Physicians." *American Journal of Sociology*, 51:282–287, 1964.

chapter 10

Afterword

In almost every known society (except the most primitive perhaps) structured inequality can be found along several continua. Furthermore, every society permits and even encourages inequality and stratification according to some ideology, custom, or even law which legitimates the system.

Because the Constitution of the United States was based on the formally written doctrine that all men are created equal, our country has a great deal of difficulty in viewing itself as a nation containing subgroups that are not equal. In point of fact, America has often denied that inequality exists within its boundaries. Today, however, denial has become all but impossible.

There is more open acknowledgment that some groups in the United States are better off than others. The "war on poverty" is one piece of evidence that proves there is official recognition of inequality along class lines. The feminist movement, the gay liberation movement, the black civil rights movement, and other smaller social protest groups are additional evidence that class is not the only important form of social discrimination in this country.

We have been forced to recognize the truth about our social system because the information about inequalities in educational and occupational opportunities, political participation, and so on, has been made manifest through the social sciences. It cannot be denied. We have learned that under certain social conditions no amount of individual motivation can help change the power structure. Deprived persons—whether poor, female, minority group members, or elderly— can no longer be blamed for the circumstances under which they are forced to live. Nobody *deserves* to be unequal. We have come to a point in time when we must acknowledge the fact that there are great inequities in our society, and that these inequities are rooted in our social structure, not in the deprived groups and not in the individual members of those groups.

Of course we can continue to refuse to believe the evidence. Myrdal concluded that Americans suffer from a national schizophrenia, and that this has led inexorably to a moral impasse (1944). However, Myrdal may have been incorrect. Rather than suffering from moral uneasiness, Americans may have a remarkable ability to rationalize experiences, to make "A" seem like "B" when it is comfortable to do so. Pareto claimed that people rarely behave rationally, and yet they constantly try to convince themselves and others that they do (Aron, 1970:119). Thus, in spite of the empirical evidence surrounding us that the United States is a country with definite class and caste discrimination, many Americans will continue to disregard or refuse to accept these inequalities.

There are three ways in which Americans who acknowledge the existence of inequality can deal with this knowledge. One argument is basically functionalist (see Chapter 3). Those who adhere to it feel there is no reason to become excited about inequality because it is natural. Some people in every society have to lead and to occupy the highest positions, and some have to do the more menial work. Those who do the best job will rise to the top by natural selection; the inferior ones inevitably will sink to the bottom. Implicit in this stance is the notion that our social institutions are basically sound, and that in any case no changes in them can change human nature.

A second and perhaps even more common way of dealing with admitted inequality is to state that something is already being done to change the situation. All one need do is observe the improvements and be patient. Massive change, after all, requires time. Rome wasn't built in a day. Those who chose this way of looking at inequality point to the advances that have been made by underprivileged groups through open enrollment programs in colleges; laws abolishing discrimination on the basis of color, religion, sex, or age; reduced voting requirements; and programs designed to help the disadvantaged child. These people fail to see just how very slow progress has been.

Moreover, they also are unaware or refuse to recognize that many of the programs presumably designed to abolish inequality are mere tokenism, misdirected in focus, or inadequate in scope. While Americans may verbalize a desire to achieve equality, the actions taken to achieve that goal belie the claims. Inequality has not, is not, and probably will not be abolished, not because people are different from one another, not because they are inferior to one another, but because those who are in a position to abolish it have systematically chosen not to do so.

The third argument for coping with inequality is that there is something seriously wrong with the American social system and its institutions, and radical changes must be implemented immediately. Advocates of this position acknowledge that people are not equally endowed biologically so that some inequality is inevitable, but not to the extent that it presently exists. They also admit that there has been some progress for some groups. Nevertheless, inequality is basically a product of culture, and they demand a complete reorganization of the American social structure.

To review the three positions, there are people in the United States who claim that nothing can or should be done to remove inequity among groups. There are also those who want to make gradual changes without causing any confusion or instability. Finally, there are people who believe that American social institutions require close scrutiny and radical changes, in order that much greater equality can be achieved at a much faster rate. The question, then, is: Are these the only alternatives, and which course is the United States likely to pursue in the future?

We reject the idea that these are the only alternatives available.

Regarding the first, Americans cannot deceive themselves much longer into believing that inequality is defensible on the grounds that it is natural and inevitable. Clearly all blacks are not inferior to all whites; all women to all men; all the aged to all the young; all those of "ethnic" origins to all those of "native" origins; and all those born in lower-class families to all those born in middle- or upper-class families.

Nor is the middle-of-the-road second alternative likely to be the best solution. Social engineering remedies such as the war on poverty, Headstart, and open enrollment have not proved viable. For one thing, these programs are usually too grandiose and too vague, making it nearly impossible to implement them. Further, most of them are inadequately funded, so they become stop-gap rather than real reform measures. Finally, such programs are helpful to too few people and they take too long to show any real results.

The third solution, which is perhaps most appealing, is too idealistic and out of reach because it is too vast and too extreme for most Americans. Few Americans will give up their almost sacred institutions willingly. An example of this is school busing. When the notion was first introduced, who could have foreseen that opponents would offer such arguments as the "traditional right of the child to attend a neighborhood school." In point of fact, if we really look at tradition, most American children have gone and still go to school by bus, especially outside of large cities. The school bus is an American institution itself! This alternative, then, is too dependent on rationality to be constructive.

It seems that the future of inequality can best take shape as some compromise between all three alternatives. It cannot be ignored or taken for granted. It cannot be changed gradually. It cannot be changed suddenly and radically. Leonard Reissman offers "three major components that generally will shape the future of inequality" (1973:119).

The first component is class, which underlies the American social stratification system, its inequality, and the institutions which support it. However, contrary to long held popular myth, the system does not have built-in self-correcting changes which keep it open and provide everyone with equal opportunity.

The result is that most people in all classes find themselves there through little fault of their own. Rich and poor alike have come to inherit their positions rather than to achieve them through their own efforts. . . . Changes have been occurring in the structure of classes and class mobility and, as a result, we have been moving closer to an institutionalization of inequality in American society even though we still retain the traditional rhetoric of equality (Reissman, 1973:119–120).

Still, according to Reissman, American classes have not become solidified. Many factors such as the liberation movements and the new awareness we have gained since the Watergate affair may still intervene to reshape the present pattern so that rational changes can still be made within a context that is familiar and acceptable to the majority of citizens.

The demographic trends which tend to segregate Americans constitute the second component which will be significant for change. Reissman speaks here of the segregation of inner-city blacks and suburban whites, but his notion is applicable to ethnic and religious ghetto areas within cities, and to such geographic entities as retirement and leisure towns or apartment complexes which are built solely for the elderly. Such geographic segregation leads to isolation, with each sector becoming more and more isolated from and ignorant of the other. "Physical separation has come to mean social and psychological separation as well" (1973:122).

In order to prevent such segregation from spreading, traditional American policies concerning private property and local politics, which have not been altered in decades, must be discarded. Because groups live apart in their own enclaves, they define the world in their own special way and cannot grasp the perceptions of other groups. There is a vast difference between driving through a neighborhood in a car at 50 miles an hour and strolling through it. If Americans truly wish to see greater equality in this country, they will have to see more of each other. They will have to use "deliberate institutional intervention" to stop the pattern of geographic separation of groups.

The third component of change is psychological perception. This means Americans of all classes and castes must be willing to give up the stereotypical images they have of each other and learn what each group is really like. Undoubtedly, the third condition is somewhat dependent on the other two, especially on the second. However, it is also the most difficult. We can open our schools, our purses, and our geographic boundaries. Can we open our minds?

It seems unlikely. Class and status community boundaries are becoming more rigid, as revealed by such indices as income differentials and styles of life. Geographic distances are widening and cities are becoming blacker and poorer while suburbs are becoming whiter and richer. Psychological acceptance is still very far from reality. Unfortunately, it appears that class inequality will continue unchanged. Indeed, it will probably become even more entrenched.

Some kinds of caste inequality may lessen. Women are clearly making the greatest progress of all American caste groups, and if the Equal Rights Amendment is passed, legally it will go a long way toward removing the stigma of being female. Ethnic and religious discrimination should also weaken because there is far less immigration to America at the present time than there has been in the past, and second and third generation ethnic group members tend to assimilate fairly quickly and well. The question of age discrimination is uncertain. Most likely there will be little change in the status of old people, unless there is a radical change in the Social Security system and the delivery of health care programs. The group least likely to gain equality in the forseeable future is that of the American blacks. American prejudice is so deeply rooted, and oppression has been so complete and so long-lasting that the probability of black absorption into the mainstream of American social life is not a hopeful one.

Inequality of all kinds in a society as heterogeneous, industrialized, and prejudice-laden as that of the United States seems inevitable for a long time to come.

Bibliography

Aron, Raymond, *Main Currents in Sociological Thought.* Vol. 2, translated by Richard Howard and Helen Weaver. Garden City, N.Y.: Doubleday Anchor Books, 1970.

Myrdal, Gunnar, *An American Dilemma.* New York: Harper & Brothers, 1944.

Reissman, Leonard, *Inequality in American Society.* Glenview, Ill.: Scott, Foresman, 1973.

index

314   Index